FOUR MINUTE
WARNING
BRITAIN'S COLD WAR

FOUR MINUTE
WARNING
BRITAIN'S COLD WAR

BOB CLARKE

TEMPUS

Front cover: Lance. Lance was an American surface-to-surface missile system. It saw service with the British Army from 1976 to 1993. (Courtesy the Vought Corporation)

Back cover: RAF Fylingdales. The AN/FPS-49 radar, each had a 25m parabolic dish, stood on a 10m-high plinth and weighed a massive 112 tonnes. (Courtesy *Scarborough Evening News*)

First published 2005

Tempus Publishing Limited
The Mill, Brimscombe Port,
Stroud, Gloucestershire, GL5 2QG
www.tempus-publishing.com

British Library Cataloguing in Publication Data.
A catalogue record for this book is available from the British Library.

ISBN 0 7524 3394 6

Typesetting and origination by Tempus Publishing Limited
Printed in Great Britain

Contents

Acknowledgements

This book would not have come to fruition had it not been for the enthusiasm and expertise of many of my colleagues and friends, I would like to thank them all. Thanks are also extended to all the organisations, representatives and individuals who have allowed access to the many sites visited in the last year.

Individual thanks go to the following: Michael Parrish of the Kelvedon Hatch Museum and Rodney Siebert of the Hack Green Museum; Chris Walker of the North Wilts Military Survey; Roy Canham, Wiltshire County Archaeologist; Nick McCamley, author of Cold War Secret Nuclear Bunkers, who helped solve some of the finer details; Bill Baker of the Avon Fire Brigade, who allowed access to the refurbished ROC Group HQ at Lansdown, Bath; the *Scarborough Evening News* for the splendid pictures of Fylingdales; Mike Fuller for flying the USAF airfields in difficult conditions, Liz Wild for access to the Reading War Room; Don Todd and Keith Watson for access and stimulating discussion at Upper Heyford; Debbie Edmonds of English Heritage; Kelvin at Country & Metropolitan for access to Becca Hall; Tony Peach and his band of merry Royal Observer Corps members – long may they keep the flag flying!; Pete Sherburne and Jim Askew for their advice on military matters; Simon Hailwood, Senior EPO for South Gloucestershire Council; Michelle Dean, Community Safety Officer for West Oxfordshire District Council, and John Kelly, Oxford EPO; Erith Demolition for allowing access to the GCHQ Oakley site; and the owners of all those sites in the middle of nowhere who struggled to understand why I found concrete so interesting, but allowed me to photograph them anyway.

And last but by no means least, thanks go to my good friend and colleague Colin Kirby for putting up with my frequent absences during one of QinetiQ Archaeology's biggest projects; Barry Huntingford, who has met the task of reading the draft text with good humour and made the story of Britain's Cold War legible; John and Christine Clarke for help with locating the Yorkshire sites and pictures; Campbell McCutcheon of Tempus Publishing Ltd for giving me the opportunity to put my thoughts down on paper; and finally Sarah and the kids who live in a house full to the roof with archaeology including now artefacts from the Cold War. A big thank you to everyone. If I have forgotten anyone, and that's highly likely, I apologise profusely. Any errors are ultimately my responsibility.

Preface

My Cold War

Growing up in Scarborough hardly sounds like the front line, but that was the point of the Cold War, it had the potential to include everybody. Very few 'traditional' front lines actually existed with the obvious exceptions of the Berlin Wall and the 38th parallel and, of course, the Iron Curtain. Almost every area of Britain had one site or another which was deemed to be a potential target, and my part of the world was no exception. So, what was my Cold War? Well I was a child of the '60s with all the usual things a young lad wanted: a train set, Dinky toys, Thunderbirds (in fact anything Gerry Anderson!) and of course Airfix kits. By the mid-'70s I had developed more than a passing interest in history, aircraft and war films; many of my models were eventually to become war casualties!

On moving to Grahame Secondary School on the outskirts of the town I came into contact with a number of 'like-minded' individuals, joined the 739 Sqn Air Cadets and never looked back. From my house I could see RAF Staxton Wold to the south and Irton Moor listening post, known locally as the wireless station, to the north. Just up the road was the North Yorkshire Moors and situated prominently on it were 'the Golf Balls', so, as you can see, I was sitting right in the middle of some prime military targets.

Being a member of the Air Cadets opened up many of these sites as we witnessed first hand the Nation's Defences. I still vividly remember our summer camp to RAF West Raynham in 1978, home of the impressive Bloodhounds. I even got to 'target' a blip on the radar with the predictable shout, 'Don't push that one !', from the launch crew after I had done it, all to much hysterics. But we were the exception to the rule; nobody else seemed to acknowledge the fact that we were at war. This was one of the interesting phenomena of the Cold War, that it was treated by most as background noise to their everyday lives. I may be wrong but I cannot recall my parents ever talking about anything which we now see as significant, even if the IRA atrocities did feature occasionally, but apart from that life just ticked along.

Life was, however, punctuated by many low flying jets; the Vale of York was a designated flying area and we got the lot. Over the years the procession was as good as any air tattoo you could see today. Formations of Vulcans, occasionally four deep, Lightnings practising dog fights and even the prototype Tornado with its Phantom and Buccaneer escorts. The Americans were also much in evidence, F-111s often whipped down the Vale and the agile A-10s could always be relied on to put up a good display, especially for a group of lads on a country lane on their bikes. I can still feel the excitement of the display and the customary salute signing off the spectacle. We slept safe in our beds.

Many of us from 739 joined the services in the early 1980s at the height of the 'Doom Boom', not to fight the Warsaw Pact or become part of NATO but to have a career. Scarborough didn't offer much so we moved out. Pilots, commandos, radar specialists, engineers, we covered the whole spectrum. I have to say, from a personal perspective, ten years in the RAF did not give the impression we were at war with a superpower. Granted it was in the background and the occasional exercise or Tacival brought into sharp perspective the NBC threat but the main problem was home-grown terrorism. By the time I arrived at St Athan, my last posting, Spetsnas was just a distant memory, then the wall came down and everything changed, including my career. I left the RAF and went into civil aviation.

The events across Europe rekindled my interest in history; I had just witnessed one of the most significant periods of the twentieth century coming to an end. My wife and I spent the next two years visiting most of Eastern Europe; I needed to know what it had all been about. What we discovered was a world of second bests; by the time we got to Moscow the whole country was pretty much upside down. As we looked at Lenin, still guarded around the clock in his empty mausoleum, my mind wandered back to all those pictures of queuing Russians waiting in the snow for a glimpse of his hallowed remains. The world had indeed changed.

In 1994 two major events happened in my life: I became a father and I picked up a contract at Boscombe Down, six week's worth and I'm still there now! Two years later I had become a qualified archaeologist (something I had started years earlier) and part of the archaeological team on site. Since then I have investigated, with my colleague Colin Kirby, many aspects of Boscombe Down's archaeology, including the part it played in the Cold War. This has developed into a bit of an obsession, one that appears here in print as my view of the Cold War and Britain's part in it.

Introduction

The Cold War was like no other conflict yet experienced. It was more than a struggle between two superpowers, it was a war of ideologies, the capitalist West and the communist East. The Cold War leached its way into every facet of British life to the extent that it was not really considered a war at all. But a war it was; thousands died over the period 1945–1991 as the superpowers fought for supremacy, often by proxy, in Korea, Vietnam, Afghanistan, Angola and the Horn of Africa. Oppression also accounted for many lives in the uprisings in Czechoslovakia, Hungary, Poland, Lithuania, Latvia and those trying to cross the Berlin Wall. The period was punctuated by an arms race which pushed the world to the edge of destruction, as both East and West amassed arsenals of nuclear weapons far beyond what would be needed to destroy, quite literally, everything. So what part did Britain play in all this?

Britain had come out of the Second World War a broken country, the Empire had been signed away and most of the financial reserves spent on equipment that was now redundant; the only consolation was that it had been on the winning side, part of the 'big three'. By the mid-1950s, Britain had become more entrenched in the NATO alliance, but the obsession with 'the bomb' meant that it was running up a huge debt in an attempt to stay at the world top table. The Cold War from the United Kingdom's point of view can be seen as a two-sided story, one of 'Protect' and 'Survive', to use the title of the famous public information leaflet from the late 1970s. In this book, international events are used as a backdrop for each chapter, demonstrating that the British Cold War was almost totally driven by reaction to external situations.

Protect

The story of how the Government went about protecting the United Kingdom from Soviet attack encompasses some of the most monumental periods of defence design. The development of radar was taken to new heights, as was the development of aircraft and submarines, but it was never a smooth ride. Many projects fell by the wayside or were out of date before they were finished; the Rotor project from the 1950s or the Blue Streak missile stand as testament to that. But there were successes, the V-force and Bloodhound missile for instance. The first part of this book will consider the defence story of Britain's Cold War, looking at the development of the independent deterrent, radar, including Airborne Early Warning and the Ballistic Missile Early Warning System at RAF Fylingdales. A little-explored subject, chemical and biological warfare, is also investigated, but this and other defence-related subjects are still difficult to research due to information restrictions. American involvement also drove certain aspects of Britain's Cold War, the most controversial being the locating of nuclear forces such as Thor missiles, B-47 and later F-111 bombers, and ground-launched Cruise missiles at Greenham Common and Molesworth. Popularly a period of spies and subversion, one aspect of the Government's 'dirty-tricks' department, GCHQ, will also be discussed here.

Survive

How was the British population prepared for nuclear war? Early in the conflict it was recognised that public involvement would be essential if anyone was to survive a nuclear exchange; Civil Defence and the Royal Observer Corps were both manifestations of this. However, when in 1952 the world went thermonuclear, the futility of civil protection on a large scale became apparent and was steadily run down and by the 1970s it was clear the population would be left to their own devices. The story of the Government's own survival was in stark contrast to this and included some of the most spectacularly protected structures in the Western world. Unfortunately the plans for reinstating water, gas and electricity were less well thought out, comprising a collection of *ad hoc* directives that would have clearly collapsed in the first instance. The second part of this book is dedicated to exploring the organisations and directives that were intended to ensure our survival after the nuclear holocaust. Using contemporary documentation it has become increasingly apparent that even the best-laid plans have flaws, and with regards to the British population they were rather large ones.

Code Names

Defence, by its very nature is a closed, secretive world. Research and development is at the core of that world and accordingly often has the highest security classification. However, in the past it has been possible to deduce what type of project is under way by the project code given. This was especially the case with radar throughout the Second World War, when Professor R.V. Jones, part of British Scientific Intelligence, deduced many German programmes using the code name. After the war the Ministry of Supply devised a system that came to be known as the 'Rainbow Codes' to cover the precise details of the many defence projects then under way. The two-unit code comprised a colour followed by a noun, neither relating to the project in any way.

Other countries used a multitude of code types for projects and tests, some of which did give the game away. For instance the two American nuclear shots, carried out at Eniwetok Atoll in late 1952, gave more than a hint of what was to come. Known as the Ivy series, the first, Ivy King, was a kiloton yield weapon whilst Ivy Mike became the world's first megaton range device. British codes, however, were somewhat more obscure. Radar projects alone demonstrate the bewildering array of permutations available: Blue Joker, Green Garlic, Indigo Corkscrew, Orange Poodle and Yellow River, to name but a few. By the 1960s this method had been replaced, as indeed had the Ministry for Supply, with a two-letter three-number system, such as WE-177, the free-fall nuclear bomb, or JP-233, the runway denial package developed for Tornado.

Iron Curtain

At the end of the Second World War Germany was divided into four military zones controlled by America, Britain, France and the Soviet Union. Berlin was also partitioned in a similar way giving the 'big four' control of the German capital. This had been partially agreed at Yalta, on the Black Sea, in February 1945, and finalised at Potsdam in July that same year. But this outwardly apparent agreement was built on shaky ground, with issues throughout the late 1930s and war years setting up a political climate of mistrust and resentment between East and West, a climate that would prevail until the Soviet Union dissolved in 1991.

The Soviet Union had signed a non-aggression pact with Germany prior to the invasion of Poland and actively participated in the annexation of Latvia, Estonia and Lithuania. As the German Army marched into Poland in 1939 Stalin's troops entered from the east, taking territory up to the Brest–Litovsk treaty line. This boundary had been set by agreement between Germany and Russia in late 1917, as the Bolsheviks pulled what was left of their army out of the First World War. Now Poland was removed from the map as it was absorbed into the Empires of the two unlikely bedfellows. When, in 1941, the German Army invaded Russia, an uneasy alliance was forged between West and East in the fight against Fascism. By the end of the conflict a new world order had emerged, one dominated by the two 'superpowers'. As the process of rebuilding Europe gathered pace the old political systems gave way to more liberal and unrestrictive governments, spurred on mainly by the champion of democracy – America. However, Stalin had other plans and pursued a policy of subversion, hampering any chance of democratic government in the countries he had 'liberated'.

It became increasingly clear through 1946 that the Soviet Union intended to keep control of as much of Europe as it could. Stalin had, from 1942, demanded the Anglo–America alliance open a second front to ease pressure on the Red Army; this did not happen until D-Day in June 1944. Moscow considered this as an attempt to weaken the Soviets for possible attack once Germany had been defeated. Now with most of Eastern Europe under Soviet control Stalin had a buffer in place that protected the Russian borders. The main problem was that Europe's traditional political drivers, France, Germany, Italy and to a lesser extent Britain, had collapsed, creating a power vacuum. Even with tens of thousands of American troops in Europe the chance of force being used to remove Soviet troops was unlikely, especially since any fight would not be on Russian soil.

Poland now signalled the problems that were to come. The Red Army had installed a communist administration in Lublin in 1944, intending to run the country on a pro-Soviet footing after the war. This was in direct opposition to the requests by the Polish Government in Exile for autonomy. Moscow's intentions became clear when, in August 1944, the Warsaw uprising saw Freedom Fighters and the Resistance fight for two months with the German Army, the Red Army refusing to advance in support of the Poles and the uprising being crushed, removing the majority of groups who would oppose Soviet rule. By the end of the Second World War Czechoslovakia, Rumania, Hungary, Albania, Bulgaria and Yugoslavia along with the Baltic States, Poland and parts of Germany were under the influence of communist-orientated groups, the majority directly influenced by Moscow. Britain had entered the conflict in 1939 to stop Central Europe being dominated by one power; after the collapse of the Third Reich the Soviet Union did just that.

The withdrawal of American troops from Europe, intended to be complete by 1947, now started to cause alarm. Churchill considered, rightly, that Britain and indeed Western Europe now faced a new enemy. In a telegram on 12 May 1945 he warned Truman of the problems now facing the post-war Continent. This was the first time Churchill was to use the 'Iron Curtain' phrase, suggesting Moscow could very well be deciding the fate of Europe behind it. The following year at a lecture at Fulton in Missouri Churchill exposed the danger publicly:

'From Stettin in the Baltic to Trieste in the Adriatic an iron curtain has descended across the Continent. Behind that line lie all the capitals of the ancient states of Central and Eastern Europe. Warsaw, Berlin, Prague, Vienna, Budapest, Belgrade, Bucharest and Sofia; all these famous cities and the populations around them lie in what I must call the Soviet sphere, and all are subject, in one form or another, not only to Soviet influence but to a very high and in some cases increasing measure of control from Moscow.'

Winston Churchill, 5 March 1946.

Many thought Churchill, by now out of office, was over-exaggerating the situation, but events throughout 1947 were to indicate otherwise.

Britain had, since 1944, been attempting to defeat a communist guerrilla uprising against the Greek royalist government. Also, India and Palestine were exerting large financial penalties on the Government's already poor reserves. By early 1947 Britain admitted to Washington it could no longer maintain its imperial position, the money was just not there. On 12 March Truman went before Congress and demanded financial support for Greece and Turkey, citing a major communist advance in the Mediterranean if both countries were left to their own devices. By the end of the year this had become the 'Marshall Plan', encompassing many other bankrupt European countries. Throughout 1947 Moscow reaffirmed its grip on the 'liberated' Eastern European states. Rather than demobilise troops and remove equipment from the occupied countries, Stalin now set about installing communist governments committed to Moscow, turning many into police states and aligning economic policies and reform with those of Russia. The rest of the world could only speculate at the motives, but many considered them to be a prelude to Russian advancement into the rest of Europe. By the end of the year Churchill's Iron Curtain was almost impenetrable. The Cold War had arrived.

Protect *v.t.* Keep Safe, defend, guard, (person or thing from or against danger, injury, etc.). *Oxford Dictionary*

one

The Bomb

From the end of the Second World War Britain embarked on a number of expensive defence projects, but none were as technically difficult or controversial as the production of nuclear weapons. This came at a time when the country was bankrupt and the United States was embarking on a policy of 'non-proliferation', so why did it happen? It would appear that Britain's obsession with the 'bomb' had everything to do with world power status, something that was dwindling away as the Empire slowly disintegrated. To gain membership to the nuclear club a number of highly complicated obstacles had to be jumped, made all the more difficult for Britain since there was no help from across the Atlantic. However, these obstacles were cleared and Britain developed both a fission and fusion capability by 1957, becoming the third country to do so. This chapter will follow those political events that forced independent development of both warheads and describe the weapons in which they were employed. Also described are the delivery systems the British jointly operated or purchased from America.

Trinity

On 16 July 1945 the world entered a new and dangerous age, the testing of the first atomic device, Trinity. The Los Alamos team, headed by General Leslie Richard Groves and scientist Robert Oppenheimer, provided the United States with the power of life or death over any chosen city. Churchill was consulted on the possible use of the weapon as had been agreed at the 1943 Quebec Conference and on 4 July he gave it his formal blessing. At the Potsdam Conference, in Berlin, following the afternoon meeting on 24 July, Truman explained to Stalin and Molotov that the Americans were in possession of a new and powerful explosive. Stalin was unimpressed, suggesting it be used as soon as possible, convincing Truman that the USSR did not fully comprehend the situation; nothing could have been further from the truth.

The Soviet Union had pledged to declare war on Japan on 15 August 1945, and whilst it was recognised this would speed up capitulation, it would also complicate post-war sovereignty issues. The Russians had already reneged on agreements made regarding the future of Poland and the Baltic States, and a major Soviet influence in Japan would be an unacceptable price to pay for their involvement. Moreover, an American invasion of the Japanese mainland had been scheduled for 1 November 1945, but casualty estimates ranged from 40,000 to one million men; this too was clearly unacceptable. With the bomb America now had the power to finish Japan before Stalin advanced too far and without major loss of Allied life. Truman had only one option, however distasteful – use of the atomic weapon was authorised.

On 6 August, 'Little Boy' razed the town of Hiroshima to the ground. The explosion, at around 600m and with the force of 13,000 tonnes of TNT, killed an estimated 100,000 civilians immediately; many more thousands would die in the ensuing months and years from the effects of radiation poisoning. Just two days later Stalin declared war on Japan and invaded Manchuria, conscious that Hiroshima could well signal the end of hostilities and his aspirations for a foothold in the Pacific. On 9 August 'Fat Man' was released over Nagasaki adding another 80,000 dead and injuring at least 60,000. Convinced there was no defence against this deadly new weapon, the Emperor of Japan indicated his intention to surrender on the 10 August and terms were signed four days later.

During the Potsdam Conference Churchill was voted out of office, being replaced by Clement Attlee. Difficulties for the British were now on the horizon. The former American President, Roosevelt, had agreed to collaborate with Great Britain on a number of projects, including nuclear weapons. Unfortunately this had been a verbal arrangement with Churchill. Now both men were gone and with them, as far as Washington was concerned, went any secret wartime agreement, especially those that had not passed before Congress or the Department of State.

The Manhattan Project had been shrouded in secrecy. Yet this had not stopped security breaches and in 1946 a major Russian spy was uncovered, Alan Nunn May; unfortunately he was a British scientist, and he would not be the last. It transpired that Stalin had received practically all the information needed to start his own programme a clear month before the Trinity detonation. The discovery of espionage so close to the United States nuclear project was to damage British chances of information and co-operation throughout the late 1940s and early '50s.

Many in Truman's administration displayed open contempt for what they considered to be shoddy security services, pointing the finger at MI5 and MI6, but spies were not the end of the story. By 1 August 1946 Britain had been sidelined by the McMahon Act, which placed nuclear development under the control of the Joint Atomic Energy Committees. More importantly for the British the McMahon Act halted all co-operation and information exchanges; the door had been firmly closed in Britain's face.

As American weapon production increased, more demand was placed on the limited natural resources available, especially uranium. One of the major producers was the Belgian Congo, and Britain's access to this resource was politically better than that of the Americans; the Joint Atomic Energy Committees (JAEC) were outraged. After denying the British programme any help it now looked like America would now have to rely on them for natural uranium ore. And if this wasn't bad enough the British had one more hurdle for the Americans to clear. They held a veto over using atomic weapons against foreign countries. This had been agreed between Churchill and Roosevelt in 1943, becoming known as the Quebec Agreement, and effectively allowed one country the right to veto the other using atomic weapons. Again the JAEC had no idea such an agreement existed as it had not passed through Congress. Now it seemed America would also need permission to use her weapons; clearly Washington needed to act.

The problems with uranium would be hard to address but the Quebec Agreement, an unratified treaty between past leaders, was much easier to deal with. Washington decided that a technology package built within the Marshall Plan should include the resumption of co-operation between the two countries, as long as Britain gave up its veto. Britain readily agreed to the package but in the event received little information, and certainly none that would help the weapons programme. On 29 August 1949 the Soviet Union successfully detonated its first atomic device a clear two years before Western predictions. Politicians in the West started talking again; clearly Britain now warranted help if it was to make a stance against perceived Russian aggression. But this was not to be, as the talks collapsed dramatically when in February 1950 Klaus Fuchs, a scientist who had worked on the Manhattan and other nuclear projects, was exposed as a Russian spy. America's security suspicions were confirmed: how could any sensitive material be shared if it could be passed straight to Soviet controllers? The talks were shelved indefinitely. Britain would now have to develop its own weapon if the world position it so coveted was to be maintained.

British Genesis

The architect of the British nuclear programme was undoubtedly William, later Lord, Penney. Penney was part of the British Mission at Los Alamos and had been a lynchpin in the development of the first atomic devices. It has been internationally recognised that the British team shaved almost a year off the programme. On returning to the United Kingdom Penney was invited to design a British atomic bomb programme, being appointed Chief Superintendent Armament Research in 1946. Sites at Harwell under Dr John Cockcroft and Risley under Christopher Hinton were opened late that year. January 1947 saw the British Government authorise the development of the first nuclear weapon and in June of that year the design process started at Fort Halstead under the direction of Penney. The department was given the title High Explosive Research (HER). However, it was soon clear that Fort Halstead was not the ideal site for developing the weapons programme and in 1950 the former RAF airfield at Aldermaston was selected to house the new HER laboratories. In 1952 it was officially named the Atomic Weapons Research Establishment (AWRE).

By the beginning of 1952 Britain was looking for somewhere to test the first nuclear device, and an American test range seemed the obvious choice. But representations to Washington requesting the use of a Pacific test site fell on deaf ears. The administration rejected the idea, and certainly didn't put the request before Congress for fear of a riot; the Fuchs affair was still fresh in the mind of many. However, the

Hurricane, Britain's first atomic detonation. (© Crown Copyright)

Australians were far more receptive and allowed the use of one of the Monte Bello islands, starting a long association with Australia and the British nuclear weapons programme. Penney remarked at the time, 'If the Australians are not willing to let us do further trials in Australia, I do not know where we would go'; luckily this was not to be. The first test was a logistical nightmare, optimistically scheduled for October 1952. Some of the major contractors were having major difficulties producing equipment to such a tight schedule. The high explosives needed for the compression system were being produced by the Woolwich Arsenal and would be ready on time. But problems were being experienced producing enough plutonium to mould the test device's core. The Windscale site in Cumbria had been built specifically to produce weapons-grade plutonium, its two reactors going critical in 1951, but this left little time to produce the required amount of material for the test shot.

The device minus its plutonium core was loaded into a redundant River Class frigate, HMS *Plym*, and shipped under escort to the test site in June 1952. Windscale managed to produce just enough plutonium to be shaped and the core was flown out to the test site with a day to spare. HMS *Plym* was moored in Main Bay close to Trimouille Island where the plutonium core was fitted to the device; operation Hurricane was ready. At 9.30 a.m. local time Britain stepped onto the nuclear stage.

Super

As the development of the fission weapons moved on apace throughout the 1940s, a group of American scientists were also considering the conclusions of an Englishman, Geoffrey Atkinson, working in Gottingen in 1927. He had theorised that solar energy could be created through the fusion of light-weight atoms. By the mid-1930s isotopes of deuterium or tritium appeared to be likely candidates. This work was not wasted on members of the Los Alamos team and by 1942 Edward Teller was considering the possibility of making the theory work; the difference was he would eventually attract the financial backing of the United States Government. Initially the concept of the fusion device had been dismissed as too complicated and expensive, especially since to trigger such a bomb successfully required an extremely efficient detonator. But the USSR's successful detonation of an atom bomb on 29 August 1949 set the ball rolling for development of the 'Super', a thermonuclear device.

Things didn't run smoothly at first. Requests by both Congress and the Military as to how long it would take to develop such a weapon were met with dismay by the majority of the scientific community. Practicalities suggested that the size of such a weapon would make it undeliverable. Also, tests were now being conducted with high-yield fission devices, around 500kt, which would more than do the job if used. Further, Rabi and Fermi, part of the lead A-bomb team, suggested such a weapon 'was wrong on fundamental ethical principles'. Truman, however, was swung by the argument that the Russians would develop a thermonuclear device and Washington could not stand back and allow them to take the lead. A Soviet development programme was a certainty, not least because Klaus Fuchs, the spy at the centre of the A-bomb, had also worked for a time in 1946 with fusion theory. On 31 January 1950 Truman, after a ten-minute meeting with advocates of the device, approved the development of the thermonuclear weapon.

Physicist Teller and mathematician Stanislaw Ulam soon came up with the idea of a primary and secondary charge, basically an A-bomb to set off an H-bomb. By 1951 Teller had devised the 'sparkplug', the ultra-efficient burn of nuclear material had been discovered. Put simply, a cylindrical mass of thermonuclear material, deuterium, has a sub-critical stick positioned down the centre. The shockwave from the primary detonation then converges on the centre of the cylindrical mass. As it reaches the centre the wave decelerates, creating heat. This turns the plutonium stick super-critical, causing it to explode and forcing a shock wave outwards, pushing against the implosion. Equilibrium between both waves, if reached within the deuterium fuel, would cause a megaton-yield explosion. Radiation implosion had been discovered and the stage was now set for a new period of test and development. It would take the British team four long years to reach this stage.

Testing of the first megaton-yield thermonuclear device proved to be a logistical nightmare. The secondary device was to contain liquid deuterium with a boiling point of 23.5 Kelvin and to stop it vaporising prematurely a large cryogenic plant had to be built. The final device weighed in at 82 tonnes and was housed, along with the cooling plant and other test equipment in a four-story-high 'shot house', which could have been quite easily used to park aircraft. Over 500 monitoring stations were established and around 11,000 personnel had to be billeted for the duration of the tests. On 1 November 1952 at 07:14 'Ivy Mike' detonated with a yield of 10.4 megatons. The small island of Elugelab at Eniwetok Atoll, part of the Marshall Islands, was replaced by a mile-wide crater 200ft deep. The Soviet Union tested an air-deliverable weapon just nine months later and by 1955 both sides had true thermonuclear devices. Churchill was later prompted to describe the situation as the 'delicate balance of terror'.

Grapple

All Britain could do as both superpowers ran to the thermonuclear finish line was spectate; clearly if it was to remain a major player on the world stage something would have to be done. In 1954 it was decided that once again Britain would have to go it alone, developing a totally indigenous hydrogen bomb. Many in the Government had mixed feelings, but this did not deter Churchill from approving the plan, even at a projected cost of £10 million. Ironically this was ultimately to lead to closer ties with the United States, form the backbone of the 1957 Defence White Paper, which was so detrimental to British Air Defence, and see the formation of the Campaign for Nuclear Disarmament.

The Grapple series of atmospheric tests, between 1957 and 1958, at Christmas Island and Malden Island in the Pacific, ushered the United Kingdom into the thermonuclear age. However, more importantly they were used to demonstrate Britain's capability to the world before an expected moratorium on atmospheric

The nuclear stores at Upper Heyford. Special weapons were stored here from the 1950s through to the signing of the INF treaty in 1988.

tests came into force. The first of a number of two-stage designs, 'Short Granite' was dropped by Vickers Valiant XD818, piloted by Wing Commander Ken Hubbard, on 15 May 1957 at Malden. The device, carried in a Blue Danube aerodynamic fairing, achieved a yield of around 300kt, well below the intended 1-megaton yield for one ton in weight; but the concept had been proven, and development continued. Incidentally, Valiant XD818 is now the only surviving complete example of its type and currently resides at the Royal Air Force Museum, Hendon.

By October 1957 the build-up for additional tests at Christmas Island were well under way. Equipment for the new shot 'Grapple X' was being flown out in a number of chartered Australian aircraft, whilst personnel were flown, this time on the newly acquired de Havilland Comet, out to Edinburgh Field, just outside Adelaide, before being ferried to Christmas Island in rather older Hastings transports. On 28 October an instrumented inert bomb was dropped over the island as part of a full scientific rehearsal. Weather delays put the live drop back three days, but on 8 November 1957 Grapple X got the green light. At 8:45 Valiant XD824, piloted by Squadron Leader B. Millet, dropped Britain's first true thermonuclear device, achieving a yield of 1.8 megatons. By April 1958, the largest ever British test, 'Grapple Y', achieved a yield of 3 megatons. America started to take notice.

Moratorium and Membership

Whilst the technological prowess of the United States, Soviet Union and, later, United Kingdom became self evident there were many who considered the escalation of nuclear testing to be just as dangerous as the weapons themselves. As early as 1954 the effects of fallout were overtaking the test debate, especially as massive amounts of irradiated material was now being introduced into the atmosphere. One salient example was the crew of the Japanese fishing vessel *Lucky Dragon*, caught in the fallout of the 'Bravo' 15-megaton shot. Twenty-three sailors suffered radiation poisoning culminating in the death of one crew member. World opinion was gathering pace as first, Indian Prime Minister Jawaharlal Nehru, closely followed by Pope Pius XII and Albert Einstein, called for a cessation of testing. Rather surprisingly, by 1955 even the Russians were voicing concerns over the amount of testing being carried out. Clearly a test ban at this time was in the Soviet Union's interests. The British, having announced their intention to develop the H-bomb, would need to prove the device before they were accepted as a true world power. If a cessation of atmospheric testing could be pushed through then Britain would be unable to complete the development; especially important since Russia would be the ultimate target of the device. Whilst pressure mounted the tests went on.

1957 proved a turning point in nuclear development and control; forty-two atmospheric tests, including the British 'Grapple' series, were undertaken that year, introducing even more deadly isotopes into the atmosphere. Steadily growing opposition was now being voiced from a scientific as well as moral standpoint, including Albert Schweitzer, the famous doctor and theorist, who warned of the genetic effects to human development of continued testing. In Britain a rising tide of public concern began coagulating into organised demonstrations spurred on by three major events. The 1957 Defence White Paper called for 'massive retaliation' if Britain was attacked and the doctrine sent a shockwave through both Parliament and the public. Britain's newfound thermonuclear position appeared to make the country even more of a target rather than acting as a deterrent. Finally the safety of the nuclear industry was called into question with a major radiation leak from the plutonium plant at Windscale in October. Macmillan covered the leaks up until it was realised that milk over a large area was contaminated, forcing widespread milk bans. The nuclear genie was now well and truly out of the bottle.

The beginning of 1958 saw the formation of the Campaign for Nuclear Disarmament (CND) including the first Easter march to Aldermaston from Trafalgar Square, attended by thousands. A shift in American nuclear policy also allowed the United Kingdom, by mid-1958, to fully support a cessation of tests. The Grapple shots were now complete, ensuring Britain remained at the big table and had the thermonuclear kudos to back it up. But more importantly, Eisenhower, recognising the potential of the United Kingdom's development programme, had amended the 1954 Atomic Energy Act in Britain's favour. Harold Macmillan, heading the Government from January 1957, needed, after his predecessor's disastrous Suez campaign, some form of American support, especially if a new US missile system (discussed later) was to be deployed in Britain. Macmillan recognised that some form of 'appeasement' towards the Americans could do no harm and in the long term Britain would see the benefits. On 3 July 1958 Eisenhower signed the 'Agreement for Co-operation on the uses of Atomic energy for Mutual Defence Purposes' (ACMDP). The door that was so unceremoniously shut by the McMahon Act in 1946 was finally re-opened. Internationally, in October Khrushchev and Eisenhower agreed on an informal moratorium on testing which, of course, Britain would also observe.

Throughout 1959 Washington looked for ways to verify a potential test ban, primarily through inspection teams, but the Kremlin favoured self-regulation. Khrushchev was concerned that American or NATO inspectors 'would have discovered that we were in a relatively weak position, and that realisation might have encouraged them to attack us', he noted later. Khrushchev proposed that any inspection would need a unanimous vote from all signatories, however each would also possess a veto; Eisenhower saw the proposal as unworkable and the discussions stalled. When talks resumed in April 1959 the scope of the proposal had been altered, giving Khrushchev the opportunity to give up the veto. Underground tests were also not included in the proposals, giving all sides the chance to silence opposition on atmospheric testing whilst carrying on with development. Macmillan's support for the ban was vindicated as the ACMDP agreement opened up the Nevada nuclear test site to Britain, and by 1962 tests for a new air-deliverable bomb, ultimately to become the WE-77 series, were under way at the facility.

Paris

In February 1960 the nuclear club gained another member when the French conducted its first shot in Algeria. Ironically, it was proposed to sign the Test Ban Treaty at the Paris summit in May that year, but with agreement within reach, the talks dramatically collapsed before they had even started. On the most hallowed day in the Soviet calendar an American CIA-operated U-2 aircraft took off from Pakistan on a reconnaissance mission. Unfortunately for the pilot, Francis Gary Powers, and the outgoing Eisenhower, the aircraft suffered a technical malfunction forcing Powers to fly lower than normal. A surface-to-air missile battery shot the U-2 down. After initially denying the flight, Eisenhower was forced to admit American responsibility. No apology was forthcoming so Khrushchev abandoned the Paris summit.

Testing now resumed. On 30 October 1961 the Soviet Union detonated the world's biggest weapon; at 58 megatons the atmospheric burst was the equivalent of all the ordnance used in the Second World War. Sabre rattling now started apace. Concern over the tests grew around the world, as it was determined that the continued test shots were releasing strontium-90 into the environment. Scientists from the newly formed pressure group 'Physicians for Social Responsibility' documented the element in the teeth of children across the world. And if this wasn't enough, a new and more deadly situation was to unfold, which would ultimately heat up the Cold War almost to melting point – Cuba.

The possibility of all out nuclear war over Cuba reached its peak in late October 1962 when it looked increasingly like an American invasion of the island would be undertaken. In the end a naval blockade appeared more favourable, at least giving Kennedy more options; but Khrushchev had authorised the Soviet Commander in Cuba to use tactical nuclear weapons if necessary. On 22 October President Kennedy appeared on national television exposing the threat posed by Soviet missiles in Cuba, the military went to DEFCON 3 and the world held its breath. By Saturday 27 October it was make or break. Luckily an agreement was reached with the Soviets involving the removal of missiles from Cuba, whilst the Americans would remove its Jupiter missiles currently based in Turkey. This would not happen immediately, as America intended to save face, and the arrangement was kept secret for many years.

All sides were visibly shaken by the ordeal and unsurprisingly negotiators were back at the table by June 1963, at the invitation of Khrushchev. Agreement was finally reached that year and the 'Treaty Banning Nuclear Weapon Tests in the Atmosphere, Outer Space and Under Water' was signed in Moscow on 5 August. This agreement was more involved with the proliferation of weapons than trying to completely ban them as Britain, America and Russia already had all the information they needed to develop their arsenals. Also the ACMDP agreement of 1958 between Britain and America had given British scientists the opportunity to exchange information with their US counterparts. Warheads under development would, from now on, be carried out below ground at the Nevada site; Britain's last test, 'Bristol', culminated twenty-five shots over a twenty-nine-year period.

Gravity Weapons

The British nuclear development programme produced two fission devices that were capable of being air delivered, Blue Danube and Red Beard, the latter being a 'true' weapon. Blue Danube gave Britain the credibility of being a nuclear power with a deliverable, if cumbersome, device. However, Red Beard allowed Britain to achieve global status, deploying the weapon with both the Royal Air Force and Royal Navy. Two fusion bombs were built in the late 1950s, Violet Club and Yellow Sun, replacing the two fission devices with the Royal Air Force, but the Navy arsenal continued with Red Beard until its eventual replacement in 1972 by the WE-177. This compact free-fall weapon continued in service with both the RN and RAF until well after the Cold War. Free-fall bombs are unpowered devices delivered by air and, in the case of nuclear weapons, have a retarding system, such as a small parachute, slowing the bomb's decent and allowing the aircraft time to escape the resultant blast.

Blue Danube

Blue Danube was Britain's first operational nuclear weapon, coming into service in 1953. It carried a physics package very similar to that used in Operation Hurricane with a nominal 10-kiloton yield utilising an implosion device. Once placed within an aerodynamic fairing the free-fall bomb was 7.5m long, 1.5m in diameter and weighed just over 4,500kg. In fact the weapon was so big that retractable tail fins were fitted so that the Vickers Valiant had ground clearance for take-off. Once the bomb had cleared the aircraft the fins were extended by a pressurised gas system, mounted in the tail fairing. A number of other devices were also carried on board, designed for any eventuality, and all pushing the weight and size of the device up. A parachute retardation system allowed the drop aircraft time to vacate the area. Detonation was initiated through a radar-operated height trigger but it also carried a barostatic and timer mechanism in case of radar jamming or failure. As a last resort the device could be detonated on impact by a series of inertia switches. As an additional safety measure the plutonium/u-235 core was only inserted into the physics package during flight, primarily in case of crashing during take-off.

    With the introduction of the new weapon came issues with storage and maintenance. Nuclear warheads are complex and require almost constant monitoring if they are to remain serviceable and effective. Storage facilities were built at two existing sites, Faldingworth, Lincolnshire and Barnham, Suffolk, to maintain Blue Danube and act as distribution centres in times of crisis. As the all-up weight of the bomber fleet increased, due to weapons, fuel and the introduction of the 'V' force, runways now had to be capable of carrying an aircraft weighing up to 90 tonnes. Upgrades to ten existing airfields were also carried out providing 'Class 1' bomber bases with runways up to 2,700m long and 60m wide for the new nuclear force. From 1958 a network of dispersal sites was also developed; aircraft would be fully armed and then dispersed around the country, moving them away from what were considered to be 'prime target' airfields. These included Boscombe Down, Leeming, Filton and Ballykelly.

    Drops were carried out with dummy Blue Danubes at AWRE Orfordness, establishing the ballistic capabilities of the weapon. Naturally, this was not without its problems. The very first test drop from a modified Valiant refused to release from the bomb rack, the bomb bay doors were closed and the aircraft returned to base. On arrival the bay doors were opened for the 'after flight' inspection whereupon the

The V-Force. Victor, Valiant and Vulcan, Britain's independent deterrent.

bomb promptly fell out onto the concrete! Luckily this casing was full of ballast, but a live Blue Danube complete with inertia switches may not have been so forgiving. Any live bomb-release problems from then on necessitated ditching the aircraft. The first operational test drop was delivered by a Valiant on 11 October 1956 as part of Operation Buffalo at Maralinga, Western Australia, with a nominal yield of 3 kilotons. Blue Danube was not built in large quantities and, whilst giving Britain its own capability, should be seen as more of a development vehicle for future research. It was withdrawn from service in 1962, being replaced by the more compact, lighter, Red Beard.

Red Beard

Whilst still a free-fall weapon, Red Beard was far more versatile than its predecessor. The detonation concept was very similar to Blue Danube, but the introduction of a far more effective implosion device allowed for a smaller physics package. This improvement allowed the outer fairing to be scaled down to a more conventional size, 3.3m long, 90cm in diameter and weighing 907kg. The tactical advantages were obvious. Here was a bomb that could be carried by a number of current aircraft types including, for the first time, those of the Royal Navy (RN).

One of the major issues surrounding nuclear weapon deployment had been how to operate from British bases around the world without upsetting the country concerned. Now Red Beard came into its own, it was possible to have a truly global capability without the bomb having to be stored for any length of time on foreign soil, especially after 1959 when the Royal Navy had started to take delivery of the device. Red Beard was carried on a wide range of aircraft types including the Scimitar, Sea Vixen and Buccaneer with the RN, whilst the 'V' force and Canberra were used in the RAF. This was a true tactical weapon. Interestingly, a Controller Air Clearance document issued in 1960 specifically notes that the Scimitar should only carry nuclear weapons in '…extreme operational emergencies…'. Considering its track record (over half of the Supermarine Scimitars crashed whilst in service), this was probably a wise move.

Violet Club

Violet Club entered service with the Royal Air Force in 1958 as a stop-gap weapon, covering the final development phase of 'Yellow Sun'. The device was basically a Blue Danube ballistic casing with an upgraded physics package. It was not a thermonuclear device in the true sense of the word, having an estimated yield of around 500kt. It appears that only five were produced and these were decommissioned a year later.

Yellow Sun

The aptly named Yellow Sun was Britain's first true thermonuclear device developed for the British deterrent. The weapon had a number of upgrades throughout its time in service, culminating with the Mk II, which had a yield of well over 1 megaton. The aerodynamic fairing measured 6.5m by 1.2m and the whole device weighed 3,175kg. Test results from the Grapple trials provided British scientists with the information on how to produce an extremely efficient implosion device and by Yellow Sun Mk II the physics package had been drastically reduced in size; the fairing, however,

Yellow Sun, Britain's first true thermonuclear weapon. (Courtesy Royal Air Force Museum, Hendon)

WE-177, the longest serving British design, in service from 1963 to 1998. This weapon was used by both the Royal Navy and Royal Air Force.

was retained. By 1958 the fruits of the new US–UK agreement on information sharing allowed the British team to reduce the package size yet again, assembling a warhead very similar to the American W-28, known as Red Snow. The series were on charge from 1959 until their replacement with the much smaller WE-177 series starting in 1972.

WE-177 Series

The WE-177 was Britain's longest serving nuclear weapon; the free-fall bomb saw service with both the Royal Air Force and Royal Navy. Requirements were first explored during the late 1950s for a versatile lightweight bomb that could be carried on the new proposed generation of aircraft, primarily the Tactical Strike Reconnaissance aircraft, TSR2. Trials of the warhead design were carried out at the Nevada test range in March 1962 under the code name Pampas, forced underground by the imminent Test Ban Treaty, finally signed in 1963. The ballistic casing of the WE-177 was not too dissimilar from the current conventional 500lb iron bomb still in use today.

Construction of the weapon fell to a number of well-proven defence manufacturers and departments. Hunting Engineering became the design authority for the ballistic casing, whilst the AWRE developed and tested the warhead. Other major components were developed and built at the Royal Ordnance Factories in Cardiff, Burghfield and Chorley whilst testing was undertaken at RAE Farnborough and RERDE Fort Halstead, the birthplace of the atomic weapons programme. Three variants

TSR-2. This aircraft was to be the mainstay of the nuclear force, carrying WE-177 free-fall bombs and possibly air-launched Blue Water missiles. (Courtesy Pete James)

were produced, 'A' in 1963, 'B' in 1965 and 'C' 1972. Specific information about the weapons' performance is still classified; however, two warheads are identifiable. The fission, or single-stage version, of the WE-177 was 2.8m long, just over 40cm in diameter and weighed 270kg. The fusion type was 3.3m long and weighed 430kg, these increases were to facilitate the thermonuclear physics package. It is a sobering thought that WE-177 was only a tenth of the size of Blue Danube but had ten times the destructive power.

Deployment

The intended carrier for WE-177, TSR2 was cancelled in April 1965 as part of swathing defence cuts recommended by the Labour Government, but deployment went ahead and the weapon saw long service with both the Navy and RAF. The Navy replaced its stockpile of Red Beards throughout 1970–1971 with Type 'A' single-stage WE-177. The small size of the weapon allowed WE-177 to be carried on many more surface vessels, extending the tactical strike and depth-charge capability to many more theatres. It has been suggested that HMS *Sheffield* was carrying the depth-charge low-yield version of WE-177 during the Falklands campaign in 1982. Naturally the MOD refused at the time to confirm or deny this, yet a salvage operation was carried out on the *Sheffield* soon afterwards to recover 'sensitive material'. Clearly something was worth the effort.

WE-177 was deployed internationally in Cyprus, Germany and the Far East as well as being ship-borne, which naturally caused much debate and consternation, as many governments did not like the idea of playing host to Royal Navy ships that could be carrying nuclear weapons. A large number of British aircraft carried WE-177 including the Vulcan, Buccaneer, Jaguar, Sea Harrier, Sea King and Tornado from 1966 until 1995. The final weapon was decommissioned at AWE Burghfield in March 1998. Interestingly, since the end of the Cold War the WE-177 has become the most prolific nuclear weapon on display to the public; examples can be seen at the majority of the aircraft museums around the country.

Mobile Surface-to-Surface Systems

The British army operated a number of nuclear-capable tactical battlefield weapons throughout the Cold War. The majority were American-produced systems and warheads operated under the dual key arrangement. British designers struggled throughout the 1950s to develop a home-grown surface-to-surface system, including Blue Water, but in the face of rising costs these were cancelled in favour of the American proven, although often inferior, designs. Surface-to-surface weapons are those fired from a ground base and are intended to hit another ground site some distance away.

Blue Water

In the mid-1950s English-Electric, later to become part of BAC, undertook a development project contracted by the Ministry of Supply to develop a mobile surface-to-surface guided missile for the army. Project Blue Water involved considerable inward investment by the company, culminating in the building of a new plant at Stevenage and a substantial increase in the workforce. The missile was designed to be air transportable and fully mobile on the battlefield, carried by a Bedford three-ton truck, which also contained the launcher. The initial trials suggested the missile was underpowered and in 1959 the Ministry of Supply lodged a new contract for a solid fuel motor with Bristol Aerojet (BAJ). The final development version had a range of 80km carrying a version of the Red Beard warhead and was even considered as an air-launched missile for the TSR2; but the project was cancelled in 1962 in favour of the American-designed system Honest John.

Corporal

The MSM-5 Corporal was Short Range Ballistic Missile (SRBM) developed from an earlier sounding rocket programme built by the Douglas Aircraft Company. The system was further developed by JPL/Firestone with the first test firing in 1952 and the missile entered service with the US Military in 1954. The system had the capability to deliver a 60kt fission warhead over 120km. Corporal was guided through a ground station with updates being passed to the missile during flight, but the major problem with this being the possibility of jamming the signal. Future updates made the missile a fire-and-forget system, increasing the effectiveness by an estimated 50 per cent. Corporal entered service with the British Army on the Rhine (BAOR) as part of the 47th guided Weapons Regiment Royal Artillery from 1957 after a two-year evaluation at Larkhill, based at the Napier Barracks, Dortmund. In 1964 this was changed to the 47th Missile Regiment.

Honest John

Honest John was a stored liquid-fuel tactical ballistic missile developed and built by the Douglas Aircraft Company. It was the first of a long line of unguided, spin-stabilised missiles that were developed for the US Army. The first tests were undertaken at the Redstone Arsenal in 1951 and the system was deployed to Europe with the US Army in 1954. The missile was transported in three parts, casing, fins and warhead, and assembled prior to launch, striking targets at a maximum range of 25km. Honest John saw service with 24th and 50th Missile Regiment Royal Artillery (Msl RA) in Germany with the British Army on the Rhine (BAOR) as part of the NATO commitment, and occasionally on the mainland. The system was removed from service in 1975.

Lance

Lance was a surface-to-surface missile system capable of carrying conventional, chemical and nuclear warheads. Developed from 1962 by the Vought Corporation, the first successful test launch was conducted in 1965. Lance replaced Honest John in service with a number of European armies and by 1972 it was sanctioned to carry a nuclear warhead. After a long period of evaluation, 1966–1975, Lance was commissioned to replace the British-operated Honest John. Throughout 1976 the 50th and 24th Msl RA were supplied with the missile system along with all support equipment, including the M752 launcher and M432 command vehicle. In 1977 the two missile regiments were amalgamated to become the 50th Msl RA based at Northumberland Barracks, Menden in Germany. The 6.15m-long missile had a 10–110km tactical range. The British-held version carried telemetry testing equipment and the nuclear warhead that was run on the dual-key system. As Lance was a mobile unit members of the 69th US Army Field Artillery were attached to each deployed weapon, unlocking the warhead prior to launch. By the end of the Cold War Lance was the only land-based system employed by NATO in Europe. Lance was replaced by the Multi Launch Rocket System (MLRS) in the early 1990s, by which time the nuclear capability of the army had been removed. The 50th Msl RA was disbanded in 1993.

Other Army Ordnance

The British Army operated a number of unusual nuclear weapons throughout the Cold War, two of the most bizarre being the Atomic Howitzer and the nuclear land mine Blue Peacock, although the land mine clearly had very limited use.

The Atomic Howitzer

The British Army employed the Atomic Howitzer, with shells being provided by the Americans who, between 1963 and 1991, produced around 1,000 W48 nuclear artillery shells, before they were finally withdrawn. The yield was very minimal, being around 0.02–0.04kt, presumably the object was to damage troops on the battlefield rather than completely destroy large areas. BAOR was equipped with the M105 Abbot 155mm howitzer up until the last year of the Cold War when it was replaced in 1990 by the AS90 39 calibre self-propelled howitzer; the nuclear capability, however, was retained for another year.

Blue Peacock

Blue Peacock was a prototype atomic demolition mine intended for use with the British Army. The requirements were first suggested in 1954, and by 1955 a series of objectives had been set for this most unusual weapon. Theoretically a well-placed Blue Peacock would cause major devastation to installations and infrastructure, basically scorched earth on a scale as yet unknown, but its most attractive quality was the amount of contamination it would cause, closing off large areas '…for an appreciable time…'. The major problem with the weapon was its size, using a physics package similar to Blue Danube the whole unit had an all-up weight of seven tonnes.

The idea was that the weapon would be transported to a forward position prior to a Soviet invasion where it would be left on the surface, buried or submerged in a lake or canal. After arming the device the army would retire to a safe distance and wait. Triggering the device could be achieved by a number of methods; it could be by landline command from a distance of 5.5km or via an eight-day clockwork timer. However, if the device was discovered a lethal combination of failsafe mechanisms were proposed. Tilt switches were incorporated making it impossible to move, also the hull was pressurised, so if a panel was removed or the device was shot at it would explode after ten seconds. As with all nuclear devices the physics package temperature needed to be kept constant, subsequently it was shielded from the cold by glass-fibre pillows; bizarrely, it was suggested live chickens would also do the job in an emergency!

By 1957 voices in Government were showing concern over the project; the political fallout, stationing such a weapon in Europe, had the potential to be more damaging than the fallout created by the device itself. It would be very difficult to convince other NATO members that irradiating large tracts of their territory in an attempt to stop Warsaw Pact forces reaching Britain was acceptable. With that in mind Blue Peacock was cancelled in February 1958, and must go down as one of Britain's less-credible nuclear developments.

Into the Missile Age

The delivery systems of the late 1940s and early 1950s had one major problem, they were manned flights to the point of target. This left sorties vulnerable to interceptor and missile attack, with the opportunity for success severely limited. Some form of unmanned vehicle was clearly required and the concept of the Intermediate Range (IRBM) and later Intercontinental Ballistic Missile (ICBM) was born. However, missile delivery systems were not a new idea, Germany had used a hydrogen/kerosene powered rocket, the V2, to drop one-ton warheads on Western European cities during the latter stages of the Second World War. Although these weapons did nothing to stem the eventual defeat of Germany, they did demonstrate the potential of ballistic missiles, a potential both East and West were eager to liberate for themselves. Missile systems fall into two broad categories, surface-to-surface and air-to-ground; this section will describe the major systems that Britain developed or considered as part of its nuclear deterrent.

V-2. Britain test fired three V-2s as part of Operation Backfire in October 1945. Many of the scientists involved in Backfire went on to work for the British Government. (Courtesy Royal Air Force Museum, Hendon)

Fixed Surface-to-Surface Systems

Operation Backfire

Britain's ballistic missile programme can be traced back to three test firings of captured V2s at Altenwalde in the British zone of post-war Germany. By the end of the war, over 8,500 engineers, designers, technicians and scientists had been captured, primarily from the sites at Peenemunde and Nordhausen. Both had been liberated by the Americans but ended up in the Russian sector, allowing both major powers access to the advanced ballistic missile programmes. Britain had had prior access to the technology when a V2 crashed in Sweden in late 1944, but it was almost completely destroyed by the impact. British intelligence could only speculate as to how the missile operated but it did indicate the importance of owning such technology in post-war Europe. Thankfully British teams were given the opportunity to salvage equipment from Nordhausen before the Russians took over, but not before the majority had been removed by the Americans and shipped back to the United States.

The first attempted test firing was on 1 October 1945, but was unsuccessful due to a faulty ignition system. A day later the first successful firing of a ballistic missile under British control took place. This was followed on 15 October by the third and final launch, this time in the presence of Russian and American officials. Present as part of the British/German launch team was Walter Dornberger.

Dornberger was one of the main players in the German rocket programme, overseeing most of the development, trials and subsequent deployment of the V2. He surrendered to American troops on 2 May 1945. After the Cuxhaven test firings he was moved to Special Camp 11 at Bridgend, South Wales; the site was used to house ranking officers prior to conviction or repatriation. Much to the Americans' annoyance Dornberger was named as a war criminal by the British for his part in the V2 launches against London and using slave labour in rocket manufacture, charges that were dropped at the beginning of 1946. But the British did not release him from custody until mid-1947, when he promptly emigrated to the United States, eventually to become a leading figure in the Bell Aircraft Company. It is highly probable that the British Government would never have brought charges against Dornberger, it seems more likely that the period of his internment at Bridgend was used to intensively debrief him. Throughout his internment the United States had made frequent applications for his release; it was already clear that America knew how to treat its 'special' prisoners of war. Other, less important, captured German staff were relocated to Britain after the trials, housed at the Rocket Propulsion Department (RPD) at Westcott. These internees received an official grade 'German Scientist' and went on to work alongside the British teams on many defence projects in the 1950s and 1960s.

Thor

Thor was the West's first operational Intermediate Range Ballistic Missile (IRBM). It was intended as a stopgap for the later generation ICBMs, designed to counter the immediate threat Russian missiles posed to Europe and interests in the Far East. The Douglas Aircraft Company became lead contractor on the development project SM-75, later designated PGM-17A. The missile was 20m long, 2.5m in diameter and weighed 4,700kg. The powerplant was a North American single-stage Rocketdyne LR-79 rocket motor, capable of powering the rocket to a speed of over 16,000km/hr. The missile was able to carry a 1.4-megaton, W-49 warhead to a maximum distance of 2,400km, the trajectory and flight path being controlled by an advanced version of the A4/V2 inertial guidance system, ensuring an accuracy of around 3.2km.

Two main reasons brought Thor to the shores of Britain. Long-range or Intercontinental Ballistic Missiles (ICBM) were some way off so America needed launch sites closer to Russia, preferably in Europe. Also the British were behind the Americans in the development of their own nuclear ballistic systems; Blue Streak and Blue Steel would not enter service until 1963, leaving the country vulnerable with only a manned deterrent.

On 15 May 1957 the Soviet Union tested the world's first Intercontinental Ballistic Missile (ICBM), known as the 'mechanism'. Less than six months later, in October, Sputnik caught the world's imagination whilst leaving the Americans looking decidedly second best. The 184lb satellite was nothing more than a radio transmitter with no real military application but it did demonstrate the SS-6 Sanwood launch vehicle as a possible contender for carrying nuclear warheads into space. Russia now had the upper hand.

The Gaither Report, published on 4 November, one month after the launch, predicted a critical threat from ICBMs by 1959. It sounded like the West had no effective way of combating any form of surprise Soviet aggression, leaving a superior American bomber force impotent in a potential first strike. President Eisenhower was pushed by Congress to commit more spending to plug the 'missile gap'. During 1958 he increased spending to the tune of $40 million, mostly directed into the missile programmes for all three services. Interestingly, it would appear that Eisenhower knew the 'gap' was non-existent and America, through effective intelligence gathering, actually had the lead in most aspects, but he chose to keep the true picture to himself. The Thor, Jupiter and Polaris projects all directly benefited from this finance initiative.

The effective range of Thor made deployment in the United States unviable and the United Kingdom became an obvious choice. The systems were offered to other nations, with Italy and Turkey accepting the United States Army-developed system, Jupiter. One major incentive involved nuclear submarine technology, the information for the nuclear propulsion systems was to be made available to interested countries. However, naturally there were conditions, not least that warheads would remain under American control, effectively a double-veto system. France was also approached, however President De Gaulle would not consider dual control, arguing it was inconceivable that France could entertain the stationing of nuclear missiles over which it had no control. This decision ultimately led to the withdrawal of France from NATO. Other countries saw the missile systems as more of a liability than protection, inviting potential Soviet first strikes, and also refused the offer.

For the British Government acceptance of an IRBM system was seen as an opportunity to win back credibility and the patronage of the United States. Suez, the previous year, had damaged the post-war special relationship, distracting eyes away from the Hungarian rising, allowing the Soviets to put it down by military force. At the Bermuda Conference in March 1957 Macmillan agreed to the stationing of the system and by February 1958 a joint government agreement had been signed, allowing for the deployment of sixty missiles across twenty sites; project Emily had begun.

Four main sites, Feltwell, Hemswell, Driffield and North Luffenham were chosen, each of which had four further satellite sites. Twenty reformed squadrons carrying the designation SM (Strategic Missile) each operated three missiles on the stations strategically positioned along the East coast. The missile, support equipment and launcher were supplied by the United States, whilst Britain provided the infrastructure and site support aspects on the bases. Royal Air Force Feltwell, 77 (SM) Squadron, was the first to receive the missile system on 19 September 1959, being delivered by C-124 Globemaster transport aircraft. But it was not until early 1960 that all twenty squadrons were declared operational.

The Thor Sites

All twenty sites were located on existing Ministry land, the four main units on permanent stations, the remaining sixteen on disused wartime airfields. Wherever possible existing infrastructure was used in conjunction with new installations, keeping costs to a minimum. The triple launch pads, which were a common feature, were built

Sixty of the American-designed Thor IRBMs were stationed in Britain between 1958 and 1963. This system covered the gap created by the late running V-force programme.

using existing taxiways and runways, allowing easy access for the missile transports. The missile launch compounds were divided into two, one containing the three pads, the other containing a small workshop for maintenance and checking of the warhead prior to fitting, known as the surveillance and inspection building. Also situated here was a small, two-bay structure known as the classified storage building, which would hold the warheads when removed for missile maintenance. The missile was powered by a liquid-propellant Rocketdyne engine which used a highly explosive, two-part mixture. The constituents, Kerosene and Liquid Oxygen (LOX), were stored at each launch pad, but they were kept separate as LOX has a nasty tendency to explode when it comes into contact with fuels, oils and greases.

Both areas were surrounded by a large double security fence, which was well lit, as were the launch pads, by floodlights. The RAF controlled access into the compound through a main checkpoint whilst the USAF 99th Munitions Maintenance Squadron controlled, via another guard post, the smaller compound. Thor was retired from service in 1963 and all missiles were removed between April and September of that year. Recently English Heritage has surveyed these sites and demonstrated that, after forty years, most have no visible remains of this important, if brief, period of Britain's Cold War history.

Blue Streak

In 1954 the British Government signed an agreement with America to develop a Medium Range Ballistic Missile (MRBM) to complement the Atlas ICBM project. Information was to be shared, allowing the technical innovations of one country to be used by the other. However, due to the McMahon Act, no nuclear information exchanges took place. Even at the project's conception Britain knew this was going to be an expensive venture, but her obsession with the bomb and the information being made available appeared to justify the cost.

Development

The specification for the new ballistic missile system was laid down in Operational Requirement (OR) 1139 issued in 1955, citing two major objectives, a missile which could strike Moscow and do it using a thermonuclear device. Both were, at the time, technically feasible but Britain had neither the funding to carry it through nor the thermonuclear device; the programme was going to be ambitious to say the least. Britain was without doubt one of the world's most innovative nations with many aerospace firsts to its name, however this project was to stretch the companies involved to the limits of their capabilities. The contracts were spread over a number of well-established companies. De Havilland Propellers and their sister company de Havilland Aircraft were to be responsible for the construction of the structural elements of the project, code named by them Blue Streak. Rolls Royce were to develop and produce the motor and the Sperry Gyroscope Company the inertial guidance system. The Government's interests were to be protected by the Royal Aircraft Establishment at Farnborough, who would also investigate the re-entry properties of the vehicle and warhead. Blue Streak was the first time British companies had attempted to build a ballistic missile system and American involvement was, therefore, paramount. The subsequent US/UK ACMDP agreement gave the chosen firms access to American development information covering the main areas of research, including wind tunnel results, motor development, inertial navigation systems and re-entry tests. Without this head start the project would have been impossible.

The management and co-ordination of Blue Streak proved to be a very complex subject, and with a large committee structure monitoring all aspects of design, test, production and deployment problems were bound to occur. Interpretation of requirements differed widely from company to company. De Havilland ran to a hypothetical production programme, whilst Rolls Royce developed a programme designed to prove a rocket engine was theoretically viable before production commenced. This was further exacerbated when it was discovered that Sperry had produced an inertial guidance system that used too much 'old' technology, new components from other contractors had been ignored and hence did not fit into the new package. The schedule demanded by de Havilland was not flexible enough to allow systems to be tested and modified; consequently problems grew or were ignored rather than rectified, effectively compounding the situation.

One other production-orientated problem was to have a major impact, a lack of trained personnel. Very few engineers had any experience with missile technology on this scale. Rolls Royce found the move from jet engine to rocket engine relatively straightforward, modifying major components in the American-designed S3D rocket motor. De Havilland on the other hand struggled from the outset, not so much with engineering problems, this firm had produced the Comet and was fully conversant with large production projects, but with the lack of manpower at its factories. It also lacked the expertise in electronics so the General Electric Company was sub-contracted to help design and install them. Owing to a lack of specialist manufacturing infrastructure the project suffered setback after setback along with the inevitable rising expenditure, and worse was yet to come.

Operational Considerations

Blue Streak had two major operational drawbacks, the length of time it took to bring the system up to readiness and the vulnerability of the weapon on the launch pad. Problems with preparing a liquid-fuelled missile for firing were nothing new, Thor had demonstrated that the propellants required could not be stored for any reasonable length of time in the missile without that system eventually becoming unusable. But Blue Streak was, from the outset, to be a defensive weapon, so hypothetically bringing the system to readiness was not perceived to be critical. However, if it was to be effective, the missile could not stand outside, especially under attack; it had to be housed in some form of robust protection.

The American Titan was stored below ground but had to be fuelled and then raised into the firing position outside the silo, taking about twenty minutes to bring it to readiness. Time was a luxury that America possessed, the Ballistic Missile Early Warning System (BMEWS) proposed by the Gaither Report, would give a fifteen- to thirty-minute warning to the US. Britain was not in such a position and could expect a strike to arrive within two and a half to ten minutes of detection. Clearly any new missile system had to withstand a strike and then be capable of delivering its payload after the dust had settled. The Air Ministry issued an addendum to OR 1139 on 29 August 1958 detailing requirements for underground launch facilities, calling for a system that could withstand a 1-megaton explosion within half a mile of a site and remain operational. They were to be placed in groups of five to ten using a central technical and domestic site. Each installation was to be dispersed far enough away from the next to permit the loss of only one site in the group in the case of a 20-megaton blast. And each silo was to be self-supporting for a minimum of three days in times of crisis, and be able to deliver its missile without help from off-base crews.

One major difference between contemporary American sites and those required by the British was that Blue Streak was to be launched from the silo, not elevated to a firing position first. Code named K11, the silo was destined to become the blueprint for most future Western ballistic missile structures. A circular subterranean seven-story silo was proposed which contained fuel, crew areas, engineering shops and storage areas. Next to this was the missile in a tube surrounded by acoustic tiles to stop the whole thing shaking apart on launch. The efflux from the engines was directed around a 'U' shaped tube that exhausted to atmosphere close to the exit for the missile. The whole structure was surrounded by a 1.6m-thick concrete wall, in turn surrounded by 2cm of mild steel to dampen the effects of the electromagnetic pulse (EMP), which would otherwise have rendered all electronic equipment inoperative. The top cover, which sealed the launch tube and efflux vent, was to weigh 400 tonnes, mounted on rails, presumably explosively opened in times of emergency. Sites would be predominantly along the east coast, preferably on Ministry-owned land, but bore holes were sunk at Upavon as well as Duxford to test the geology prior to construction, suggesting some sites were to be placed further away from the coast. Tests were made using scale models at Westcott and from these were produced the designs for the silos that are now deposited at the Public Records Office (AIR 2/17377). One silo was estimated by the Air Ministry to have a price tag of £2.3 million and it was considered a minimum of sixty would be required to give adequate retaliatory coverage.

The End of the Road

By 1958 the costs were becoming astronomical. The estimated figure at the start of the project had been £150 million; by 1960 it had already cost £60 million and was projected to reach around £450 million. Clearly the Treasury was getting shaky feet as it tried to shave money off the development costs. Harold Macmillan discussed the problem in Parliament, suggesting a reduction in funding which would not be too visible; clearly Britain needed a way out without accepting, in the eyes of the world, that she was just not up to the job. America had been developing a ballistic missile with an air launch capability code named Skybolt since 1958 and in 1960 President Eisenhower agreed to sell the missile to the British. The end was in sight as far as Blue Streak's military role was concerned, but the launcher went on to become the first-stage component of the European Launcher Development Organisation and saw three successful launches of the Blue Streak. The project was terminated in 1970.

Stand-off

Stand-off missiles are a logical step beyond a conventional bomber force. The missile utilises the aircraft as both transport and launch platform. The concept was not new; towards the end of the Second World War the Germans had been experimenting on such devices, using them effectively against Allied shipping. The idea was, however, resurrected prior to the rise of the Intercontinental Ballistic Missile (ICBM). Britain developed one type, Blue Steel, which became a major part of the deterrent force. However, as with many other weapon types, events conspired against further successful developments.

Skybolt

Skybolt was Strategic Air Command's (SAC) preferred weapon for the B52H Stratofortress, built by the Douglas Aircraft Company. It carried a W-49 thermonuclear device (a similar warhead to that fitted to Thor) just over 1,600km. The idea was that this was well outside the range of the Soviet air defence network, keeping the aircraft platform out of danger. The missile would then reach a maximum speed of 14,400km/hr before hitting the target with total impunity. And it was a solid-fuel system, so had none of the problems of generation seen in the Thor and proposed Blue Streak systems.

   This seemed the ideal system to the British Government. Here was a missile that would carry out the same task as Blue Streak, but did not require underground protection or suffer from ever-rising costs. And, if indeed Skybolt was to be ordered, savings could be demonstrated in other areas. The current Blue Steel stand-off missile required some much-needed upgrades and a new generation of launch platform was required to replace the Vulcan and Valiant. Skybolt was the obvious choice. Blue Streak and the Blue Steel upgrade were shelved and trials were undertaken to ascertain the suitability of existing aircraft. The Vulcan was considered the most compatible aircraft in the British fleet, B2s were still in production at AVRO's Woodford factory, and structural modifications were made to the design allowing for Skybolt to be mounted on wing pylons.

The concept of Skybolt was ambitious but not impossible, although the development of such a weapon was not critical to the United States security; her arsenal already contained similar systems. This put the project in an unstable political theatre which wasn't helped by the fact that the first four test firings, at Eglin in Florida, failed. The US Defence Secretary, Robert McNamara, recommended President Kennedy cancel the programme, especially since Minuteman and Polaris were in advanced stages of development. Kennedy informed Macmillan on 19 December 1962 of his decision to cancel on the day a Skybolt was successfully launched and struck a target 1,600km down range. It appeared Britain would be left high and dry yet again. She now had no surface-to-surface missile system and the air-launched Blue Steel was severely limited after the U-2 incident demonstrated high flying aircraft's vulnerability to Soviet anti-aircraft missiles.

Blue Steel

As early as 1954 the Government had noted a requirement for a propelled controlled missile and in 1956 A.V. Roe Ltd won the development contract for Blue Steel. Powered by an Armstrong Siddeley Stentor sustainer motor, the stand-off missile could carry the proposed 1-megaton Red Snow warhead 160km into enemy territory. The hope was that the launch platform could be kept out of the range of the constantly upgraded Russian Air Defences. Blue Steel would have followed other cancelled British designs had it not been for the collapse of the Skybolt project. As it was the Blue Steel Mk2, with an extended range and bigger powerplant, never left the development stage. As with all British projects, more than one company was involved in the development of the missile. Contributors included Elliotts, EMI, Handley Page, Hunting and staff from the RAE and WRE.

Trials, Tests and Tribulations

The first airborne trials were conducted at Aberporth, West Wales, where ironically two scale models were dropped from Valiants, the only V bomber not designated to carry Blue Steel. Throughout 1957–58 aerodynamic investigations were carried out before full-scale drops of test missiles at the ranges at Woomera, Australia. The original concept required an air-burst weapon, the most destructive type of detonation, however the possibility of Blue Steel malfunctioning after launch was also considered.

To counter this a number of inertia switches were fitted to the missile, which it was hoped would initiate detonation on contact with something solid. Tests were carried out by A.V. Roe Ltd at the Proof & Experimental Establishment (P&PEE), Pendine in 1960. Five rounds were fired along the rocket sled track reaching an impact velocity of 1,990ft/sec, striking test shapes. It was determined that the inertia switches would operate in time 'to allow a proper weapon yield before warhead damage occurred'. Clearly all avenues were explored; if Blue Steel was intercepted or the guidance system malfunctioned then it had the potential to be just as potent as if it reached the designated target.

Blue Steel was powered by a two-stage rocket motor, the Stentor. This liquid-fuelled motor had a boost stage that powered the missile up to around mach 2, after which a smaller sustainer motor took over. One large drawback, indeed a problem with most British concepts of the time, was the fuel, a kerosene–High Test Peroxide (HTP) mix. HTP is an oxidising agent that allows the fuel to burn in the upper, oxygen depleted, atmosphere. But if allowed to degrade it becomes highly volatile and consequently it could not be stored for long periods in the missile. This seriously increased the amount of time needed to prepare a Blue Steel for flight and made any missile ready for use very dangerous indeed.

Blue Steel was a complex weapon, demonstrating the innovative aspects of British weapon design. It was to all intents and purposes a fledgling cruise missile carrying its own automatic pilot, inertial navigation system and generator for flight control movement. The complexity of testing such weapons systems often required the construction of specific installations, and one such site, connected with Blue Steel, still survives at Boscombe Down. The various flight control systems were, in part, tested along with a functioning engine at the Aircraft & Armament Experimental Establishment in Wiltshire during the late 1950s. A large circular earthwork bank was constructed, standing 5m high, and placed centrally to this was a large gantry containing a missile cradle; the cradle could be positioned in any attitude. A single-story concrete control room was built next to the earthwork to house the test equipment required to monitor and control the missile during test runs. This, in turn, had a 1m-thick concrete blast wall encased in half-inch metal plates built in a section cut out of the bank, just in front of the control room. Clearly, careful consideration was given to any possible event! This site is now part of a conservation area at Boscombe Down and also retains the original lifting 'A' frame and assembly shed, making this whole complex of structures unique.

Into Operation

By October 1962 Blue Steel was issued to 617 Squadron at Scampton and became fully operational in February the following year. In all, nine main bases and thirty-four satellite sites were used as part of the British nuclear deterrent. From any of these sites Vulcans and Victors could carry around forty Blue Steel rounds to within 160–230km of their targets. The missiles' flight computer would be constantly updated by the launch aircraft until the point of release, after which the Blue Steel would be on its own. After free falling for around 100m the rocket motor would start and accelerate the missile to around twice the speed of sound and up to a height of around 21,000m. It would then cruise using the sustainer engine until it was close to the target, at

Boscombe Down. The Blue Steel test site showing control bunker, assembly shed and crane gantry. (Courtesy MOD Boscombe Down)

which point it would either assume a ballistic trajectory or fly in powered (if fuel was still available). The suggested accuracy of Blue Steel was, according to A.V. Roe, 160m, which is extremely effective for the period, especially when considering Thor had an accuracy of 3.5km.

Tactical Versatility

Traditionally the RAF had operated a high level delivery system, keeping the aircraft above the ceiling of the Soviet Union's air defence network. However, in 1960 a Soviet surface-to-air missile bought down a U-2 on a surveillance mission, sparking an international incident. The problem was the U-2 was at 21,000m at the time; in a single act the concept of high-level bombing had become obsolete. From November 1963 tests at Woomera involved low-level Blue Steel launches to try to combat this new threat. The aircraft would fly into enemy territory at around 150m or lower and release Blue Steel 40km from the target. The missile would climb anywhere between 6,000 and 12,000m before diving ballistically into the target. In 1964, after the successful completion of the trials, the tactical delivery of Blue Steel changed to low level and has become the mainstay of British offensive bombing tactics ever since.

Unfortunately this change of delivery method was to have far-reaching effects. The effective distance of Blue Steel meant that some sorties would be required to fly up to 2,400km into enemy territory, potentially limiting the success of each mission. Also the possibility of successfully launching a retaliatory strike from British soil was very unlikely; Soviet missiles would be able to take out the bomber bases well before

Blue Steel. The stand-off missile was in service between 1962 and 1970. Air launched from Victor and Vulcan aircraft it was capable of hitting the target at twice the speed of sound. (Courtesy NMSI)

the aircraft were clear. Finally, although the Vulcan could withstand the extra fatigue caused by low flying, the Victor could not. Britain now had a potential 'bomber gap' to add to her problems. By 1968 the Victors had taken up new roles, primarily as tankers, and by December 1970 Blue Steel was decommissioned. The deterrent mantle passed to the Navy and the RAF was left to develop a theatre nuclear role.

Submarine Launched Ballistic Missiles

Submarine Launched Ballistic Missiles (SLBM) became the weapons of choice for both superpowers during the Cold War. Tactically they had far more advantages than any land-based system; jet bombers were in the air for extended periods, could be detected by radar and more importantly be shot down. The ground silos of the ICBMs were all well documented through years of satellite reconnaissance and the majority could be destroyed if struck first, but the submarine was a completely different situation altogether. And once nuclear power plants were fitted, the submarine became almost impossible to stop. Britain built SLBM systems in conjunction with the American government and continues to rely on this silent, secret weapon for the ultimate protection today.

Polaris

The possibility of Britain acquiring Polaris technology was first agreed at Nassau during talks between Macmillan and Kennedy in 1962. Kennedy had recently cancelled Skybolt, leaving Britain with a very denuded deterrent. Macmillan had

Polaris. With the introduction of Polaris, in 1969 the independent deterrent moved to the Royal Navy. The RAF now assumed a tactical role.

abandoned both Blue Streak and the Blue Steel upgrades, entering heavily into the development of Skybolt, and now that programme had gone Britain was struggling. A submarine-launched ICBM had many attractions, not least that it is almost impossible to locate once deployed. The main drawback with a bomber fleet is that they need airfields to operate from, potentially the first targets in a pre-emptive strike. Submarines, on the other hand, could be anywhere in the world and came to epitomise the possibility of the 'no-notice' strike which so underpinned the public's fears throughout the Cold War.

The first successful test firing of a Polaris missile was carried out in April 1956, with the first systems entering service in 1960 aboard USS *George Washington*. The missile launch system was an ingenious piece of equipment. Polaris was ejected out of the submarine silo by compressed air and then a solid-fuelled rocket motor fired when clear of the water, powering the missile into a ballistic trajectory.

Britain, as part of the US/UK Polaris Sales Agreement signed in 1963, developed many parts of the system. The submarines were built by Vickers Armstrong in Barrow-in-Furness and Cammell Laird in Birkenhead. Each company built two boats. The design followed an earlier Valiant Class Fleet Submarine but was greatly modified to accept a sixteen-bay missile compartment and a nuclear reactor. The Resolution class submarines had a length of 130m, beam of 10m and draught of 9m, with a submerged displacement of 8,400 tonnes. The pressurised water reactor (PWR) was developed by Rolls-Royce at Derby, and was proof run at Vulcan, Rolls-Royce's reactor facility at Dounreay, Scotland, going critical for the first time in January 1965. The turbine system was developed and built by English Electric and was capable of giving the submarine a speed of 25 knots.

The Polaris missile was developed by Lockheed, having its first successful underwater test launch in 1960 at the ranges near Cape Canaveral. It was powered by a solid rocket motor which had distinct advantages over its liquid-fuelled predecessors and was capable of delivering a 1-megaton warhead over 1,600km. Updates in the American missiles increased the effective range to over 4,000km carrying multiple re-entry vehicles. Polaris systems were gradually replaced by Poseidon and finally Trident in the United States. The missiles were supplied to the United Kingdom along with the launch tubes and fire-control systems by the American manufacturers, but Britain was responsible for producing the all-important warhead.

A new type of deterrent required a new base and a working party set up in 1963 looked at a large number of sites around Britain. Many sites were discounted because they lacked a deep-water entrance. Eventually a shortlist of ten was produced. These were Portland, Devonport and Falmouth in England; Milford Haven in Wales; and Loch Ryan, Gareloch, Loch Alsh, Fort William, Invergordon and Rosyth in Scotland. Gareloch was the final choice and the first new naval base to be built in Britain since 1909 was started in 1963. The site, subsequently named Faslane, was complemented by a new weapons storage facility at nearby Coulport. It was not until June 1968 that HMS *Resolution*, carrying sixteen Polaris, conducted its first deterrent patrol. And by the middle of 1969 the responsibility for Britain's retaliatory capability had passed from the Royal Air Force to the Royal Navy, where it remains today.

Chevaline

In 1967, a full year before the first operational deployment, it was recognised that the Polaris system would require a substantial update if it was to remain a credible British deterrent for any length of time. The American Navy had begun upgrading some Polaris systems by introducing the new, longer range Poseidon missile. However, the Labour Government of 1967 opted to update the existing deterrent. Known as Chevaline, this project became a political 'hot potato' for subsequent governments for over a decade.

Feasibility studies were carried out by AWRE Aldermaston into the possibilities of designing and fitting an enhanced warhead system into the existing weapon. Chevaline was to modify existing Polaris missiles to carry two warheads and develop a suite of deployable penetration aids to confuse the Russian Anti Ballistic Missile (ABM) systems. It also needed to produce a hardened warhead and decoys. Edward Heath's Government continued to support the upgrade whilst considering a possible Anglo–French nuclear collaboration, primarily used to look at ways of allowing Britain's entry into Europe rather than cutting costs.

In 1974 a new Labour Government entered office and immediately reassessed the future of the Chevaline project. The party's manifesto had committed them to not buying any new generation nuclear systems and it had to be seen to uphold that principle. A group of senior cabinet officials concluded that Chevaline was not a new system, and was important if Britain wanted to stay at the nuclear top table, and

Chevaline was one of the most costly projects of the whole British nuclear programme. The large black object is one of two warheads carried by the SLBM.

the development was given the go-ahead to the tune of £250 million. A year later the Treasury insisted the project be reviewed yet again as costs had already risen to £400 million; clearly the seat at the table was becoming very difficult to hide in the figures. By September 1975 Chevaline went into full development, ensuring Britain's independent deterrent well into the 1980s.

Contracts and the project were run in strict secrecy. The financial aspects had been approved by the inner cabinet and as such had not received Parliamentary approval. However, a large number of companies were involved in the research and development. These included AWRE Aldermaston who developed the warheads, RAE Farnborough who developed the hardened re-entry vehicles and Hunting Engineering at Ampthill who designed and manufactured the warhead carrier. Smaller but no less important companies such as Bristol Aerojet (BAJ) at Banwell were also involved.

BAJ had been formed through a strategic partnership between Aerojet General, Sacramento and the Bristol Aeroplane Company (BAC), formally incorporated in December 1958. The site at Banwell designed and manufactured a variety of rocket casings, working on such systems as Blue Water, Black Arrow, Bloodhound and Thunderbird along with solid-propellant development. BAJ was sub-contracted in 1971 by R.P.E. Westcott to develop a large solid-fuel casing for the fledgling Chevaline project and development was to absorb over 50 per cent of the company's production capability. MOD research and development contracts were obviously both lucrative and essential to some smaller defence firms.

Public Admittance

The existence of Chevaline was revealed to Parliament in 1980 by Francis Pym, Margaret Thatcher's then defence minister. The project had become far too costly to hide in the cabinet budget any longer. The price tag had now reached an astronomical one billion pounds, but rather than cancel Thatcher continued with the programme. The fact that Chevaline had been financed in secret caused much consternation in both Parliament and the press, and although Thatcher saw this as an opportunity to discredit the former government, it has to be remembered that both Labour and the Conservatives had been involved in the project. Deployment of the first Chevaline–Polaris upgrade was aboard HMS *Renown* in the summer of 1982. The system was retired from service in 1998 and the dismantling of Chevaline warheads now forms part of the Atomic Weapons Establishment (formally AWRE) nuclear warhead arms control programme.

Trident

In June 1980 the Government signed an agreement with the Carter administration to replace the Chevaline system with the new version of Trident, subsequently announcing this to Parliament the following month. The warhead development again fell to AWRE Aldermaston with the first seeing completion in September 1992. Trident II has the capability to engage twelve targets at once at a maximum range of 6,500km to an accuracy of a few metres. The first Vanguard class submarine was launched in 1993 carrying sixteen Trident II D5 ballistic missiles and has become the cornerstone of Britain's post Cold War defence policy.

two

Air Defence

The development of an air defence network saw some of the biggest capital works of the Cold War; millions were spent developing systems that we now take for granted. This chapter follows those developments from the conception of the Rotor project through to the latest state-of-the-art systems employed today.

The major cause for concern in post-war Western Europe was that the Soviet Union would use its vast forces, still in the East, to expand the communist ideal. Politically this had been hinted at during the Potsdam Conference in 1945 and the fact the Soviets had set up puppet governments in many 'liberated' countries underpinned these fears. The Labour Government, elected in 1945, had promised social reform and this was not going to come cheap. Britain had come out of the war bankrupt, rationing was still widespread and further expensive defence projects were unpopular. In 1946 the National Insurance Act ensured that the 'Welfare State' was in place; the Government would now care for the population 'from the cradle to the grave', and defence spending was now redirected to fund these initiatives.

By 1948 new storm clouds were gathering over Europe. In March restrictions were placed on the movement of supplies through Soviet-occupied Germany to Berlin and by 24 June the borders were permanently closed. The only way in now was by air and the following day the Berlin Airlift began. As a direct consequence the Civil Defence Act (1948) was passed in Britain; an eye was now on the resurgence of a possible European conflict. In direct defiance of the Soviet Union the West supplied Berlin with every item possible and stationed long-range United States bombers at three British bases, threatening grave consequences. To encourage European governments to stay with the West a system of aid to help with recovery, the Marshall Plan, also started that year. Aid came in many forms and whilst not strictly a financial package it did take the pressure off the United Kingdom's failing economy to the tune of $3.2 billion.

The Berlin crisis shook the West and by April 1949 the North Atlantic Treaty Organisation (NATO) had been formed; now aggression against one member state would invite attack from all. But NATO stood for more than that, it also gave signatory countries the protection of the United States. Britain became over the next few years a major repository for American weapons systems. The West's fears were confirmed in August of that year when a reconnaissance B-29 picked up the unmistakable signature of an atomic bomb, clearly the USSR had become a nuclear power. Defence chiefs could sit back no longer, any doubts they had had over projects such as radar updates were no longer an issue, also the financial climate was better thanks to the Marshall Plan. Britain now needed a credible air defence network, not only for the defence of the nation, if American protection was to remain then it would also need to be seen to be defended. An upgrade to Britain's radar network, the 'Rotor' project was quickly agreed, as was the reorganisation of the Gun Defended Area network, and a renewed impetus was also given to the development of anti-aircraft missile systems. These projects proved prudent as on 25 June 1950 Britain became involved in the Korean War, viewed by many in Government as the prelude to Russian strikes in Europe.

Radar

No air defence system is effective without radar and throughout the Cold War the advances made in the latter years of the Second World War were improved beyond all recognition. Cold War radar was key in locating enemy incursions into British air space, guiding interceptors to the threat and if need be allowing anti-aircraft missiles to find and destroy the target. A great number of bases were constructed or refurbished, principally along the east coast, often receiving modification to equipment before the previous systems had been commissioned; such was the pace of development.

Genesis

Towards the end of the Second World War thoughts turned to the defence of a post-war Britain. Events throughout the late 1940s, especially the Berlin crisis, were to radically shape that thinking. Air defence was recognised as being woefully poor, especially in the area of detection. Two post-war studies laid out the options open to Government. A report prepared by the Chiefs of Staff in mid-1945 suggested a reduction in coverage, utilising outdated equipment to protect specified areas only. Estimated time for full reactivation of a capable detection network was to take up to two years; clearly Britain would be extremely vulnerable was this report to be followed. Late 1945 saw the publication of the 'Cherry Report' in which a call was made for a fully integrated network, run by Sector Control Centres. Each centre would organise air defence after assessing the information from a number of radar stations within the sector footprint. Unfortunately all this would involve large investment, money Britain didn't have and money the Labour Government was unwilling to find for yet more defence projects; the existing air defence network was effectively placed in care-and-maintenance.

Berlin was the wake-up call, the spectre of war once more manifested itself in central Europe, the prospect of air-raids became all too apparent as did Britain's unprepared and outdated detection network. By 1949 thirty-six stations were up and running, forming a 'defended area' along the east and south coasts, but the reality of the situation dictated that major development and the overhaul of the entire network was urgently needed.

Operation Rotor

The largest and most far-reaching upgrade of Britain's radar network was the Rotor programme. Aircraft speeds had been steadily increasing as jet engine technology advanced, cutting down the response time from detection to interception. An advanced detection system was clearly now required. In 1950 a plan was formalised by the Air Council that required the re-establishment of an effective air defence system.

The Rotor programme had three main stages encompassing the vast task of producing a full report and control capability for air defence. It included a massive civil engineering project as bunkers, sometimes three storeys deep, were constructed underground. It also incorporated a bewildering array of old and new radar technology to obtain the coverage needed for total air defence coverage.

Rotor 1

A number of phases were envisaged within Rotor 1, which essentially satisfied the original requirements set down by the Air Council. Twenty-eight Chain Home (CH) stations were to be completely refurbished, including accommodation for staff in the immediate locality of the base. Eight Centimetric Early Warning (CEW) stations were to be completely refurbished along with six Chain Home Extra Low (CHEL) sites along the east coast. Eleven protected Ground Controlled Intercept (GCI) stations were to be built in the most vulnerable east and south. Fourteen semi-sunken GCLs were to be built in the Midlands and the west. The construction of such a varied number of structures required standardisation and plans were drawn up as part of the original programme to cover this. Nine 'R' type structures were designated to cover all permutations of surface, semi-sunken and sunken bunkers, a further six were added as part of the post-1953 revision.

The Rotor Guardhouse

The most distinctive of the buildings of the project has to be the guardhouse constructed at most Rotor sites. To the casual observer the structure appears to be a normal bungalow with a dormer roof, but the building, on sunken sites, controlled access to the control room constructed below. This is in contrast to the majority of structures built throughout the Cold War where function and protection far outweighed any attempt to conceal, camouflage or consider aesthetic possibilities. The guardhouse was simple in layout comprising a rest room, store, armoury, toilets and a guardroom.

At the back of the structure was a rectangular building which had either a flat or apex roof, which covered the entrance shaft to the main bunker. To gain access to the shaft, personnel would first have to pass through the guardroom, via a turnstile, thus controlling entry to the site. At the back of the shaft cover were two large metal doors; these allowed large pieces of equipment to be introduced into the bunker, an occurrence that did happen from time to time. The guardhouse structures were mainly made of brick, but local stone was sometimes used, primarily to have less of an impact on the local environment. Under

The guardhouse at the Goldsborough Rotor site near Whitby. Access to the control bunker was via a staircase at the back of the building.

the apex roof was a protective concrete cap, which would afford some protection to the occupants during air raids; it also supported four 500-gallon water tanks. Internal steel shutters could also be lowered to protect against blast and small arms fire.

The Radar Systems

Four principle radar systems were used in Rotor 1: Chain Home, Chain Home Extra Low, Centimetric Early Warning and Ground Control Intercept. The majority of which were upgraded wartime systems, but continuous development by Marconi and other British and American companies ensured that the system specification was in a constant state of flux.

Chain Home

Chain Home had its beginnings before the outbreak of the Second World War. Developed at Orfordness and Bawdsey, it went on to be the backbone of British air defence throughout the period. Sites were easily recognisable by transmitting (steel, 107m) and receiving (timber, 73m) towers at each unit. Twenty-eight stations were identified for reuse within the Rotor programme giving long-range early warning readings. These sites were the least changed by the post-war refurbishment, seeing mostly equipment upgrades, although some sites, such as Ventnor on the Isle of Wight, did incorporate CEW units as well.

Chain Home Extra Low

Chain Home Extra Low (CHEL) was developed to counter the problem of low flying aircraft, and supplemented the existing network from 1941. The radar unit was smaller

The Rotor site at Bempton near Scarborough. Radar plinths and to the right an escape hatch from the bunker below.

than its predecessors comprising a 7m dish that could be mounted on a gantry or the back of a normal service lorry. The system was able to detect aircraft flying as low as 17m above sea level, a required part of the later Rotor programme.

The network of CHEL stations all needed to be situated at least 80m above sea level and as close to the coast as possible, thus allowing a sweep unaffected by topographical obstacles. Subsequently six wartime stations, Crosslaw, Fairlight, Foreness, Goldsborough, Hopton and Truleigh Hill, were considerably upgraded to accommodate the new system. On each station a single-story sunken bunker was built, designated R2, which housed the staff involved in the operation of the Type 14 or 54 scanners.

Centimetric Early Warning

Eight Centimetric Early Warning (CEW) stations were also brought back into service. The CEW system was more versatile than the other wartime developments as it could provide medium to high altitude detection as well as low level. Rotor refurbished sites received an R1 type sunken single-story control bunker incorporating a combined filter plotting room for fighter control. Two radar units were operated on each site, a Type 13 plan positioning unit and a Type 13 height finder. This arrangement was complemented on a number of sites by Type 54 scanners and occasionally range was extended by additional AN/FPS-3 American-developed units. Twelve sets of the AN/FPS-3 had been acquired from the United States as some British-built equipment was starting to have seriously delayed lead times by 1952.

Ground Control Intercept

Ground Control Intercept sites were based on a system developed during the Second World War, giving direction to fighter squadrons and anti-aircraft batteries. Information was drawn from CEW and CHEL sites, using this and the information gained from their own radar, fighters would be guided onto the target.

Rotor stations had a number of different structures and radar units located on site. Firstly, depending on the station's geographical position a number of bunker designs were available. East coast stations, such as Holmpton in Yorkshire, had a two-story sunken bunker designated R3, accessed through the Guardhouse then down a 60m tunnel. Less vulnerable sites such as Hack Green in Cheshire were two-story semi-sunken R6 types, whilst some stations had little protection; Charmy Down near Bath used Seco huts to house equipment and staff. The heart of the GCI was similar to other control bunkers comprising a two-story plotting room containing the large general situation map, weather information and fighter readiness boards. From these positions it was possible to bring a number of defensive assets to bear on any intruder.

A number of radar sets were incorporated into the system and included a Type 7 control unit that had all the turning mechanism in a specific structure below ground, designated R7; a Type 13 on which the head moved in the vertical plane giving an accurate height of the target; a Type 14 working in the horizontal plane giving a distance fix in plan form; and a Type 11 and occasionally a Type 54 scanner. Also

Charmy Down. Unfinished radar plinths at the Ground Control Intercept site near Bath. This site was abandoned when the Rotor system was modified.

Kelvedon Hatch. Air filtration plant. (Courtesy J.A. Parrish & Sons)

included was an Identification Friend or Foe (IFF) aerial interrogating any contact for a signal indicating the aircraft's intent.

Sector Operations Centres

To control the overall situation the United Kingdom comprised six sectors, each containing a Sector Operations Centre (SOC). These sites had no radar equipment, relying totally on information supplied from other stations, both in their sector and beyond. Four purpose-built SOCs were located at Barnton Quarry, Scottish; Skipton, Northern; Bawburgh, Eastern, and Kelvedon Hatch, Metropolitan, whilst sites at Box, Southern and Longley Lane, Western reused existing structures. The new-build bunkers were designated R4 within the Rotor design framework. Central to the SOC was a three-story operations room surrounded by segregated watch cabins, all with a view of a general map and tote board. On these a picture of the general situation and operational readiness of fighter squadrons would be displayed, aiding senior staff co-ordinating any response to an enemy incursion.

Rotor, as can been seen above, was an ambitious plan often run to very tight, unachievable deadlines. The majority of the work was projected to be complete within four years. As with any project requiring the development of new technologies the programme suffered some serious setbacks. The construction of the infrastructure, estimated to have cost £24 million, had some major problems, including the lack of steel for reinforcing concrete bunkers and building support gantries. The General Post Office worked on little else throughout 1952–54 and was constantly frustrated with the lack of progress by other contractors. Compounding the problem was the lack of ventilation.

Dehumidifiers for the underground bunkers were slow to be fitted, leading to Marconi and the GPO replacing many equipment sets due to degradation within a damp environment. The radar and communications networks cost an estimated £28 million.

Beyond the logistics of the station building, technology also became a headache early on. Wartime equipment was initially refurbished allowing Marconi and other contractors time to develop the new generation radar systems and display consoles that had been requested. However, the wartime kit was far beyond its best, causing the programme to be eighteen months late, so late in fact that some GCIs were fitted with AN/FPS-3 Radar sets, bought new from America, just to plug the gap. To add insult to injury Marconi announced that all refurbished kit would be totally obsolete by the end of the decade. If a credible replacement couldn't be found then the whole network would be ineffective within five years. The situation looked grim, but a technical breakthrough was to turn the whole situation around.

Rotor 2

Rotor 2 proposed that all the refurbished wartime equipment would be replaced by 1957 with new longer range and more accurate radar sets and displays. In 1954 a new long-range early warning radar 'Green Garlic', a development on the Type 14 unit, became available, subsequently to be known as the Type 80. This system revolutionised the thinking behind Rotor, having a vastly improved range and the ability to fulfil the roles of a number of earlier sets. Practically overnight the majority of the Rotor stations became obsolete. The Type 80 could discriminate between two targets at over 175km, a very important factor when dealing with inbound bombers potentially carrying atomic weapons. The unit also possessed far more power than its predecessors making it far less susceptible to electronic countermeasures. Type 80s had a far greater range, up to 300km, than the Chain Home network, especially the tower stations, meaning fewer sets could be positioned along the coast. And most importantly to the Treasury the radar had an immediate cost saving element at a time when budgets were being closely scrutinised.

The first operational Type 80 came on line at RAF Trimingham in 1955 just three years after the Centimetric Early Warning R1 site had opened as part of Rotor 1. Seven sites were chosen for upgrade and all received the new system by 1957. Installation required a purpose-built single-story modulator building containing a rectifier room able to convert AC to DC current along with the transmitter modulators and switch gear. The scanner was an enormous metal antenna 8.5m high and 25m wide which stood on a rotating cabin housing the transmitter and receiver equipment along with the IFF equipment racking. Power was passed to the drive motors through a slip-ring arrangement connecting the rotating parts to the modulator building. The whole structure stood astride the building on a steel gantry 9m high.

In April 1956 the Rotor stage one stations were finally placed under the control of the Royal Air Force. Almost total coverage was now afforded to the east and south coasts and the Atlantic approaches were now receiving basic coverage. Also, most of the Type 80 sites had now received the new scanner system. Fighter Command, however, dealt the new Rotor stations a fatal blow. The GCI system was found to be

Bempton. Type 80 modulator building. The Type 80 revolutionised the British radar network.

causing information blockages, often slowing the network to a standstill, changes were once again in the pipeline.

Modified Plan and Plan Ahead

By 1958 a major revision of the air defence network, known as the 'Modified Plan', was proposed. The Modified Plan called for better links between controllers and fighter aircraft from fewer sites whilst still providing adequate defence for the nuclear deterrent bases. Cost, as always, dictated how many changes would be made to the existing system and required some major streamlining before the Treasury would agree to even more defence spending so soon after Rotor. In the face of the perceived threat from the hydrogen bomb and ballistic missiles, coupled with the rearmament of the services post-Korea, the disastrous Suez campaign and the increasing reliance on the nuclear deterrent, the task was certainly going to be up hill.

The Type 80 radar, much heralded for its ability to overcome jamming, also became virtually obsolete overnight, primarily due to a French discovery. The technical staff at Compagnie Generale de Telegraphie Sans Fil invented a form of microwave oscillator that came to be known as the Carcinotron. Suddenly the Type 80 looked fallible and it was proposed that the radar be sidelined in favour of a new system. Clearly if the French could develop such a system so could the Soviet Union. One radar set already in development, Blue Riband was considered. This high-powered system could simply 'burn' through any countermeasures. But Blue Riband was eventually cancelled in favour of a network known as Winkle, a microwave system that flooded airspace and received any disturbances at three receiver sites. To complement Winkle,

Type 80 sets would be reduced to a supporting role for a new tactical radar, the Blue Yeoman, all to be integrated into an automated data handling link connecting main control centres via radar sites to the fighters. The estimated cost of the whole upgrade had been set at £30 million by the Air Ministry; however, this soon topped £100 million, primarily due to the development of the computerised data system. The Treasury and other Government departments were not impressed and in late 1958 the proposals were drastically slimmed down, becoming 'Plan Ahead'.

Plan Ahead reduced the air defence network down to a bare minimum. If, as had been predicted in the 1957 defence White Paper, the bomber fleets on both sides were to become redundant by 1965, then only a small network was required. The new network was now to comprise three central Radar Tracking Stations (RTS), Staxton Wold, Neatishead and Bramcote, coupled to one Master Control Centre (MCC) at Bawburgh. Each RTS would be equipped with a Type 84 and Type 85 radar system, full IFF system and be able to track at least 200 plots per site. Type 80 radar sets were to be retained at Saxa Vord and Buchan to afford coverage across the north of the country. Both sites would transmit verbally to Staxton Wold where the information would be integrated into the data link and so on to the MCC. The main Air Defence Operations Centre was to remain at Bentley Priory; from there the situation could be monitored and discussed through a voice link with both the MCC and RTS.

The next step was to gain Treasury approval, and despite some adjustments the plan was eventually approved in principle. However, the adjustments were fairly fundamental. Firstly the Government wanted an integrated system, no more development of radars to suit each service in turn. Secondly, after discussion at the Defence Committee on 16 September 1960, the Prime Minister, Harold Macmillan, demanded this should be a joint Air Defence–Air Traffic Control system, especially if the plan wished to attract funding. The Linesman/Mediator system was born; radar from both sides of the fence would, from now on, be inextricably linked.

Mediator

Whilst Mediator is outside the scope of this book, it is worth briefly outlining the project as it had a direct effect on the process of air defence and protection within the British Isles.

Civilian Air Traffic Control (ATC) had, up until the early 1960s, been a fairly *ad hoc* affair, using a collection of low-powered and experimental radar, coupled with pilot visual reporting. Aircraft had primarily been, until the late 1950s, a collection of piston-drive types, requiring a flight corridor height of no more than 11,000ft. But in May 1952 the world's first turbo-jet commercial airliner, the de Havilland Comet, entered service, requiring a much higher operating ceiling to gain maximum engine efficiency. Unfortunately, due to a series of accidents, the Comet was not a bestseller, and others were catching up fast, and in 1957 Boeing launched the first of a series of highly successful aircraft, the 707, changing the face of air travel forever. This also prompted a change in air navigation; Boeing 707s operated at around 35,000ft, much higher than previous aircraft and well inside the military areas, raising the civilian air corridors above Britain was now essential.

In 1962 the Air Traffic Services organisation was established, co-ordinating the layout of the proposed network. The task of setting up Mediator was far more complex than its military counterpart; Linesman (discussed below) was after all a slightly modified but existing programme (Plan Ahead). But Mediator required the modernisation of three ATC Controls, West Drayton, Prestwick and Preston, whilst encompassing all the existing radars covering the flight corridor approaches. The four joint service–civil air traffic control radar units based around the country also required new data links and a flight plan processing system. As would be expected the enormity of the task, akin to the earlier Rotor project, meant that the target date of 1968 was completely unachievable.

In 1967 the Southern Air Traffic Control Centre was moved from Heathrow to West Drayton, starting the centralisation of the system. But it was not until 1971 that the new suite of control screens and computers were ready for use. The prime contractor, Marconi, provided the majority of the equipment for the West Drayton control centre and the Flight Plan Processing System. Mediator led to the formation of the now familiar Civil Aviation Authority, primarily on the recommendation of the Edwards Committee in 1969, forming both a regulatory and reporting body for the civil side of ATC. By 1975 Mediator was complete, over budget and in need of updating, but, apart from software enhancements and some basic system introductions, this was not to happen until the opening of the new air traffic control centre at Swanwick, Hampshire, on 27 January 2002 at a cost of £623 million.

Linesman

Linesman, although linked with the proposed Mediator network, already had a head start on its partner. The primary advantage over Mediator was the similarity of Linesman to Plan Ahead and, whilst the latter had stalled due to governmental concern, was already well advanced in both the planning and procurement stages. The three Plan Ahead identified RTS sites were to be incorporated into Linesman at minimal cost to the bases' infrastructure and each station was to comprise the same radar systems, Type 84, 85 and HF200. This would be complemented by the passive system, Winkle, and the whole network would be directed from the Master Control Centre at West Drayton, designated 'L1' close to the London ATC Centre. A fully automated recognised air picture dissemination system was also installed at HQ Strike Command at High Wycombe. And the system would also link the UK network into that of the NATO Air Defence Ground Environment (NADGE), adding to what was hoped would be a comprehensive European air defence network. Subsequently, by 1969 the links between NADGE and Linesman were downgraded, yet the concept of co-operation was not lost and would reappear in the years to come. Linesman was finally operational in 1974. But by then planners had already started to investigate a replacement, the United Kingdom Air Defence Ground Environment (UKADGE).

Linesman Equipment

The Linesman network comprised a number of radar sets that were often mirrored on each site. The size of the scanners made the sites quite conspicuous; RAF Staxton Wold, overlooking the Vale of Pickering near Scarborough, is a classic example of

Staxton Wold. The revolutionary Type 84 radar. (Courtesy *Scarborough Evening News*)

this. The station, elevated 120m above the vale, was in clear view of the thousands of holidaymakers using the A64 to travel to the seaside every year. Described below are the standard three types from that site:

Type 84 L-Band

Type 84 radar sets were already in the advanced stage of development by the conception of Linesman, due to orders for the now defunct 'Plan Ahead'. The system was designed and developed by Marconi at the Chelmsford site and comprised a pair of 18.2m x 6.2m parabolic reflectors, built in sections using aircraft construction techniques to ensure a standard accuracy. The high-powered 'L-Band' radar used a 2.5-megawatt magnetron as a transmitter giving a typical range of 400km, up to a height of 7,000m, rotating at four revolutions per minute. The first of five sets was installed at RAF Bawdsey in October 1962 to prove the system and facilitate the training of radar technicians. Three more Type 84 sets were installed at Staxton Wold, Neatishead and Boulmer by 1964 and finally one was installed in Cyprus.

Staxton Wold. The HF 200 Height Finder with the Type 85 behind. (Courtesy *Scarborough Evening News*)

Type 85 S-Band

Type 85 started out life as project Blue Yeoman, under development at the Royal Radar Establishment (RRE) at Malvern. Contracts for the construction of the system were awarded to Metropolitan Vickers in 1958, replacing the procurement contract for Blue Riband, which had been cancelled earlier that year. The parabolic reflector was similar to that used in the Type 84, as were the drive gear and mounts, making a substantial saving in the production costs. However, this system required a specific building, which did incur large costs. Designated the R12, one was constructed on each RTS site to house the generators, switch gear and a massive cooling plant to reduce the heat expelled from the system's electronics. Twelve transmitters were fitted vertically in front of the reflector, but only two were operational at any one time. The system was able to use any combination of transmitter frequencies, including fractions of each and instantaneously switch to another wavelength if jamming occurred. The principle being that the hostile aircraft would not be able to locate all frequencies used, enabling the radar to operate under the majority of conditions.

Height Finder 200

The major problem with the Types 84 and 85 was that they only gave distance to a target, the ability to note the height still required a separate radar system; by the time of Linesman this was the Decca Height Finder 200. The scanner measured 10m by 2.5m and was situated on a 15m-high conical tower, containing the hydraulic systems for the nodding and rotational aspects of the radar. When a target was illuminated by either the Type 84 or 85 the HF200 would be turned onto that track. The scanner was capable of between 20–30 cycles per minute giving adequate height data to the RTS and MCC out to a maximum of 280km and up to 17,000m.

UKADGE

Discussions within the Air Ministry in 1970–71 recognised that the old doctrine of total nuclear response under 'Trip-Wire', the main reason for dispersed Linesman sites, was inappropriate in the current climate. NATO had, by 1967, changed its defensive posture to one of 'Flexible Response' where a gradual escalation in hostilities would precede any nuclear exchange. Clearly more conventional and chemical air strikes could be expected and a modern air defence system fully integrated with NATO was now required for the United Kingdom. The implementation of the United Kingdom Air Defence Ground Environment (UKADGE) plan started in the mid-1970s continuing right through to the 1990s.

Linesman, for all its modern approach, had some major failings, especially when it came to low-level detection (below 300m). Also, the fixed radar assets were susceptible to attack from the air or through saboteurs. Interestingly the United States had forewarned of this during the Plan Ahead discussions, suggesting the Air Ministry stick to smaller multiple sites, but due mainly to cost the dispersed arrangement was eventually implemented. Command of the network was to be retained at the current Linesman sites, West Drayton and High Wycombe, whilst Control and Reporting Centres (CRC) would be created at Buchan, Bishops Court, Boulmer and Neatishead. The crucial difference here was that if any of the CRCs were knocked out one of the other sites could take over as each had a large degree of autonomy. Fast low-level aircraft still continued to be the major flaw in the radar network and a number of solutions were tabled to counter the threat. Consideration was given to placing radar on some of the larger North Sea Oil Rigs, similar to the Texas Towers operation off the eastern coast of the United States between 1955 and 1964, to extend the range of the coverage. Some quarters wanted to see the revival of the Royal Observer Corps recognition role, whilst the concept of Over-The-Horizon-Radar had already proved to be technologically unworkable and was rejected. In the end it fell to the ageing AEW Shackleton (next chapter) to extend the coverage beyond the horizon.

NATO financed substantial upgrades to facilities during the 1980s including the protection of sites at Buchan, Neatishead and Ash, including the installation of comprehensive decontamination suites; clearly the military considered the use of chemical weapons a distinct possibility, not the image they promoted to the public. It was also proposed to replace the vulnerable fixed radars as quickly as possible; but due to development problems with the mobile sets, Neatishead did not loose its Type 84 until 1993, other sites being slightly earlier. The 'new' network comprised three main parts: Sector Operation Centres (SOC), Control and Reporting Centres (CRC) and mobile radars dispersed to areas from the vulnerable fixed radar sites.

Tactical Control in the 1980s

By the mid-1980s Strike Command oversaw a complex series of sites fully integrated with NATO Supreme Air Command Europe (SACEUR). Interceptors included a bewildering array of aircraft from all periods of the Cold War including Hunter, Phantom, Lightning, Hawk, Jaguar and the new Tornado F3 Air Defence Variant. Surface-to-air missiles included the Bloodhound Mk2, complementing the fighter cover and for close airfield support there were the Rapier squadrons. Information was collated from a number of sources including Navy air defence (upgraded after the Falklands Campaign), and Airborne Early Warning from the ageing Shackleton fleet or one of NATO's other member states. For attacks from the west, Strike Command used data links with the Royal Navy along with passive radar sites situated on the west coast and in a real crisis could also use information from the BMEWS at Fylingdales. This information was passed to one of the three SOCs at Boulmer, Buchan or Neatishead, whilst filtering of civil aircraft was carried out, using the Identification Friend or Foe (IFF) system at High Wycombe.

Opportunities to test out the operational effectiveness of the network did occur (up to three times a week in the 1980s, and more during NATO exercises) courtesy

'Bear' – the Tupolev TU-95 regularly skirted British airspace in the 1970s and '80s, often three times a week.

of Russian reconnaissance missions, usually a Tupolev TU-95 'Bear' flying on the edge of British airspace. Strike Command maintained aircraft on Quick Reaction Alert (QRA) twenty-four hours a day for just such an occurrence, that would be scrambled and placed on an intercept course. The intruder would then be shepherded back out into international airspace. These impromptu meetings between East and West were often good-humoured affairs with crews waving and often holding up pinups whilst the aircraft flew alongside each other.

Of course, on transition to war things would be very different. All aircraft movements, civil and military, would come under the direct control of High Wycombe. Airborne Early Warning patrols would give extended coverage across the North Sea, whilst Phantoms and later Tornados would patrol the same areas using Victor K2 and VC10 tankers to extend duration. Close coastal support would be afforded by Lightnings, Hawks, Jaguars and Hunters and if that failed the Bloodhound Mk2 batteries would be activated. Bloodhound no longer afforded point protection, being used more as a 'wall' down most of the east coast. If any aircraft got through the layered defence then the Rapier batteries dispersed at strategic points around the many airfields would, hopefully, finish them off. The Western approaches would be covered by point air defence Harriers from the Fleet Air Arm using a combination of carrier-borne and land-based aircraft.

Beyond the Cold War

Since the end of the Cold War some radical changes have been undertaken in air defence. The SOCs have been reduced to one site, Neatishead, that now performs the role of Command and Control, whilst other sites have lost their fixed radar installations relying on the mobile '90 series' sets. In times of crisis these will be moved to less-vulnerable dispersal sites, the information being disseminated by microwave data link via satellite. The majority of the early warning network is now covered by the Boeing Sentry, giving 'real time' information and performing, in many cases, the control and command task. Interestingly, it was as flying Fighter Controllers onboard Sentry that the first women flew in operational conditions for the RAF. The intercepting aircraft, primarily Tornado F3s, also require minimal control once the target has been identified, a very different situation from the hundreds of personnel operating the numerous Rotor-period sites devised in the 1950s.

Lightning. The supersonic English Electric Lightning, capable of over twice the speed of sound, regularly intercepted Russian aircraft testing British air defence reaction times.

F-3. The Tornado F-3 Air Defence Variant (ADV) has been the mainstay of the RAF interceptor fleet since 1985. (Courtesy Pete James)

three

Airborne Early Warning

One major disadvantage with the ground-based Rotor equipment was the fixed range, primarily because it had no 'over the horizon' capability. Units could be moved around the country to protect specific areas (a requirement of Operation Vast) but, as Britain is an island, their range was severely hampered. One way of countering this was to put radar in the air, extending the coverage by the range of the aircraft. This was recognised as a distinct advantage throughout the Cold War, especially as hostile aircraft speeds were increasing beyond the sound barrier. The concept is still a major part of today's national defence. Three aircraft platforms stand out during this period, Shackleton, Gannet and Nimrod; all performed various duties beyond Airborne Early Warning but will be described here in that role. Theirs is a story of often poor decisions that dogged British Defence throughout the Cold War period.

Genesis

Airborne Early Warning (AEW) owes more to Royal Navy requirements than any other service; practically all aircraft employed within this operational role had their origins in submarine detection and carrier defence. The first of the Cold War AEW platforms deployed with the Fleet Air Arm (FAA) was the Douglas AD-4W Skyraider, a variant of the successful ground attack aircraft. This carrier aircraft, designated the Skyraider AEW 1 by the FAA, was first placed on charge from November 1951 and fifty of the type operated until it was phased out in 1960. The key point here is that it was equipped with a chin-mounted AN/APS-20 radar, which was to give an incredible forty years of service before it too was phased out in favour of the Boeing Sentry electronics package (described later).

Avro Shackleton

The Shackleton's origins can be traced back to the Second World War, the first of the lineage being the AVRO Manchester, later to become the famous Lancaster, which in turn was developed as the Lancastrian civilian airliner then into the Lincoln. The first Shackleton flew on 9 March 1949 and entered service as a Maritime Reconnaissance (MR) aircraft with 120 Squadron, based at Kinloss, on 5 April 1951. The aircraft was powered by four Rolls-Royce Griffon engines with contra-rotating propellers. Three major electronic upgrades were initiated during the twenty years it operated in the anti-submarine role. This included the addition, on MR3 aircraft, of two Bristol Siddeley Viper turbojets to assist take-off. Unfortunately this reduced the fatigue life of the aircraft and by 1971 all Shackletons had been withdrawn, giving way to the Nimrod MR1.

This was not the end of the Shackleton story. As the Royal Navy became more reliant on land-based AEW aircraft it became apparent that a longer range and duration was needed than the carrier-borne Skyraider and Gannets could provide. Subsequently twelve low-fatigue-life Shackletons were converted to AEW2s becoming operational on 8 January 1972 with No. 8 Squadron RAF at Lossiemouth. This was considered an interim solution until a purpose-built radar platform could be developed. One familiar piece of equipment featured in this conversion, the AN/APS 20 radar; both scanner and radome from decommissioned Gannets were fitted underneath the flight deck of the aircraft.

Fairey Gannet

Towards the end of the Second World War the Admiralty had recognised the need for a specialist anti-submarine aircraft, preferably carrier based. On 19 September 1949 Fairey flew the 'Type Q' prototype powered by an Armstrong-Siddeley Mamba turbojet. The first deck landing of a turbo-prop aircraft was made on HMS *Illustrious* on 19 June 1950 and soon after an order was placed for 100 aircraft, by now known as the Gannet. Early in the production run the radar requirement was changed, so that aircraft entering service from 1954 now had a retractable radome fitted to the lower fuselage. The last Fairey/Westland Gannet anti-submarine MR aircraft was replaced by the Westland Whirlwind helicopter in the early 1960s.

The Airborne Early Warning variant, AEW3, entered service in 1958 with some radical modifications to the MR aircraft. Firstly an AN/APS-20 radar was chin-mounted in a fairing under the aircraft. This led to the structure of the airframe being re-designed to counter the extra fatigue placed on it. A larger tail fin was fitted to counter the adverse yaw effect of the radome. The Gannet AEW3 also had foldable wings to allow for carrier-borne storage.

Hawker Siddeley/BAe Nimrod

A replacement for the Shackleton was given top priority in the mid-1960s and led to Hawker Siddeley (later BAe) winning the contract to develop the HS 801, destined to become Nimrod. The aircraft was based on the Comet 4C airframe, but was essentially a brand new aircraft, although the first two examples were converted Comets. The first prototype flight was on 23 May 1967 with the first production model flying a little over a year later. Forty-three aircraft were delivered to the RAF as Nimrod MR1, operated by 42 Squadron, RAF St Mawgan and 120, 201, 206 Squadrons, RAF Kinloss. By the early 1980s thirty-two were upgraded to MR2 with enhanced communications and tactical avionics. All MR types were, and later marks still are,

AVRO Shackleton. First flying on 9 March 1949, this elderly aircraft was to see service throughout the Cold War.

Fairey Gannet. The Gannet entered service as the AEW3 variant in 1958; it was both carrier and land based.

employed in the anti-shipping/submarine role as part of the NATO commitment.

South Atlantic Wake-up Call

In 1964 the new Labour Government initiated major defence cuts including the decommissioning of the aircraft carrier fleet. The decision caused a major outcry. Denis Healey, then Secretary of State for Defence, was in favour of phasing out the carriers by the mid-1970s and placing no orders for new ones, relying instead on shore-based fixed-wing aircraft. The First Sea Lord, Sir David Luce, and Minister of Defence for the Navy, Christopher Mayhew, resigned over the proposals finally announced in the Defence White Paper published on 22 February 1966. By 1978 when the last carrier, HMS *Ark Royal*, was laid up for the final time, the Gannet also ceased operation and the task of providing air cover passed to the Royal Air Force. This was to prove the ultimate folly.

On 2 April 1982 the Argentinean Dictatorship, led by General Galtieri, launched an invasion of the Falkland Islands in the South Atlantic, quickly overcoming the small Royal Marine force stationed there. Just three days later the first ships of the Falklands Task Force set sail for the Islands. Aircraft were also amassed at the small British outpost on Ascension Island, just over halfway between Britain and the Falklands. Now an unforeseen problem manifested itself, the Royal Navy had spent the last two

Flight deck director lining up a Phantom onto the catapult onboard HMS *Ark Royal* in 1978. The loss of the heavy carrier capability was to have serious consequences in the South Atlantic. (© Crown Copyright)

decades downsizing and preparing for an anti-submarine role within NATO. It no longer had the capability to cover an operation such as the Task Force.

Airborne Early Warning (AEW) was now a combination of ship-borne radar and occasional coverage from Nimrod aircraft stationed at Ascension, 12,000km away. However, the Nimrod MR2 was still essentially a submarine/surface hunter not an AEW platform, although the fitting of Sidewinder missiles for aircraft defence did lead to it becoming affectionately known as the 'biggest fighter in the world'. The situation was further exacerbated since the Navy had lost its large fixed-wing capability and with it the Gannet AEW3. The new carriers were only capable of operating Harriers, with their STOL/VTOL characteristics, or helicopters, so coverage was dramatically reduced. The elderly Shackleton AEW had neither the range nor speed to be involved and played no role in the campaign, further compounding the situation. Argentinean aircraft were able to get in a lot closer before detection, which contributed to the loss of a number of Navy and civilian vessels. Clearly the Labour decision of 1966 had come home to roost; it was now obvious the Navy could not rely on intermittent cover from the RAF. This led to the development of Searchwater, fitted to Sea King HAS1 aircraft, which now operate from all Navy carriers.

Recipe for Disaster

The story of British AEW is a microcosm of the Cold War, involving changing goal posts, under-funding, lack of Government foresight, advances in technology and lack of partnership in the NATO ideal. The replacement of the Douglas AD-4W Skyraider with the Gannet AEW3 from 1958 fulfilled the Royal Navy's requirement for a carrier-borne platform. But the slow decline of the aircraft carrier fleet sealed the fate of the Gannet and by the early 1970s the task had moved to the RAF, operating Shackletons from bases at Malta, Gibraltar, Cyprus and mainland Britain. These aircraft were 'updated' Maritime Reconnaissance aircraft having a refurbished communications suite and the, by now familiar, AN/APS-20 radar, which had already seen service with the previous two aircraft. Increasingly the aircraft was used in a supporting role for RAF air defence as well as affording cover for the fleet. The Shackleton stop-gap was intended to cover just a few years whilst the Government procured a new purpose-built aircraft, but this was not to be.

The Boeing Company in the United States had been developing an Airborne Early Warning aircraft from the early 1970s, later to become the E-3 Sentry, which was initially offered to NATO member states. A lack of orders from Europe prompted Boeing to revise the offer in 1977, now NATO was to be given chance to buy the system, which could then be operated by member states. One year later, after lengthy discussions, a multilateral memorandum to acquire the E-3 Sentry was signed by NATO Defence Ministers. The first aircraft was delivered in 1982 and by 1985 the full complement of eighteen had been reached. But the British Government saw the aircraft as an expensive option, involving little in the way of jobs for the United Kingdom, neither was it clear how the aircraft were to be operated. Instead an order was placed for eleven Nimrod AEW3 to be built in Britain using the highly successful Nimrod MR as a blueprint.

The AEW Nimrod. The British Government spent an estimated £1 billion before deciding to buy the E3-Sentry.

The primary contractor, Hawker Siddeley (later BAe), proposed a GEC-Marconi two-antenna system, mounted front and rear of the aircraft, giving 360 degrees of uninterrupted vision. Initial tests were conducted aboard two converted Comet 4 aircraft, flying for the first time on 28 June 1977, carrying just the forward radome. The first of eleven production models made its maiden flight in July 1980 from Woodford Aerodrome. The problem was that the stop-gap decision now meant that the Shackleton would have to stay in service well beyond the intended replacement date.

Then development hit the buffers. The first major problem was the size of the Nimrod airframe. Although the aircraft was a 'new' build it still inherited the old Comet 4C dimensions, making the equipment difficult to accommodate. Secondly the electronics were such that when running at full capacity a large amount of heat was generated. To dissipate this, fuel in the wing tanks was used as a heat sink, however this only worked if the tanks were at half or more capacity. Clearly this had serious range implications. One option was to air-to-air refuel the aircraft whilst it was on station, pushing operating costs through the roof.

The processing capability of the GEC 4080M computer was also in doubt. When the various avionics systems were tested separately they operated perfectly, but when the full suite of systems was linked together the computer's 2.4-megabyte capacity crashed – repeatedly. By now the costs were, unlike the aircraft, soaring and the due delivery date continually slipped. During trials by MOD(PE) in 1984 the aircraft only managed three hours of full avionic operation during an incredible eight flights. Also the range for all the equipment was far below requirements. By 1986 it was becoming increasingly apparent that the Nimrod AEW3 would never reach full operational deployment and the Conservative Government pulled the plug. The estimated cost ran to a staggering £1 billion. All the while the Shackleton fleet, albeit reduced by a combination of airframe fatigue and cost cutting, soldiered on.

Sentry

At the same time the Government announced the Nimrod AEW3 cancellation it indicated its intention to purchase six Boeing E-3A Sentry aircraft, the type offered back in the mid-1970s. The projected date for the first delivery was March 1991; the remaining Shackletons with their, by now, antiquated AN/APS-20 radar would have to last a few more years. The order with Boeing covered six aircraft, spares, systems trainers and associated ground equipment, also a number of specialist modifications such as a refuelling probe and an enhanced maritime radar system. The MOD exercised its option for one more aircraft and in 1991, as the Cold War came to a close, the Royal Air Force finally got a modern Airborne Early Warning platform.

The Shackletons were finally retired in 1991, an incredible fifty-two years after the first test flight, earning their place alongside the Bloodhound as one of the few weapons systems that encompassed the whole of the Cold War.

Boeing E3A Sentry. The first aircraft entered service with the Royal Air Force in March 1991, the last year of the Cold War.

four

The Anti-aircraft Network

The origins of anti-aircraft systems can be traced back to the trenches of the First World War, and by the Second World War it had become a mixture of rudimentary radar and proximity fused shells that proved very effective. In the early years of the Cold War the use of artillery prevailed, but the arrival of the jet bomber changed anti-aircraft tactics forever. This chapter will trace the anti-aircraft network from the days of the Gun Defended Area through to its modern conclusion – the Rapier missile.

Genesis

By the end of the war in Europe a complex network of anti-aircraft systems were in place to counter any threat from the air. This network comprised barrage balloon squadrons, search light batteries, Royal Observer Corps posts, gun batteries, both fixed and mobile, and radar sites all controlled through sector operations sectors in line with Fighter Command. The tactics were sound, having been developed through six years of struggle against a variety of intruders, including large bomber formations, low-level hit-and-run missions and towards the end the first cruise missile attacks from the V1.

On the Ground

The highly developed radar network was often the first to pick up raiding aircraft, giving RAF Fighter Command time to predict which sectors needed to be brought to readiness. Balloon squadrons would ensure that enemy aircraft had to operate at higher flight levels, making bomb aiming less accurate and giving gun crews more time to target them, whilst the ROC tracked formations and low-level aircraft as they crossed the country. RAF Sector Operation Centres (SOC) then activated the fighter group or Gun Operation Rooms (GOR) within the threatened sector who orchestrated an appropriate response.

Gunnery defences were, by the end of the war, extensive. Swindon had three heavy batteries and at least six light emplacements protecting the railway industry in the town. However, by late 1944 most gun batteries had been relocated to either the south coast or into Europe as the front moved steadily east. Positions for the defences were a mixture of fixed emplacements with adjacent accommodation and stores, and mobile sites under tents with little or no real structure around the gun. At the end of the war just over 200 sites were designated to be retained, forming the 'Nucleus Force'. But this proved to be a little ambitious and by 1947 a revised plan, 'Igloo', was put in place. Fixed guns at fifty-four sites were to be kept operational with equipment and other light-calibre weapons stored at depots around the country.

Anti-aircraft Operations Rooms

The command and operation of the anti-aircraft network remained the preserve of the Army, as it had throughout the Second World War. Thirty-three Anti-Aircraft Operations Rooms (AAOR) were envisaged to control the Gun Defended Areas (GDA) that were divided into five groups, in line with the RAF Sector Operations Centres (SOC). The majority of operations rooms were new-build structures, but a few were located at existing sites such as Fort Fareham, GDA Plymouth/Southampton, Group 2; Dover Castle, GDA Dover, Group 1 and Llanion Barracks, GDA Milford Haven, Group 4. The new structures were impressive concrete buildings that were, where possible, semi-sunken two-story designs.

Lansdown, GDA Bristol, Group 2, completed in 1954, typifies the construction techniques of the time. Built on two levels the site is now occupied by the Avon Fire Brigade, forming part of the Emergency Control network. The structure centred

Lansdown UKWMO and ROC Group 12 HQ. The ROC protected HQ is the grey-roofed structure, formally an Anti-aircraft Operations Room built in 1954. The offices on the left were built in the 1980s to house the UKWMO.

Ullenwood. Anti-aircraft Operations Room near Gloucester. Gun Defended Area, Brockworth.

around a plotting room that, in turn, was surrounded by a three-sided balcony. Rooms around this included accommodation for both male and female army officers and other ranks, a mess hall, signals office, ventilation and generators, and even a small NAAFI. From the AAOR, information regarding direction, height and potential threat was passed out to the gun sites within their GDA.

The Gun Defended Areas

Designated GDAs concentrated on two specific areas, industrial, especially defence-orientated sites, and coastal sites, including major ports. Wartime facilities were reoccupied in the majority of cases, however some new sites were constructed. Interestingly English Heritage have identified a change in layout between the old and new sites. Whilst the 1939–45 emplacements tend to be in a diamond or arch the later ones were constructed in a line, suggesting a wall of fire could be put up; clearly an eye was already on the lone bomber threat. The two main weapons employed were the 5.25 and 3.7-inch anti-aircraft guns, both modified from earlier versions, having fully automated loading, rotational and elevation systems, which increased the response time.

Advances in radar saw the introduction of fire control sets that could be mounted on site and used to accurately track the intruder, giving more lethality to the gun system. The information was fed directly to the automated gun, eliminating the time-consuming optical laying in method and any time delay from the AAOR. Upgrades to the weapons systems were also intended and two new medium/heavy anti-aircraft guns trials were conducted at the Royal Armament Research and Development Establishment. Green Mace was a 5-inch calibre rapid-fire weapon that was fully automated; the shells were fed to the breach by way of two revolving magazines, achieving a rate of fire up to ninety-six rounds per minute. Red Queen was a twin-barrelled gun developed by the Oerlikon company, who incidentally still supply rapid-rate weapons to the defence community today. Both projects were cancelled in 1955 in favour of the new, guided anti-aircraft systems being developed by English Electric and Bristol Aeroplane Company.

Construction of the Gun Defended Area network took nearly five years, by which time technology and tactics had overtaken conventional anti-aircraft thinking and the whole system was considered obsolete. It was during this period that both superpowers had tested thermonuclear devices; aircraft had also started to operate at heights that were far above gun limits. Ballistic missiles were now a reality with systems coming on line in both Russia and America, whilst Britain was developing the Blue Streak. The funding for the British project was to be at the expense of research and development in other areas, including anti-aircraft guns, and by 1955 the Army had been replaced by the RAF as the provider of air defence. The Gun Defended Area network was summarily abandoned.

Countering the Supersonic Threat

Surface-to-air Missiles

Britain had investigated the possible development of Surface-to-Air Missiles (SAM) towards the end of the Second World War, with the first test firing of the 'Brakemine' programme in 1944. The programme continued until early 1947 and proved that a SAM system was feasible, but cost was a major issue. The potential was quickly recognised by the Air Ministry who, through Operational Requirement 1124, requested the development of a comprehensive network of anti-aircraft defence systems capable of destroying an aircraft a great many miles from its target. Two companies were awarded development contracts and, in conjunction with the RAE and other Government departments, produced two very effective missiles. One, the Bloodhound, is a classic example of a Cold War weapons system.

Red Shoes – Thunderbird

The Royal Artillery did not give up their claim on air defence on stand down of the GDA network. As part of the Stage Air Defence plan the Army intended to retain its in-the-field capability with a new medium-range weapon, code named Red Shoes, destined to become Thunderbird. The development contract was awarded to English Electric who had recently built a plant at Luton to explore and develop rocketry principles. The missile was powered off the stand by four Gosling boost motors, manufactured by Bristol Aerojet at Banwell, and then sustained in flight by an Albatross solid motor. The original Red Shoes concept had been a liquid-fuelled motor; however, by the turn of the 1950s solid fuel had become a reality, making the operation of Thunderbird in the field a lot simpler. Field trials were carried out at the RAE range at Aberporth, West Wales, and acceptance trials were completed at Woomera by the end of 1959.

Green Mace was capable of firing ninety-six 5-inch calibre shells per minute.

Thunderbird Mk I entered service with a number of heavy anti-aircraft batteries throughout 1959–60, replacing the 3.7-inch mobile and fixed guns, by now in storage or used for ceremonial duties. The deployed system exceeded requirements with the missile capable of reaching at least 40km, twice that specified. The system was replaced by Thunderbird II in 1966. This had an extended range (75km), had a better low and high level capacity, between 1,500–22,500m and reached well over mach 2. The warhead was a continuous-rod high explosive charge which could be detonated by radio control or proximity fuse, all in all a very effective weapon.

Batteries

A Thunderbird operating regiment was usually made up of two batteries and each battery comprised three troops. The first troop was equipped with the tactical control radar and height finder system, both run from a mobile Battery Command Post. Troop two operated the target illuminating radar and Launcher Control Post, whilst troop three carried out missile duties at the launch site. The Royal Signals and REME also supported the Thunderbird at battery level clearing and surveying launch sites and setting up communications links. Thunderbirds I and II were the first purely British-built missiles to be deployed with the Army and the Government was eager to sell the system in an effort to recoup some of the ten-year development costs. Some potential customers were Libya (also interested in Rapier) in 1968, and Zambia in 1969, not the best of choices but then when is that ever the case. The system was withdrawn from service in 1976 as it was considered Rapier performed a very similar function and was considerably more versatile.

Red Duster – Bloodhound

Red Duster was the Ministry of Supply code name for the Bloodhound development project awarded to the Bristol Aeroplane Company in 1947. The Mk I had some distinct limitations, not the least of which was the lack of mobility; the original concept had been to post the missile firing batteries on existing anti-aircraft sites. Unfortunately this thinking, albeit watered down, stayed with the Mk I and it became a fixed asset with the launcher bolted to a permanent concrete hard standing. By 1958 the first Bloodhound Mk I surface-to-air missiles were being deployed with 264 Squadron, under 148 Wing based at RAF North Coates in Lincolnshire. Four Wings were designated in all including 21 Wing, Lindholme, 24 Wing, Watton and 151 Wing, North Luffenham, with eleven squadrons operating the SAM system until mid-1964. Bloodhound, like Thunderbird, was a total air-defence system incorporating many different technologies produced by a number of defence contractors.

Bloodhound II

The development of the Bloodhound Mk II began in 1957, before its predecessor had been deployed. The Mk II addressed some of the Mk I shortcomings and delivered a far superior weapons system, allowing for greater 'kill' potential. A Type 86 Target Illuminating Radar (TIR) was used in the new system which was far less susceptible to electronic countermeasures, using a continuous wave pattern instead of the earlier pulse system employed with the Type 83 TIR. The missile was modified too, having a better propulsion system, the Rolls-Royce Thor ramjet, that could power the Bloodhound to an improved height of over 20,000m and gave an effective range of

Bloodhound Mk 2. The RAF's surface-to-air missile powered by two Rolls-Royce Thor ramjets.

around 185km at 10,000m. The low-level capability was also enhanced to counter the new radar-evading techniques being employed by both sides. Bloodhound was capable of destroying an aircraft at a height of 42m at just over 10km; it was clearly now an all-round weapon. As the missile got close to the target a proximity fuse detonated the warhead sending shrapnel from the steel rods encasing the explosives through any aircraft nearby, shredding systems and occupants alike.

Deployment

Deployment of the Bloodhound Mk II was restricted to fewer sites than those of its predecessor, concentrated in an arc from North Coates down to Bawdsey along the east coast. However, from 1970, 25 Squadron was stationed in West Germany, comprising three flights, Bruggen (A flight and HQ); Wildenrath (B flight) and Laarbruch (C flight). These were pulled back to the United Kingdom in 1975 as a gap in home defence was recognised and Rapier units were now considered more effective in the field. During 1989 the surviving squadrons, 25, 112, 41 and 85, were amalgamated and ran as flights (A to F) attached to 85 Squadron HQ at RAF West Raynham. The cost of maintaining such an elderly, if effective, weapons system was becoming apparent.

Bloodhound II was originally given a ten-year life, but the system was to remain Britain's main anti-aircraft missile until the end of the Cold War. Over a two-year period the deployment of the missile was steadily reduced, and on 28 February 1990 Parliament was informed that Bloodhound would be based at RAF Wattisham and RAF West Raynham, closing four other units. By 2 May 1991, as a direct consequence of 'Options for Change', the last remaining Bloodhound Squadrons were earmarked for stand down. Bloodhound did soldier on abroad, though, both Switzerland and Singapore were still operating the system in 1998.

Rapier

Rapier is a mobile Short Range Air Defence (SHORAD) missile system based on a 1964 development programme by English Electric, primarily at Stevenage. It originally comprised three units, a Blindfire mobile radar, optical tracker and a firing unit with four missiles. By the 1980s this had been complemented with a tracked mobile launch system that contained operational command, laser optical sighting and a four-missile firing unit all on one unit. Rapier is still deployed with the armed services around the world, but avionics and mobility upgrades mean it is almost unrecognisable from its Cold War predecessor.

Deployment

Rapier systems entered service with the Royal Air Force Regiment and British Army in June 1967 for airfield defence, countering low-level conventional threats and, under field deployment, aircraft launching stand-off weapons. After an extended 'shake-down' period, which demonstrated the system was not as robust as first thought, major modification was undertaken by British Aerospace (English Electric had by the late 1970s been absorbed). The system was combat proven during the 1982 Falklands campaign, achieving aircraft kills over San Carlos Bay.

Rapier. The mobile Short Range Air Defence missile system proved highly effective in the Falklands campaign in 1982.

Normal operational deployment from the late 1970s to the end of the Cold War was extensive. Low Level Air Defence (LLAD) squadrons were stationed in the United Kingdom, Germany and Cyprus. Strike Command, Group 11, contained three LLAD units, 27 Squadron at Leuchars; 48 Squadron at Lossiemouth and 34 Squadron posted to Akrotiri; but in times of a national emergency this would have been moved back to Northern Europe. Germany had four squadrons, 37 Squadron Bruggen, 26 Squadron Laarbruch, 16 Squadron Wildenrath and 63 Squadron Gutersloh. Detachments also included the protectorate of Belize in South America and covering Aldergrove in Northern Ireland.

Tactics

When required for airfield defence the Rapier system was deployed to designated points in the landscape, usually between 10 and 15km from base. Each firing unit was capable of covering 100 sq. km around 360 degrees, making a deployment of eight units extremely effective. Three major components comprised the system: the firing unit containing four Rapier missiles, the optical tracker unit used by the operator to guide the system onto the target, and the DN 181 Blindfire radar for low visibility or nighttime conditions. Up to eight firing units could be controlled by a mobile command unit situated in a purpose-built unit on the back of a four-tonne truck. In these forward positions the fire units were self supporting, having mobile workshops, messing and spare Rapier rounds; all were fully protected for NBC conditions.

The Rapier round was 2.2m in length, 13cm in diameter and weighed at launch 42kg. Powered by a dual thrust, Troy solid rocket motor, built and developed by Bristol Aerojet at Banwell, it was controlled by tail control fins onto the target at speeds of up to mach 2. Rapier worked on the hitile principle. Unlike many other anti-aircraft systems which were proximity fused, the round needed to physically strike the target to explode. Once launched the round was optically or radar-assisted onto the target to a maximum range of 6,800m and a ceiling of 3,000m.

In the early 1980s the United States financed three RAF Regiment squadrons to set up defensive outposts around the main USAF Airbases in the United Kingdom. Control of the squadrons came under Wing No. 6 formed and based at RAF West Raynham in July 1983. By 1985 the three squadrons, 19, RAF Brize Norton, 20, RAF Honington, and 66, RAF West Raynham, had been formed and were operational. The sites these squadrons would protect included the Ground Launched Cruise Missile (GLCM) bases at RAF Greenham Common and, had it been activated, RAF Molesworth.

Deployment as part of exercises involving NATO aircraft were a common occurrence, although sometimes the siting could be rather embarrassing. On 16 May 1994 the Cambridgeshire village of Great Stukely awoke to find an operational Rapier firing unit stationed in their midst. Alarm and complaints were such that questions were asked in the House of Commons, especially since the village was within the then Prime Minister John Major's constituency. After the reduction of USAF sites to two in the United Kingdom, Wing No. 6 was disbanded in 1995, part of the peace dividend which permeated throughout the first half of that decade.

five

Ballistic Missile Early Warning System

The Ballistic Missile Early Warning System, part of which was situated on the North Yorkshire Moors, achieved iconic status during the Cold War; it was from here that the public expected the 'four-minute warning' to be given. This chapter looks at RAF Fylingdales and some of the lesser-known projects that were intended to detect ballistic missiles.

Ballistic missiles (BM) are the most potent weapon in the nuclear arsenal. Unlike aircraft they are almost impossible to stop and by the late 1950s BM combined with the development of the thermonuclear warhead necessitated a radical rethink in the detection and warning of such an attack. The changes to the radar network under Plan Ahead (1958) could track stand-off missiles but was ineffective when used to detect missile launches. Some development had been under way in Britain as to how to counter the threat of such an attack, however this was at a very basic stage. The V2 attacks of the Second World War had demonstrated that only the destruction of the launch site or passive defensive measures were possible. By 1953 it was recognised that a defensive network against ballistic missiles was required, but the Defence Research Policy Committee also recommended that the air defence missile projects currently under way should investigate the possibility of shooting down a BM.

The Ministry of Supply instructed English Electric and Marconi, in 1955, to research two main areas: Anti-Ballistic Missile Missiles (ABMM) and Anti-Ballistic Missile Early Warning (ABMEW), to counter the threat. Whilst the Air Ministry took interest in the projects, they quickly concluded that the ability to destroy ballistic missiles was some way off. The technology just wasn't available, and subsequently funding was reduced. In 1956 the Tripartite Conference, comprising Britain, Canada and the United States, pointed out that whilst work on the Rotor sites could bring them up to a level capable of detecting incoming missiles, the possibility of building a complete network capable of detecting a launch, tracking trajectory and predicting the target had some real technological problems to overcome.

The main problem was how to track a nuclear warhead once released from the missile. It was well known that a number of decoys would also be released at the same time and this, coupled with parts of the missile, would make tracking the warhead very difficult indeed. Even the University of Manchester got involved, using the massive radio telescope at Jodrell Bank to track debris from meteorites, in an attempt to measure potential background particulates, in case a system was designed. The process of research into the problem was extremely slow and then, in October 1957, the Soviet Union launched the 'Mechanism', shaking many on both sides of the Atlantic. If the Russians had a rocket capable of launching a satellite into orbit, then it was only a matter of time before it could carry nuclear warheads to America; earlier concerns now took on a new sense of urgency. In 1958 the Whitehouse passed plans to the British Government outlining a Ballistic Missile Early Warning System (BMEWS), the development of which had been under way since at least 1956. The proposed network would entail building three sites to cover the northern hemisphere all linked to provide early warning and target prediction. The British Government welcomed the move, American companies would supply most equipment, and this was by far a better option than years of expensive development costs. The three sites were to be Clear, Alaska, Thule, Greenland, and one in Northern Europe. The construction of the first two sites got under way in 1958, but the position of the third site required far more consideration. Locations from North Scotland to East Anglia were considered and after a year of intensive ground and political work 750 hectares of the North Yorkshire Moors were chosen. Situated on Lockton High Moor the site was destined to become the most famous symbol of Cold War Britain, Royal Air Force Fylingdales.

The area had a number of attractive qualities; it was already owned by the Government and it was high enough to have a clear view of the horizon whilst being far enough inland to be inconspicuous from the sea. It was remote, helping security and keeping people out of the way of the vast amounts of microwave energy that the radars would emit. Furthermore it was far enough away from Eastern Block stations to be less susceptible to electronic countermeasures (ECM). The location had been an Army training area and required considerable ordnance clearance prior to any groundwork; several members of the clearance team were killed in accidents whilst this was under way. Construction was completed in March 1963 and the site was officially commissioned on 17 September the same year. Although the system was essentially United States-manufactured equipment, some development work was undertaken by Elliot Automation under the code name Legate. This was to tie the BMEWS into the United Kingdom Monitoring and Warning Organisation. The UKWMO now had the ability to warn the population of an impending missile attack. The 'four-minute warning' was born, although in reality it could have been as little as two and a half!

Fylingdales performed the same Intercontinental Ballistic Missile tracking, warning and target prediction function as the sites at Clear and Thule, although it was also capable of detecting and tracking Intermediate Range Ballistic Missiles, due to the closeness of Europe. The site comprised three main areas, all heavily fenced and

RAF Fylingdales. Construction of the three massive protective domes and associated protective buildings took three years to complete. The site was commissioned on 17 September 1963. (Courtesy *Scarborough Evening News*)

RAF Fylingdales. From here the progress of any suspected missile would be tracked and if necessary the 'four-minute warning' would be issued. (Courtesy *Scarborough Evening News*)

Left: RAF Fylingdales. The AN/FPS-49 radar, each had a 25m parabolic dish, stood on a 10m-high plinth and weighed a massive 112 tonnes. (Courtesy *Scarborough Evening News*)

Opposite: RAF Fylingdales. The solid-state phased array, built to replace the 'Golf Balls'. It was completed in 1992. (Courtesy *Scarborough Evening News*)

patrolled by MOD police. The technical site contained the three tracker buildings, a support area covering administration, fire security and other domestic operations, and the North Atlantic Radio System (NARS) allowing communications, through a chain of sites, to the United States.

Sentinels

The technical site contained the three scanners, each housed under a massive weatherproof radome; these gave rise to the site being known locally as the 'Golf Balls'. The AN/FPS-49 radar comprised a 25m parabolic dish and a counterbalance to cope with the weight of the massive 112-tonne array, all mounted on a 10m-high plinth. Each one was capable of spotting objects up to 4,500km distant and scanned in an arc of 75 degrees. During normal operation the site performed two tasks, two scanners were used to provide 135 degrees of surveillance coverage whilst the other monitored specific targets as they were designated. In 1964 a single tower was built to the south of the technical site, topped by an electronic counter-countermeasures (ECCM) device, primarily to overcome new powerful Soviet jamming techniques.

Each scanner was built on the top floor of a tracker building, which contained three storeys, two above and one below ground. Each building had plates of mild steel incorporated into the structure to counter the effects of the microwave effects emitted from the scanner. The scanner plinth was supported by a series of concrete pillars, which, due to the immense weight of the structure, passed through all three floors and into the bedrock. Each tracker building contained all the equipment required to

generate the massive power that enabled the system to have such an effective range. The data was processed in an annex built at the central tracker, which processed the information as it was intercepted. Having the system in triplicate meant that in the thirty years of operation Fylingdales was never completely out of action.

The three tracker buildings were connected by an enclosed, above ground, tunnel just over 1.5km long that was again steel lined. There was an entrance at each end that had a designated Ministry of Defence police post present, however this would be augmented by the Army around the perimeter in times of international tension. The tunnel or 'Utilidor' as it was known was the only way to access the trackers and scanners and was capable of surviving blast damage, although a direct hit would probably have cracked it open. As with most protected structures from the Cold War a positive internal pressure was maintained throughout the utilidor and tracker buildings to stop the ingress of fallout or chemical agents into the structure. The radomes were not, however, blast proof and would have been fairly comprehensively damaged had a strike on the site been successful; a fact the designers were aware of as access to the golf ball from the room below was via an airlock.

The radome around the scanners was originally constructed from five- and six-sided, 150mm, cardboard honeycomb sections between polyethylene-coated fibreglass outer covers. But cardboard is flammable and when, in the 1970s, the site at Thule was damaged by fire the structures at Fylingdales were modified to be more fire resistant. A lattice aluminium framework was covered by a glass-fibre reinforced Tedlar skin in tension; incidentally, Tedlar went on to have a distinguished career as the covering now found on the walls of aircraft toilets! When the site was finally demolished in 1994 one thousand pieces of fabric, cut from the material, were attached to certificates to commemorate the thirty years the Golf Balls had watched the Northern Hemisphere.

As with all technology during the Cold War, Fylingdales was soon showing its age, and by the early 1970s it was recognised that some upgrades would be needed, especially in the computer systems, if it was to continue effectively. One other major problem manifested itself during this period; ICBMs could now be launched from submarines, hypothetically, whilst Fylingdales was watching the Northern Hemisphere one shot from a submarine in the Irish Sea could destroy the site unannounced, clearly something of a rethink was needed. The answer came in the form of the 'Pyramid', a Solid State Phased Array Radar (SSPAR). Between 1988 and 1992 the SSPAR was constructed on the old NARS site; this too had become obsolete due to a growing reliance on satellite communications, and once completed the golf balls were removed. The old technical site is now being returned to moorland through the guidance of the North Yorkshire Moors National Park Committee whilst the SSPAR is destined to become part of the National Missile Defence programme or 'Son of Star Wars'.

Over-The-Horizon Radar

The systems in place at RAF Fylingdales had a greater range than any other land-based British radar site, but this still had limited 'vision' due to the curvature of the earth. This problem had been well known since the inception of radar and a number of development programmes throughout the Cold War investigated ways of overcoming this. The ability to see over the horizon would have major implications; applications included locating ships and low-flying aircraft, but more importantly was the possibility of greater warning of a missile attack. The division between low-flying aircraft and ballistic missile locating is blurred throughout the 1950s and 60s, primarily due to the application of radar technology. The following projects were designed to counter aircraft first and then see development through to BMEWS, so it is appropriate to describe them here.

Orange Poodle

The Royal Radar Establishment (RRE) developed an experimental radar, code name Orange Poodle, in 1952–53, primarily to explore Over-The-Horizon Radar (OTHR) theories for the Government. The trials were aimed at detecting moving objects, aircraft or ships, below the radar horizon (beyond the curvature of the earth), using the ground-wave effect. Marconi became lead contractor on the project and developed the transmitting equipment, slinging a broadside array between two timber towers at the Chain Home site, RAF Downderry, on the Cornish coast. Small-scale trials in 1953 demonstrated that the concept had potential, designated aircraft were tracked and the equipment was able to discriminate between sea waves and the target. Unfortunately the system, when tested against basic jamming equipment, showed that it would be very easy to disrupt a network of sites if they were commissioned. Subsequently Orange Poodle was scrapped, but the concept and requirement for OTHR continued.

Blue Joker

Another way of seeing over the horizon was to elevate the radar, in similar fashion to equipment mounted on aircraft. Airborne Early Warning was already under development by the mid-1950s but was directed to the Maritime Reconnaissance role rather than total air coverage of the mainland. Also aircraft are expensive to keep in the air and any radar system, if it were to be effective, would need a massive fleet of aircraft to give twenty-four-hour coverage to the entire United kingdom. The answer came in the form of one of the earliest types of air transport, the balloon. It was proposed that a balloon tethered at around 1,500m with a transmitter suspended below would considerably extend the range of land-based stations, possibly up to 80km, a distinct advantage.

Development of the balloons started in 1953 at the RAF Balloon Squadron at Cardington, the same site at which the R101 airship had been built, and by 1954 Metropolitan-Vickers were awarded the development contract for the radar. A ground-based location at Drum, Caernarvonshire, was also selected to test the radar unit before it became airborne. A system of multi-balloon configurations was tested including a triple unit utilising a barrage and then two purpose-built envelopes. Each balloon was capable of 1,400kg of static lift, which was expected to raise the 8 x 2.5m aerial to the required 1,500m. To ensure the equipment was retained a composite cable, which also had to carry the power for the aerial, capable of resisting up to 13 tonnes was developed.

Interestingly the cover story was quite a simple one. Weather balloons were frequently launched from the site, so Blue Joker did not appear to be anything unusual. Some weather considerations were, of course, necessary. The stability of a balloon at Blue Joker's operating heights did require the input of the Meteorological Office. The records demonstrate that in 1956 a number of balloons were lost during weather trials; concern was also voiced that the aerial and cable constituted a serious lightning hazard. By 1960 the Air Ministry was demanding some serious changes to the system, including how Blue Joker would cope with missile detection. The Government was concerned that the detection system was not likely to complement the BMEWS and, seeing as missiles were now considered to be the major threat, cancelled the project in October 1960.

This was not the end for Over-The-Horizon Radar, however, and whilst the British now played little or no part in further development in the 1960s, the Americans continued to develop ways of overcoming the problem. Two joint projects were destined to be conducted in Britain in the late 1960s and early 70s and a third was programmed for the early 1990s, only to be abandoned due, primarily, to international events.

Cold Witness

Project Cold Witness involved having separate transmitter and receiver sites spread widely around the world with the target monitoring area somewhere central to the arrays. As a high-powered signal bounced between transmitter, ionosphere and receiver, using the forward scatter principle any missile passing vertically through it would cause a disturbance in the wave. This complicated and politically sensitive network saw partial success, the results were encouraging enough to warrant the design of a similar system which, it was proposed, would be based in Britain in the 1990s.

Cobra Mist

Project Cobra Mist used a single rather than double or multi-array sites and was built at the old AWRE site at Orford Ness, Suffolk. The AN/FPS-95 radar was originally intended to be built in Turkey, where it would have had a very deep effective range into the Soviet Union. The proposals placed before the Turkish government in 1964 caused some consternation. The country had already been embroiled in the Cuban Missile Crisis by agreeing to have US Jupiter ballistic missiles based there; the Government was not about to get involved in another major international crisis and refused the request. The search for a test site resumed and in 1966 the British Government offered the use of the AWRE test range.

Ground clearance was required before any building work commenced. The site had been a bombing range from late 1917, even seeing the ballistic checks for Blue Danube and Red Beard casings in the 1950s. The AN/FPS-95 system comprised a large fan arrangement covering just over 1 hectare, eighteen 'strings' 549m long were laid out between two masts, one 55m, the other 13m in height. Banks of harmonic filters were built to counter the background noise, which was expected to be encountered, and a large operations unit was built to house test equipment and the staff running the trials. The last transmitter string was fully installed by 10 July 1971 and commissioning checks commenced later that year. The project was up and running by 1972, but trials were delayed by such diverse occurrences as the miners' strike and bad weather blowing down masts in the array. To overcome the background noise the radar was capable of producing a very high transmitted output that could peak at 10 megawatts, yet the average power output was set to 600 kilowatts. Even with this enormous power capability the background noise could neither be filtered nor identified and after almost a year of research into the problem the United States government decided to abandon the project. On 30 June Cobra Mist was decommissioned and the site cleared of the aerial arrays, and the BBC World Service now utilises the buildings and harmonics bank that now sits within a National Trust nature reserve.

Beyond The '70s

By 1984 the idea of OTHR had been resurrected and in November 1988 the British Government was back in negotiations with Washington as to the best way forward. On 20 April 1990 a 'Memorandum of Understanding' between the United Kingdom and the United States was signed covering a joint, two-year trial, of a US Navy developed OTHR based in Britain. The radar was to use a similar principle to that employed on the Cold Witness project of the late 1960s, but the trial was to use two sites in the recipient country rather than be too ambitious and spread itself all over the globe.

RAF Blakehill Farm. Trials were being undertaken at the GCHQ site much earlier than was announced, however the end of the Cold War saw many projects such as Over-The-Horizon Radar shelved.

To be effective the system needed separate transmitter and receiver sites far enough apart to allow the ionosphere to be utilised; accordingly two Ministry of Defence sites were chosen, St David's, Pembrokeshire, and Blakehill Farm, Wiltshire. The project was intended to be up and running by 1993 and if trials were successful then the system would become permanent, with more sites proposed for other NATO countries. Some idea of the scale of the undertaking can be seen in the proposed planning applications for the sites. The transmitter station at St David's would require an 85m-long array with the total site, including restricted areas, encompassing 45 hectares. Thirty-five aerial masts, sixteen of which would be 45m high, would make up the array at St David's alone. The receiving station at Blakehill Farm was even bigger, requiring an antenna array 2.5km long and the enclosure of around 75 hectares of land.

A control centre was to be built at Blakehill Farm that would be run by the joint British and American team, estimated to be around sixty military staff. Whilst at St David's a temporary building and around fifteen equipment containers would be sited, staffed by nineteen civilians only. Financially the cost of setting up the project was estimated to be around £11 million, with Britain preparing the sites, designing all structures and carrying out all construction work. Operating costs for the two years were set at a further £3 million per year. The arrays would be built and shipped over to the UK by the American government. Construction was to start in late 1991 at both sites, but international events took over as the perceived Soviet threat melted away. First was the attempt to remove General Secretary, Mikhail Gorbachev, in August 1991, which ultimately led to his resignation on 25 December and by 31 December the formal dissolution of the USSR had taken place. Projects such as the proposed Over-The-Horizon Radar were shelved.

What makes this project interesting is the very open nature of the records available at the time. In a series of debates in the Commons, between 30 March and 31 October 1990 the entire project was discussed and some very deep factual information was disclosed. This included staff levels, array types and even an eight-figure National Grid reference (SM 7907-2551). What makes this all the more incredible was that, during the same discussions, MP Alan Clark was quizzed as to the locations and operational periods of both Cold Witness and Cobra Mist, both projects by now twenty years old; his reply: 'This information is classified.' Clearly the bureaucracy of 'openness' still had a long way to go. As for St David's and Blakehill Farm, both are now, like Orford Ness, nature reserves, St David's owned by the National Trust and Blakehill Farm by the Wiltshire Wildlife Trust.

Over-The-Horizon Radar continued to be developed by the United States and the Australian governments and both countries now operate advanced networks of the system.

six

'Gas – Gas – Gas'

One of the most controversial and least understood aspects of the Cold War has to be the development of chemical and biological weapons. Members of the armed services were acutely aware of the potential threat that such an attack posed; however, civilian understanding was almost non-existent, especially after the Civil Defence stand down of 1968. That was not to say the public were unaware of the concept of 'gas' warfare. Two generations had lived with storeys from the trenches or carried gas masks throughout the blitz, but the Cold War threat was radically different. The history of the subject is very diffused, being difficult to recognise defensive from offensive development, but for all the research it is interesting to see that Civil Defence really does not feature at all. Both topics will be discussed separately here, but some aspects do overlap. Also, the information regarding biological agents is extremely difficult to obtain, primarily because it encompasses current pharmaceutical research.

Genesis

The origins of the current chemical and biological programmes can be traced back to the early 1940s, although the chemical story has much to do with the weapons deployed in the First World War. During the Second World War the German Army developed, to an operational level, the nerve gas sarin and tabun whilst Britain retained vast stocks of mustard, phosgene and tear gas. However, both sides refrained from use of the agents for fear of the other side retaliating in kind. This was due, in part, to the Geneva Protocol of 17 July 1925, forbidding the offensive use of such weapons. The British Government ratified the treaty in 1930; interestingly it took until 1975 for the United States to follow suit. By the end of the war Britain had stockpiled nearly a quarter of a million 25lb shells charged with mustard gas and three million aircraft bombs. This was complemented by 71,000 bombs captured in Germany and stockpiled for possible use in the Pacific Theatre.

West Oxfordshire Emergency Centre. Filter systems such as this were fitted to most Government sites by the mid-1980s. They were capable of removing fallout and a number of chemical agents. (Courtesy West Oxfordshire District Council)

Chemical Development in Cold War Britain

Post-war Britain considered the development of a chemical weapon capability paramount. The reasons were two-fold: the threat of retaliation to a potential aggressor and the development of protective clothing and detection systems for the services were the main objectives. The occupation of Germany gave both East and West the opportunity to investigate nerve agent technology. Two plants, Raubkammer near Munster and Dyhernfurth in Silesia, had been involved in the production of sarin and tabun, and it soon became clear that the Germans had been far more advanced than first thought. The British conducted trials at the Raubkammer factory with the help of captured German scientists, but the majority of testing was to be undertaken in the United Kingdom.

Britain considered the development of chemical weapons paramount to national security, especially since the Russians had dismantled the captured Dyhernfurth factory and rebuilt it in the Soviet Union. From this the Government concluded that the Russians clearly had a nerve agent based capability, and most dangerously it was probably more advanced than the British. Until this period the equipment used by British forces was designed to counter the threat of agents dating from the First World War. Post-war evaluation of the developments in Germany proved that the equipment, whilst still relevant against some chemicals, would not protect against a nerve agent. To explore other avenues of protection Britain would have to develop its own chemical agent to enable accurate assessment of any new clothing and respirators.

Offensive Field Trials

The development of chemical weapons was undertaken in the utmost secrecy, all decisions being taken at Cabinet level or above. It was considered imperative that any potential enemy had no idea what the British arsenal contained, combining defensive and offensive thinking. Beyond the military it was considered that the less the public knew about the subject the better. Two wartime production and research sites, Porton Down and Sutton Oak, were initially used to develop the United Kingdom's Cold War capability; but in 1949 a new more isolated research establishment opened at the former RAF Portreath in Cornwall, subsequently renamed the Chemical Defence Establishment, Nancekuke.

Field trials at Porton Down suggested that a programme centred around sarin was Britain's best course of action. The majority of the groundwork had been covered by the German war programme and this was the most likely direction the Russians would be taking, bearing in mind they had access to the same agent. Twenty tons of sarin were produced between 1951–56 for use in a number of trials and under the Tripartite Conference Exchange the information was shared with Canada and the United States.

It is during this period that one of the darker episodes of British Cold War research manifested itself. The many different facets of research conducted by departments based at Porton Down and Nancekuke needed, in some instances, human involvement. Volunteers were routinely recruited from all parts of the Armed Services, indeed this policy survived up until the late 1980s where personnel were invited to attend trials for a period of twenty-eight days. At this point it has to be stated that the majority of trials were concerned with how protective clothing would stand up to continued use and the physical effects of wearing kit for prolonged periods of time. In the early 1950s it would appear that sarin was also used in tests involving volunteers.

On 6 May 1953, Ronald Maddison, an RAF engineer, died whilst participating in trials at Porton Down. It is still not clear exactly what happened but forty-five minutes after having 200mg of a sarin-based solution dripped onto a patch of clothing the young airman was dead. A closed inquest was set up, finding that death was due to misadventure. Recently the Wiltshire Coroner, on the findings of the Wiltshire Constabulary, applied to have the ruling quashed, citing poor documentation and withheld information as a basis for an unsafe finding. Wiltshire Constabulary has also conducted an investigation into over 3,000 other volunteer servicemen, known as Operation Antler, who had passed through Porton Down on similar trials programmes between 1939–89. A new inquest into Ronald Maddison's premature death was opened on 5 May 2004 at Trowbridge in Wiltshire. Already the Government has received criticism from the proceedings as it has been revealed that tests using Sarin resumed shortly after the airman's death.

The extensive test ranges at Porton Down saw the development of a number of offensive techniques throughout the early 1950s. Nerve agent delivery, if it were to be deployed, could be in the form of artillery shells, anti-tank shells and bombs for aircraft. However, a change in Government policy in the mid-1950s, led in part by the push to develop a ballistic nuclear capability, meant only 1,000lb bombs were tested and stockpiled, whilst the others never left the development stage. Between 1951–55 trials using a live agent were conducted in Nigeria, primarily to explore the rate of evaporation and effects of strong sunlight on the chemical.

One important discovery came as the result of research by Imperial Chemical Industry (ICI) in the early 1950s. Investigations into the effectiveness of insecticides had lead to the discovery of an extremely potent number of agents, which became known as the 'V' series. One, 'VX', was extremely significant and was subsequently identified as having military potential. Interestingly, whilst Britain developed VX as part of its research programme, the Government also sold it in large quantities to the Americans, generating much needed financial revenue to fund further research.

Offensive chemical research was downgraded throughout 1956–57, the focus now became one of defence against attacks on British soil, but this was on a much reduced scale as funds for projects were now redirected. Any release of a chemical agent close to populated areas had the potential to cause massive casualties and it was clear that this needed to be researched. To ascertain an agent's movement, tests were carried out with the Meteorological Office using a zinc particulate, which was safe and could be tracked.

From the 1960s a diverse number of projects were undertaken at the Chemical Defence Establishment, primarily chemical orientated, but some investigations into CS gas for crowd control and smoke screens were also carried out. However, the main thrust was to understand how chemical agents could be combated, their dispersal properties and the amount of time they took to degrade once delivered. Trials involving the use of sarin were conducted on animal and human subjects up until 1989 at Porton Down.

Chemical Defence

To adequately protect service personnel from chemical attack a new set of protective equipment had to be developed. The majority of Cold War chemical developments, both East and West, produced by the mid-1950s a series of odourless, fast acting agents that required minimum exposure to cause major trauma and death. Nerve agents were set to become the most potent development; just one droplet on the skin could kill within one minute, blister agents too could leave the victim covered in large fluid-filled untreatable sores and lungs too scarred to function. To counter this any protective clothing would have to be worn for long periods, as it would take too long to don during an attack, give all over protection and not impede normal duties. What transpired by the late 1970s was a charcoal lined two-piece suit, gloves and over boots, the S10 respirator, atropine combo-pen (to act as an antidote), detector paper and the decontamination kit including a fullers earth blotter. Secure decontamination procedures were also developed reducing the chance of contamination entering a building. The concept of protection became known as NBC – Nuclear, Biological, Chemical. Protective clothing and equipment could be effective against all three to a greater or lesser degree. The services were well provisioned for any eventuality, so what about the population?

Wearing NBC Individual Protection Equipment (IPE)
You have to be able to:
a. Recognise all items of NBC IPE.
b. Put on IPE so that it fits correctly.
c. Stow the relevant items properly in the haversack.
d. Attach Detector Paper (one colour) to your IPE.

S10 Respirator
and Canister

NBC Gloves
Inner and Outer

Mk 4 Protective
Suit

Mk 4 NBC
Overboots

Mk 5 NBC
Overboots

Right: NBC Suit. Over thirty years of research and development has produced some of the most effective protective clothing, but in stark contrast the civilian population would be given nothing. (© Crown Copyright)

Below: Airfield Refuge. One HAS in each clutch at Upper Heyford was converted into a personnel refuge, in case of surprise attacks.

The concept of Civil Defence and protection against chemical and biological agents would appear to follow the development programmes dictated by Government. From the end of 1949 through to 1956, offensive capabilities were being explored and whilst this could attract weapons in kind if ever used on another country, they were still not fully understood. Even so information to civilian organisations was comprehensive. The Civil Defence Training Booklet issued as part of a course held for British Transport staff in 1951 dedicated seventeen pages out of sixty-four to chemical warfare. Included was a full rundown of known chemical types, precautions, symptoms, respirator drills and protective clothing suggestions. When the end came for Civil Defence in 1968 so did the information given to the public on chemical warfare. From then on in it would seem the Government chose not to keep the public up to date with findings and events.

Service Personal Protection

Every serviceman was issued with a copy of 'Survive to Fight' an *aide-mémoire* covering just about every aspect of how to protect yourself in NBC conditions. The opening paragraph graphically describes the situation, as seen by the services after over forty years of research:

> *NBC weapons may be used in any future conflict, whatever the level. We have the necessary equipment to enable us to survive their attack provided we know how to use it. If we are to survive and continue to operate we must be thoroughly familiar with the drills and procedures; they cannot be learnt at short notice but must be constantly practised. They are individual skills which we all must be able to carry out correctly first time, without reference or supervision.*

'Survive to Fight' JSP 410 (1988).

Clearly it was imperative that a well-practised series of procedures needed to be followed if the individual was to survive a chemical attack. The services had all the necessary protective equipment, and most was personal issue, to ensure a large rate of survival. Just looking at the RAF one can see the level of competence maintained. Training was constant with six-monthly courses known as Ground Defence Training (GDT) at station level. All personnel would fire weapons and take a stint in the 'gas chamber', often a the Second World War temporary brick structure or air-raid shelter, where full NBC suites would be donned and the personal issue respirator was checked by filling the room with CS gas. Up to the end of the Cold War, tactical evaluations (known as Tacivals), conducted by a mobile inspection team, routinely turned up at RAF bases and called no-notice exercises; these always included air attacks using chemicals, long periods wearing full protective gear and a nuclear fallout situation as a conclusion. Clearly, forty years of research at Porton Down and other sites had brought about a comprehensive array of techniques to combat chemical and biological attack. But this was in stark contrast to the civilian situation.

Command Centre Greenham Common. The GCLM Command Centre was considered a prime target, the use of chemical agents was a very real threat. This picture shows the inlets for the filter system. Houses in Newbury, a few miles away, had no such luxury.

Civil Personal Protection

One contemporary publication with advice on how to 'Survive to Fight' was the *Civil Protection Training Manual*, which graphically illustrates the level of readiness in mid-1980s civil protection.

> *The use of chemical agents against targets in the UK cannot be entirely ruled out. These agents could be delivered by bombs, missiles or spray, and their effects would be to kill or incapacitate when inhaled or in contact with the skin. Deliberate attacks on civilian population areas are not likely, but chemical agents can drift and contaminate areas up to several kilometres downwind of the intended target. Whilst the Government believes the best way of dealing with this threat is to obtain a comprehensive international ban on such weapons, it is examining ways of detecting and monitoring the presence of chemical agents and of warning the population who may be in danger. It is also considering what protective measures can be taken and what advice given to the population on precautions that can be taken in the home.*

Civil Protection: Community Adviser Training Course (1986).

This clearly gives the population the impression the Government considered chemical weapons would not be used; but this was not really the deciding factor. It is only when the situation is paralleled with the development of nuclear weapons and protection against their effects that the picture becomes clear.

Wiltshire County Standby. Filters for the air-conditioning system were designed to remove fallout and small amounts of chemical agents. (Courtesy Wiltshire County Council)

Preparation for war with nuclear and chemical weapons was a major part of the late 1940s and early 1950s; the surviving literature covers extensive protection regimes for both. This was more to do with a statement to the enemy than the process of protection; it demonstrated a willingness to go on after any form of attack. Britain had always aspired to produce its own nuclear weapons and went on to do just that, making no secret of it. Part of the deterrent was the construction of protected shelters for Government, clearly indicating the intention to launch retaliatory strikes. Preparing the population through the large Civil Defence network helped strengthen this persona. The development of an offensive chemical capability brought with it the defence posturing needed to make it credible. The Geneva Protocol (1925) forbade the use of such weapons as a first strike option but, as it was clear the Soviet Union had the potential and will to develop such agents; the ability to survive a strike on the United Kingdom and retaliate in kind had to be demonstrated.

In July 1968 the Commons were told by John Morris, the then Minister for Defence, that work at Porton Down was purely defensive. A year later, Fred Mulley, as Minister responsible for overseeing disarmament, announced that a draft proposal had been tabled at the Geneva Disarmament Committee, making it illegal to use, produce and possess chemical and biological weapons. As the Civil Defence network was stood down so the chemical and biological weapons programme was to be dismantled, any work now would be purely research led. Troops in West Germany still had to be protected from the effects of agents if used on the potential European battlefield and trials of equipment carried on throughout the Cold War. This was extended to sites on the British mainland and so training continued. However, to demonstrate commitment to the Geneva Protocol and later the Biological Warfare Treaty of 1972, the Government could not be seen to be preparing for the offensive use of chemicals in any future conflict.

If the Unthinkable Happened

Chemical agents are divided into two categories: persistent, that survive as droplets which can remain dangerous for a number of hours or days, and non-persistent, that degrade or disperse to harmless levels soon after deployment. On the transition to war NBC kit would be issued to service personnel, respirators would be checked and Nerve Agent Pre-treatment Sets (NAPS) tablets issued and started to be taken. Chemical sentries would be posted up to 10km from the base, setting up monitoring posts checking wind direction, whilst keeping in constant contact with the base. Civil Protection planners would already be aware that chemicals could be used to soften up military targets and if persistent agents were used then some casualties were inevitable. If RAF Lyneham is used as an example target (which in the 1980s was highly possible) it is possible to see what loss of life a nerve agent attack using an aerosol delivery could cause.

An aerosol-delivered (sprayed from an aircraft) persistent nerve agent would have an almost immediate effect on the village of Lyneham, population 2,000, and if drifting with the prevailing wind would hit the market town of Wootton Bassett, population c.10,000, within twenty minutes. A moderate easterly wind would continue to carry the agent into the densely populated areas of Swindon. Undoubtedly casualties would be extremely high. The standard information is to stay indoors and await an all-clear, but to fully protect your shelter you would need to be able to completely seal your house. Purpose-built shelters were designed to give a positive internal pressure using filtered air, although this was not available to the general public. Also it has to be remembered that Britain had many operational military bases during the Cold War, most of which were close to populated areas; there were nearly 100 RAF sites alone in the 1980s, each one a potential target. The horrific fact is that chemical agents would account for massive numbers of civilian casualties, were they ever used.

The International Scene

The first attempt during the Cold War to rid the world of chemical and biological weapons met with limited success. Talks in Geneva built on the pre-Second World War Geneva Protocol (1925) that Britain had signed up to in 1930. The Conference of the Committee on Disarmament (later to become the Biological Weapons Convention) was formally opened for signatures in 1972, coming into force in 1975. Unfortunately there was no workable verification process within this, relying instead on government integrity. As with most issues in the Cold War this turned out to be a bad idea, one which was graphically demonstrated some years later. Estimates given in the House of Commons in July 1989 as to how much toxic agent the Russians actually possessed by the end of the Cold War suggested that chemicals could, indeed, be used in a future conflict. Russia had fourteen factories producing chemical agents and announced, after years of denial, that they possessed at least 50,000 tonnes for defence purposes; the British Government considered the figure was probably seven times that amount.

The United States had ceased the production (and import) of chemical weapons in 1968 and had not restarted the programme until 1987. However, having finally ratified the Geneva Protocol (1925) and Biological Weapons Convention in 1975, it could not be seen to develop an offensive capability, even though the Soviet Union was clearly manufacturing large quantities. The loophole came via a 1960s development. The handling of such a dangerous substance had always caused great concern, the corrosive properties of agents, once decanted into shells and bombs, encouraged pressure to build up in the case, causing a potential for leaks. Incidentally Britain used the last of its nerve agent stockpile investigating this problem. The answer was the binary chemical weapon. Two component agents were stored separately in the shell or bomb and as long as they did not come into contact with each other the handler was relatively safe; but when fired or dropped the two were mixed, producing the toxic agent.

Britain did flirt with the idea of starting up the weapons programme again during the mid-1980s, but this was quickly abandoned. From 1980 the Conference of the Committee on Disarmament had been investigating ways to eradicate chemical weapons, whilst having a rigid and intensive verification process. The negotiations were to take twelve years before a workable treaty could be tabled, presumably this would have taken longer if the true horror of chemical attacks had not been demonstrated in the Iran–Iraq war and the Kurdish town of Halabja. The drive for the banning of all chemical weapons picked up pace after these events and the Chemical Weapons Convention was opened for signatures in 1993. By 1997 this had come into force and by March 2004 161 countries had joined the list. Unfortunately this was not the end of the story – the most potent reminder of how dangerous sarin, one of the earliest forms of nerve agent, can be was graphically demonstrated on the Tokyo underground in 1995. The Aum Shinrikyo religious cult released a small amount of the agent, killing twelve and injuring over 5,000; research goes on at Porton Down primarily to counter this 'new' terrorist threat.

Biological Warfare

The cultivation of biological agents is not a complex process; the possibility of an attack is, as was seen with anthrax-contaminated letters in the USA, now a distinct possibility. Information as to how and when Britain developed biological weapons is still shrouded in secrecy, but a few documents have been released, primarily through the Freedom of Information Act, and this information is used here. Britain, in line with other powers, did develop a biological capability, considered as a weapon against economic targets, during the Second World War. This took the form of anthrax-infected cattle cake, cultivated in a mixture of salt, molasses and Marmite!

Beyond this Britain's capability was very limited, with more emphasis on the easier to produce chemical agents. The only known deployment of a biological weapon during warfare was carried out by the Japanese in China; plague-infected fleas dispersed by aircraft were dropped on a number of villages, killing many thousands of people. Even this limited use demonstrated the lethality of such weapons; clearly it would be devastating if used on a civilian population. It was suspected that the Soviet Union had a development programme investigating the potential of biological agents, so clearly a threat was present. After the war there were many stories covering suspect outbreaks including the East Germans, in 1950, accusing the United States of dropping Colorado Beetles into Germany whilst the Soviets accused them of testing plague on Eskimo communities. Even Britain attracted attention by apparently using biological weapons in the Oman crisis of 1957; the point is that any suspicious incident or outbreak triggered the imagination, such was the terrible reputation of biological warfare.

Tests into the effects of anthrax were carried out on the small Scottish island of Gruinard and at Penclawdd between 1943–45, using sheep as the subjects; however, the trials stopped at the end of the war. This halt was to be short lived as the Defence Research Policy Committee recommended in 1947 that within the next ten years Britain should have some form of biological capability. By 1948 biological experimentation had become part of the Chemical Defence Experimental Establishment's remit. A pilot plant was constructed at Sutton Oak, St Helens, in 1949 containing six 112-litre batch fermentors; subsequent larger plants would appear to have been abandoned at the planning stage. This facility was also made available to the Medical Research Council who were investigating new strains of antibiotics.

Testing Times

One of the major issues with biological development was how, and more importantly where, to release the agents. The tests in Scotland had left large tracts of land virtual no-go areas. The answer was sea trials. There were no wind restrictions, land contamination was not an issue, the site was secure and any spore or virus would not survive the conditions. Five sea trials were conducted between 1948–55, three off Scotland and two off the Bahamas. Findings demonstrated that spore survival rates were very low. At the same time inert simulants were being used to investigate dispersal in a number of trials conducted across southern England. As the tests were under way a new Microbiological Research Department laboratory was being built at Porton Down. Completed in 1951, it was at the time the largest brick building in Europe. Clearly biological warfare was considered worthy of considerable funding. However, in line with other defence areas, funding was reduced to almost non-existent levels in 1955 as the Government decided to abandon the development of biological offensive weapons. Research would now be directed at investigating how biological agents may be used on the UK mainland, whilst more emphasis was placed on development in other areas such as veterinary and medical applications.

The introduction of a biological agent to the population could be carried out covertly and tests were therefore needed to investigate spore and viral movement around specific areas. The problem was one of detection. During the '50s the Army had voiced concerns as to the speed of a biological agent, when compared with the effects of those induced by chemical weapons. To an aggressor this delay between infection and effect meant that any introduced disease could spread far beyond the initial contamination point through one person infecting another. To investigate this trials were designed to look at covert releases in densely populated areas. One 'live' test, carried out in the 1960s, included the introduction of simulants into the ventilation system of the London Underground. Notwithstanding the obvious public outcry when information of the trial was released, the tests demonstrated that a covert release would cause many casualties and could, if virulent enough, be possibly uncontrollable.

The Biological Weapons Convention

Along with chemical weapons the Biological Weapons Convention, as the name implies, sought to ban biological agents citing:

> *...never to develop, produce, stockpile, or otherwise acquire or retain, microbiological or other biological agents or toxins, whatever their origin or method of production, of types and in quantities that have no justification for prophylactic, protective or other peaceful purposes; and weapons, equipment or means of delivery designed to use such agents or toxins for hostile purposes or in armed conflict.*

Biological Weapons Convention.

Russia was a signatory of the Biological Weapons Convention and as such was bound by the terms of the treaty. But due to the verification problems and the fact that all members of the Security Council could veto inspections, no one actually knew if the Soviet Union had ceased production of biological weapons. It was not until 1992 that Russian President, Boris Yeltsin, finally admitted to the fact a programme had been running throughout the treaty period. He also confirmed that there had been an incident in 1979 at the Soviet Institute of Microbiology and Virology in Sverdlovsk, central Russia, in which anthrax had been released into the environment. It is still not clear what happened, either there was an explosion or a technician servicing a filter system neglected to fit the new filters. Either way anthrax spores were released into the atmosphere and contaminated a populated area close by. At least sixty-six people are thought to have died and many countless more were injured. At the time the outbreak was put down to the ingestion of contaminated meat, but what it did confirm was that any new treaty would require stringent verification processes if it was to be credible. Biological weapons are now at the top of the agenda as they are seen to be within the capability of both rogue states and terrorists; unfortunately the treaties ignored by signatory countries in the Cold War now look less effective than ever.

seven

Americans

One American airbase became, in the last decade of the Cold War, the focus of intense media attention: Greenham Common. The site near Newbury continued to make the headlines throughout the 1980s as first peace protests and later a permanent peace camp sprung up around the perimeter. Public disobedience and mass demonstrations were flashed around the world as the Government tried to quell the situation. But Greenham Common was not the only American base in Britain (in fact sixty-seven were either fully operated or used as standbys throughout the Cold War), nor had the site always been a missile base. Whilst to describe the many facets of American armed involvement in Britain would produce volumes it is worth considering some of the aspects here. This chapter will focus on two sites, synonymous with the Americans involvement in Britain's Cold War, Upper Heyford and Greenham Common. Public opposition is also discussed at the end of the chapter.

American military detachments were commonplace throughout the Second World War earning Britain the title of the biggest aircraft carrier in the world. However, as the front moved eastwards towards Germany many of the aircraft were redeployed at forward captured and temporary bases in Europe. After the cease of hostilities the United Kingdom became nothing more than a staging post for the Continent and the majority of bases were wound down and abandoned; this dramatically changed as the first major stand-off of the Cold War set the West back on a war footing. By 18 June 1948, the situation over Berlin was at breaking point and by 24 June the Soviet Army had sealed all land access to Berlin. Clearly some form of message needed to be sent to Moscow and in July sixty B-29 Superfortress bombers had arrived at RAF Scampton and RAF Waddington, known in the press as the 'atomic bombers'. Long after the event it was disclosed that the aircraft were only armed with conventional payloads, but the die had been cast and British airfields were, from that point on, to be home to hundreds of American aircraft, service personnel and their families for the rest of the Cold War.

Strategic Air Command

The Strategic Air Command (SAC) became a symbol of American air power throughout the Cold War and interestingly its creation was ultimately led by the conflict. It has to be remembered that the United States did not have a designated air force prior to the end of the Second World War; air combat groups were controlled by either Army or Navy commands. In April 1945 a proposal was tabled by the Special Committee for the Reorganisation of National Defense, that a new air force having parity with the army and navy should be formed. The first step towards this occurred on 21 March 1946 when Strategic Air Command was formed out of an amalgamation of the Second, Eighth and Fifteenth Army Air Forces. On 26 July 1947 President Truman signed the National Security Act and on 16 September 1947 the United States Air Force came into being. By 1951 aircraft already stationed in Britain were absorbed into the Third Air Force and SAC Seventh Air Division and a relationship was formed between Britain and America which has outlived the Cold War.

Build-up

By 1950 four redundant airfields were selected to accept a new fleet of 'very heavy bombers', all positioned further west than those already existing in East Anglia, hopefully putting them out of range of Soviet bombers. Each was required to have a runway in excess of 3,000m, parking for at least forty-five aircraft and the infrastructure to support long-term detachments. The chosen bases all dated from the Second World War, but Fairford and Greenham Common had only been temporary sites, with very little permanent infrastructure, whilst the other two, Brize Norton and Upper Heyford, were permanent but still required substantial work to bring them up to operational readiness. Further sites were also earmarked for upgrade in case the proposed fleet required reinforcement at any time and these included Elvington in Yorkshire and Bruntingthorp in Leicestershire; also the old diversion airfield at Carnaby near Bridlington in East Yorkshire received some upgrade work. All this was complemented by the existing sites at Lakenheath, Mildenhall, Sculthorpe and Bassingbourne, a base made famous by the propaganda film *The Memphis Belle* shot in 1944.

Greenham Common

In late 1950 survey teams from both Britain and America visited the site of Greenham Common in Berkshire as part of a pre-build assessment programme. By 1951 the 929th Engineering Aviation Group, a specialist construction team, moved onto the base, and on 18 June 1951 it was formally handed over to American control. An extensive two-year building programme completely changed the landscape and in September 1953 the first aircraft were arriving at the totally refurbished airfield. The work included a completely new runway, taxiway and hardstanding, three new hangars, officers' and airmen's quarters and a variety of support structures.

In 1953 a special weapons area was also built, capable of storing and arming nuclear devices, to a standard pattern that can still be seen at other USAF bases such as Lakenheath and Upper Heyford. By 1954 forty-three Boeing B-47 aircraft, the first

Greenham Common. Three hangars were built in the 1950s to accommodate the new aircraft stationed there. The one on the left is a replacement after the original was destroyed by fire.

Boeing B-47 Greenham Common. This aircraft was the workhorse of the USAF nuclear strike force in Europe during the 1950s and '60s. Crews were often on constant readiness.

of many types to visit the base, were stationed at Greenham Common. These large long-range aircraft were capable of delivering two nuclear devices deep into Soviet territory at speeds in excess of 600mph, and at low level. However, this was a short-lived first detachment as the all-up weight of the B-47 (79,378kg) was soon causing damage to the new runways. Whilst repair crews strengthened the runway the aircraft were based at RAF Fairford, another SAC-controlled airfield in Gloucestershire. After Greenham Common was re-opened it played host to B-47s, this time on 'Reflex Alert', a state of constant advanced readiness, and KC-97 tankers designed to extend the range of the bomber aircraft from both the home airfield and those stationed at Lakenheath.

The Convair B-36 Peacemaker also used the airfield as a forward operating base in response to the international Hungarian uprising of October 1956. This flying leviathan had massive proportions, the wingspan alone was 70m, the aircraft was powered by six rear-facing piston props and four J47 turbojets, and was capable of carrying a 72,000lb bomb load. The type was originally conceived in 1941, when it looked like Britain might lose its struggle with Germany, as a bomber with the capability to reach Europe from the United States. The aircraft had an unhappy association with Britain. Aircraft incidents included a crash near Chippenham on 7 February 1953 and one just short of the runway at Boscombe Down in January 1952. Internationally the B-36 didn't fare much better; the aircraft achieved notoriety on 13 February 1950 when it was the centre of America's first 'Broken Arrow' (the loss of a nuclear weapon) over Canada. Greenham Common hosted the last visit of the B-36 in September 1957. During this period the runways were again upgraded, this time to accept the new B-52 bombing fleets, but the aircraft only visited the site for training and familiarisation flights. With the introduction of 'Reflex Alert' fewer aircraft were stationed in Britain, however those that were maintained a high state of readiness, often fully loaded with nuclear weapons. It was during this phase of the Cold War that a major incident occurred at Greenham Common, one that occasionally comes back to haunt the British Government.

Crash and Burn

A number of military related accidents have occurred in Britain in the last fifty years and wherever possible the Government has naturally played down the situation. One such intriguing event took place at Greenham Common on 28 February 1958. At 4.25 p.m. an airborne B-47 jettisoned its fuel-laden drop tanks over the airfield, whilst suffering an engine failure; both missed the designated jettison area, landing instead within the airfield complex. One struck the ground near another B-47 causing it to burst into flames, the other hit Number 1 Hangar, one of three Luria hangars built in the early 1950s. Both hangar and aircraft burned for nearly two days. The B-47 airframe was constructed using magnesium alloy, a light but hazardous material, that once alight proved difficult to extinguish (it is worth noting that the Westland Whirlwind in service with the RAF had the same pyrotechnic problem when on fire). The British confirmed an accident had occurred at Greenham Common in a press release and whilst admitting the B-47 was used for carrying 'atom bombs' it was stated none were involved. That was the end of the matter until high radioactive readings were discovered near Aldermaston eighteen months later. Naturally a leak from the AWRE was suspected, but on investigation it appeared to have travelled with the prevailing wind west from Greenham Common.

Now clearly one should be able to put two and two together here; was nuclear ordnance involved in the incident? Certainly the press continue, on occasion, to ask the question and CND are convinced that this was the case. Documents recently released to the Public Record Office also point to something happening that February day, something that had a profound effect on the control of incidents involving American weapons.

In June 1959 the United States government forwarded copies of press guidance notices, to be used by the 7th Air Division and 3rd Airforce, to the Foreign Office. They detailed procedures for dealing with enquiries from the press or public in the event of an American aircraft crashing in the United Kingdom whilst carrying a nuclear weapon. The document started a long discussion throughout many Government departments including the MOD, Home Office, Air Ministry and Foreign Office. All were rather alarmed that the United States intended issuing statements involving weapons accidents without British sanction. Furthermore the Ministry of Defence was concerned that any US announcement would indicate that the Government had no control over weapons stationed on British soil.

Letters between the American Embassy and British Government demonstrate that, whilst the US wanted a degree of openness in the event of an accident, the British

Greenham Common. The original hangar on this site was destroyed when a B-47 shed its external fuel tanks on take-off. This hangar is now being demolished.

preferred '...not to mention the nuclear weapon unless it made its presence felt'. In an attempt to control any possible situation the Government set up a callout list of department representatives who were to be informed prior to any press statement being released. This allowed for a co-ordinated response ensuring that the 'interests' of all departments were covered. So whilst the American administration recognised the potential risks to the public the British Government was more concerned with their credibility. The significant point to all this is that the timing of the US suggestions comes barely a year after the incident involving the B-47 at Greenham Common.

Meanwhile an investigation carried out by Ministry scientists and written in 1961 by staff at the Atomic Weapons Research Establishment, Aldermaston, did find levels of radiation, albeit small in comparison with the fallout from an exploded nuclear weapon. The point is that if a device had been on board the B-47 and had detonated the subsequent discussions would have been rather academic, as the whole world would have known in a matter of days, whilst a weapon burning would only produce particulate evidence. This report provided the basis for two further reports by the National Radiological Protection Board (NRPB) in 1986 and 1994. In 1996 Nicholas Soames, the then Minister of State for the Armed Forces, stated that:

> ...if the data in the 1961 report are correct, the indications are that the radiological impact would have been negligible.

> Rt Hon. Nicolas Soames, House of Commons Written Answers for 23 July 1996, column 208.

An interesting comment if no weapons were involved. On completion of yet another NRPB report, 'An Assessment of Radioactive Levels around the Former Air Base at Greenham Common, Berkshire', NRPB-M752, published on 19 December 1996 at a cost of £50,000 to the taxpayer, came the following comments:

> The findings of the study are entirely consistent with my Department's assurances that there is no basis to the allegations made last year about a nuclear weapon accident at the base. There are no plans to commission any further such studies.

> Rt Hon. Nicolas Soames, House of Commons Written Answers for 17 January 1997, column 259.

This is completely different to a year earlier when the suggestion was that something had happened but wasn't considered a risk to public health. Further, this was not the final word on the subject. In 1998 the Committee on Medical Aspects of Radiation in the Environment (COMARE), an independent advisory group set up on the recommendation of the Black Advisory Group commissioned by the Minister of Health, Norman Fowler, in 1983, investigated incidences of cancer in the vicinity of Greenham Common. Previously COMARE had looked into the nuclear research sites at Aldermaston and Burghfield, concluding that increases in cancer could be attributed to a number of factors, including releases from the two sites. When looking into Greenham Common the results were incomplete due to the failure of the organisations involved with the incident making records available. However, they did comment that levels were consistent with those encountered around Aldermaston and were around the National average, concluding it was unlikely a weapon was involved. An official letter written thirty-four years earlier, dated 13 July 1964, in which the following points are made, suggests otherwise:

> *These papers were sent to me by Mr Witney because he recalled that A.4 Division had had some responsibility in 1958 for giving advice to the fire service on how to deal with crashed aircraft carrying nuclear weapons. This advice is given in Technical Bulletin No. 5/1958 a copy of which I attach, together with the Air Ministry pamphlet on Rescue from Crashed Aircraft to which the bulletin refers. It was only after a good deal of enquiry that I was able to find the earlier correspondence to which the Ministry of Defence refer. This is contained in file CDA 36/26/1 which Mrs Smith took from your safe on Friday last. As it was quite clear from these papers that a much wider issue was involved than operational instructions to the fire service.*

J. McIntyre, 13 July 1964, Home Office. National Archives Ref: HO 346/189.

The point to all this is that it looks as if a weapon was on board that February day back in 1958 and in the ensuing fire some radioactive material was released. If no weapon was involved why did the Government suggest the hazard was 'negligible' in 1996, changing this to 'non-existent' in 1997? And why so many investigations when one, and then the release of documents covering the accident, would probably have finished the debate once and for all? The Government's reluctance to help subsequent investigators (COMARE in particular) continues to fan the flames and above all what prompted the protracted discussions, recently released into the public domain, on American weapons and incidents in Britain in 1958? The author views the evidence as 'suggestive'; it is up to the reader to draw their own conclusions.

1960s Rundown

The 'Reflex Alert' state was put to the test during 1962 as the Cuban missile crisis reached its climax. Greenham Common, along with most other bases, both USAF and RAF, were placed on high readiness. Across Britain and Europe aircraft now stood ready, armed with live nuclear weapons. And when on 27 October a Soviet anti-aircraft battery shot down a USAF U-2, killing the pilot, the world stood on the edge of disaster. But two days later, Khrushchev and Kennedy had agreed to remove the missiles stationed in each other's backyards, effectively defusing the situation. By 1964 Greenham Common had been placed on 'care and maintenance' as the USAF presence in Britain was reduced, partly due to the RAF 'V' Force achieving operational readiness and the ICBM network now being in place.

This was to be a temporary situation as, in 1966, France finally decided it would not entertain NATO forces on its soil. The American bases were told they had three

RAF Welford. One of the biggest USAF ammunition stores in Britain, it was used throughout the Cold War.

years to relocate, Washington decided to move within the year. A large amount of equipment was moved to Germany and Britain, causing some bases to be re-opened during 1967. Greenham Common now became a storage base under the control of RAF Welford. Welford, the site of an RAF wartime airfield, had in the 1950s been converted into a vast ammunition store for the USAF, being centrally sited to a number of SAC airfields.

The airfield was used for a number of interesting exercises in late 1968 and early 1969, primarily to investigate the problems faced by inspectors engaged in the verification of arms controls, including the Nuclear Non-Proliferation Treaty (NNPT) and later the Strategic Arms Limitation Talks (SALT). Up to eighty inspection teams from all NATO member states were involved with ground-based inspections and aerial reconnaissance. By 1970 the base was being used for annual exercises known as Flintlock, having reactivated the site for continuous flying. These culminated with the arrival of Lockheed C-5 Galaxy and Lockheed C-141 Starlifter transport aircraft, which, it has been suggested, took a large amount of the ammunition stored at Welford back to the United States when they left. By mid-1972 the base was once more back in care and maintenance, but the now empty barrack blocks were used from September to house another army, this time one of refugees. As President Idi Amin continued a programme of intimidation, murder and expulsion many Asians looked to the United Kingdom for help; those who did come to Britain were temporarily housed in the empty barrack blocks at Greenham Common between September 1972 and June 1973. The airfield was also to become the site of the International

KC-135 Tanker. Based at RAF Fairford in Gloucestershire, this aircraft formed part of the European Tanker Force.

Air Tattoo in 1973, an event held for the Royal Air Force Benevolent Fund, after its move from North Weald in Essex. The base again became fully operational in 1976 as F-111 aircraft were stationed there whilst the runway at Upper Heyford received vital maintenance; however, this was short lived and by the end of that year the site was once again reduced to a standby base.

'Glicum'

The final phase of the Cold War, seen by many as the second war, thrust Greenham Common firmly into the world spotlight. The base and the quiet market town of Newbury became the centre of NATO's attempts to counter the new Soviet SS-20 missile threat. But the base was initially earmarked for another USAF deployment, one that in hindsight would have had far less implications than the basing of Ground Launched Cruise Missiles (GLCM). In April 1977 the USAF planned to expand the European Tanker Force, intending to base at least twenty KC-135 tanker aircraft at the airfield. This caused the first of many public protests over use of the base, as residents of the by now enlarged suburb of Newbury and Thatcham complained to Parliament about the re-opening of the site. Their argument was that the KC-135, a derivative of the Boeing 707 passenger aircraft, was far too noisy to operate close to a residential area. Furthermore a fuel-laden aircraft crashing into a highly populated area would cause a major disaster. The Government eventually came down on the side of the protesters using the base's closeness to the Atomic Weapons Establishment as the main reason for stopping work that was already under way. The tanker fleet was subsequently deployed to RAF Fairford in Gloucestershire, a base first activated in the 1950s but which had stood empty for almost ten years by this point. Greenham Common was also considered as a base for the upgraded version of the famous U-2, now known as the TR-1; these were finally deployed to RAF Alconbury in Cambridgeshire, but things were to change drastically at Greenham Common.

Driving Forces

During 1977 the Red Army started to take delivery of the NATO-designated SS-20, a solid-fuelled mobile missile, capable of firing three warheads, each with a Multiple Independently Targetable Re-entry Vehicle (MIRV). As this was replacing the older, liquid-fuelled SS-4 and SS-5 and not technically introducing a new type of weapon the deployment did not contravene the existing SALT agreement. The West viewed this as anything but a weapons upgrade. The SS-20 was an intermediate-range missile and shifted the spectre of war from a global to a European one. NATO argued that a pre-emptive strike on the military infrastructure of Europe would effectively cut off the continent from the Americans. The United States would have to think long and hard before it intervened, and if it did the ICBMs, which both sides had relied on so much, would undoubtedly have destroyed most of the Western hemisphere. For two years the United States followed a twin-track policy, basically a stick and carrot approach, planning the deployment of new deterrent systems in Europe whilst negotiating with the Soviets in SALT II for arms limitations. Discussions throughout 1977 and 1978 led to the then Prime Minister, James Callaghan, agreeing in principle, at a summit

The GAMA site at Greenham Common. The Cruise missile launchers would be deployed from this protected site in times of crisis.

Greenham Common. Command Centre (top) showing the hardened end on the right-hand side of the building. The rectangular structure is a bomb and chemical refuge for staff in times of attack.

in Guadeloupe, to the basing of the new GLCM on British soil; later that year Italy, Germany, Holland and Belgium also signed up to the idea. East–West relationships now took a nosedive as the Russians argued they were only modernising old weapons systems, whereas the Pershing II and GLCM were clearly new deployments – a provocative move. Further, Moscow was to initiate another round of action against dissidents that outraged the United States, who cancelled a number of high-level visits to Russia and cancelled oil and gas exploration equipment. An agreement was reached through SALT II, signed in June 1979; but it was not ratified in Congress, primarily due to Russian belligerence in Cuba and other world hot spots, remaining instead a gentlemen's agreement. By late 1979 the international climate was decidedly frosty as first NATO announced, on 12 December, their intentions to base the new weapons in Western Europe, quickly followed on Christmas Day by a full-scale Soviet invasion of Afghanistan in support of the communist regime – the Cold War was once again heating up.

In May 1979 the Conservatives were returned to office, under the leadership of Margaret Thatcher, who immediately started negotiations to upgrade Britain's independent deterrent, the ageing Chevaline, with the new Trident-series submarine-launched ballistic missile. A deal was struck and the Government subsequently announced that Greenham Common and Molesworth were to be the bases that would house the new GLCM flights. Work started at Greenham Common in 1981 to accommodate both missiles and families of US servicemen and by late 1983 the first GLCM had arrived, manned by 501 Tactical Missile Wing. The most notable development on the base was the construction of a command HQ and six massive hardened shelters within the old special weapons area. This was known as the GLCM alert and maintenance area (GAMA), and stood within its own heavily guarded compound. Each of the hardened shelters housed two Launch Control Vehicles, four Transporter Erector Launchers and recovery vehicles. The earth and gravel-covered reinforced concrete structures were 50m long, 18m wide and 5m high. Incorporated within the gravel layer were concrete burst caps, similar to those employed in the Rotor project bunkers, to dampen out blasts from above. One shelter was designed as a Quick Reaction Alert unit, being able to deploy the launcher out onto the airfield and clear a flight of four missiles in the event of a pre-emptive Soviet attack being detected. The idea of the mobile launcher was to be able to deploy into the countryside on transition to war, making them incredibly difficult to locate. Between 1984 and 1990 there were sixty-one deployment exercises involving first just the transporters and back-up crews with minimal security, but as the Cruise Watch protests (discussed later) became more efficient at tracking the convoys an ever increasing amount of security was needed. Other bases were used as overnight staging posts, including Boscombe Down, which had eight deployment units lodging at the Wiltshire airfield between 14 March and 12 April 1989, whilst on manoeuvres on Salisbury Plain.

Upper Heyford

Upper Heyford in Oxfordshire, whilst sharing similar origins to Greenham Common, took a different route from the early 1970s, becoming one of the USAF's principle bomber bases when its name became inextricably linked with the General Dynamic F-111 swing-wing bomber. The site is an interesting mix of structures from all periods of the Cold War, making it an ideal site to demonstrate the effect USAF airbases had on the British landscape.

The Early Years

A number of specialist structures were built on heavy bomber sites across Britain during the 1950s, primarily aimed at maintenance of the aircraft whilst on the ninety-day 'Reflex Alert' detachments, the most unusual being the nose dock. These unusually shaped hangars were designed to cover the forward fuselage, wings, centre section and engines of the B-47, stationed at Upper Heyford between 1953 and 1965, protecting components and maintenance crews from the traditional British weather. Other aircraft based at the site included the RF-101 Voodoo from 1957 to 1971. Interestingly the 66th Tactical Reconnaissance Wing re-deployed to the base in 1966 from Laon in France as part of the withdrawal of American forces after the French left the NATO fold. Also present at the base throughout the 1960s was the famous F-100 Super Sabre and later a number of KC-135A tanker aircraft.

Whilst the majority of staff rotated through the site on detachment a number were stationed at Upper Heyford permanently and two types of building were used for this purpose. Firstly the original 1930s officers' quarters situated just off the base were modernised; this included the knocking through of semi-detached houses to create

Upper Heyford. Nose docks designed to cover the front fuselage and wings of the B-47, built in the 1950s.

Upper Heyford. Surplus Commodity Housing, otherwise known as 'Tobacco Houses'.

Above: Upper Heyford. The General Dynamics F-111 was, from the 1970s, the standard fighter/bomber of the USAF. Four squadrons were based at Upper Heyford alone.

Left: 77th Tactical Fighter Squadron art in one of the Hardened Aircraft Shelters at Upper Heyford.

a more spacious family living area. Around the mid-1950s these were complemented by the construction of purpose-built housing estates, often around the original RAF housing. Officially known as Surplus Commodity Houses, these spacious bungalows quickly found another name – 'Tobacco Houses'. The building work was carried out by the British Government, but they were financed by the Americans, not with money but tobacco, much the same principle as the Marshall Plan a decade before. Each semi-detached structure was designed to represent a house back home, hopefully allowing the service family to adjust to the 'smaller' way of British life. The majority are now in private hands.

Hardening Up

The landscape of Upper Heyford, along with several other airfields, both operational and standby, changed dramatically as lessons from a far-off conflict filtered through Washington and London. The change took nearly ten years to implement but when it was finished it left some of the most striking monuments of the Cold War on the landscape – the Hardened Aircraft Shelter or HAS. On 5 June 1967 Israel launched a pre-emptive strike on Egyptian airfields at the start of the 'lightning' Six Day War. Territorial gains during the conflict were impressive, but it was the tactics of the initial attack that worried NATO planners. The Israeli strike attack pilots could hardly believe their luck when they found the majority of the enemy's aircraft on the ground and parked in neat rows or under lightly protected shelters, and within hours they had reduced most of the Egyptian Air Force to component parts. This gave the Israelis air superiority, a major factor in the successes seen over the next few days; the Sinai (Egypt), West Bank (Jordan) and Golan Heights (Syria) were all now under the control of Tel Aviv. NATO recognised that if the Warsaw Pact was to launch a pre-emptive strike then their numerically superior land forces would have free reign on the plains of Europe, and a conflict would have the potential to 'go nuclear' very quickly indeed. Clearly something had to be done. Initially little changed on European airfields, probably due to America's commitments in Vietnam, however some airfields in Britain did receive a new aircraft type – the General Dynamic F-111 bomber – as part of the 'Flexible Response'. The new tactics NATO had devised to contain Warsaw Pact aggression were with attacks in kind. From 1970, the time of the aircraft's deployment, a number of structures appeared at Upper Heyford designed to cater for the Quick Reaction Alert (QRA) squadrons. The buildings were no more than asbestos-covered sheds, open at both ends and capable of taking one fully armed F-111. Whilst it has been suggested the structures were weather covers, they did perform a more important function against a situation that was becoming prevalent by the early 1970s, the spy satellite. But major changes were still on the horizon, especially after the 1973 signing of the armistice between the United States and North Vietnam in Paris. From 1977 a number of airfields were surveyed for a series of new protected buildings and by 1981 almost 300 Hardened Aircraft Shelters (HAS), along with a number of other protected structures, could be found on both British- and American-operated bases.

Upper Heyford. A later 'winged' Hardened Aircraft Shelter or HAS built in the late 1970s.

HAS

The NATO-financed structures conformed to a standard design; two types were built in Britain, but the differences are slight. This said, some Royal Air Force bases had a protected annex built at the same time to house ground equipment. Those on American bases were either 38 x 25 x 10m with a flat back jet efflux deflector through the rear doors allowing the aircraft to run up whilst still inside. Or a slightly later version with smaller dimensions 36.5 x 21.5 x 10m and with a modified jet efflux deflector designed to exploit the principle of hot air rising. Below the deflectors on both types was a generator room, giving the HAS independent power if need be. Both types had two ninety-ton concrete sliding doors fitted with napalm guards. Crew entrances were built in the forward left-hand corner of the main structure, via a steel blast door. The standard design HAS were not chemical proof, protection being through the use of personal protective equipment, but at Upper Heyford one HAS in each operating clutch was modified as an NBC refuge in case of surprise attacks. Fifty-six HAS were built at Upper Heyford in three construction phases.

Four squadrons were resident at the Oxfordshire base, 55th, 77th, 79th Tactical Fighter Squadrons and 42nd Electronic Countermeasures Squadron, all under the command of the 20th Tactical Fighter Wing. Each squadron had its own protected headquarters and operations building linked to a normal unprotected office block. These in turn were controlled from a purpose-built Hardened Control Centre (HCC) from where all aspects of airfield operations, from defence to armament allocation, were run. The structure maintained a positive pressure when in the closed down mode, much the same as the Government bunkers, making the ingress of chemical and fallout particulates difficult. The HCC at Upper Heyford also maintained a

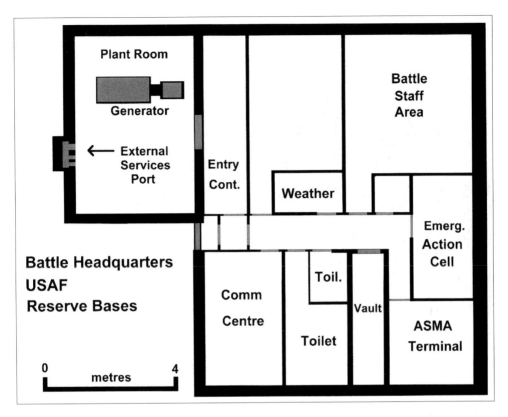

Plant Room

Generator

← **External Services Port**

Entry Cont.

Weather

Battle Staff Area

Emerg. Action Cell

Battle Headquarters USAF Reserve Bases

Comm Centre

Toil.

Vault

Toilet

ASMA Terminal

0   metres   4

USAF battle control.

Upper Heyford. Each squadron had its own hardened HQ in case of air attack.

Greenham Common. Corrugated steel clad buildings were a common sight on USAF airfields from the 1970s. These gave the appearance of civilian rather than military buildings.

WB1400 link with the UKWMO group HQ at Oxford, for air attacks and the progression of fallout if a nuclear strike did happen.

The existing nuclear weapons stores were refurbished, receiving extremely well-protected points of entry, a triple surrounding fence, camera surveillance and, later, motion detectors. Areas within the compound at Upper Heyford were also covered with 12m-high steel and timber posts that acted as a deterrent to helicopters, something that was only implemented after the bomb dump was captured by 'invading' forces (on exercise) landing within the compound. Other structures dating from the late 1970s and early 1980s were a mixture of brick and corrugated pressed steel sheet, giving American-designed buildings a distinctive appearance. At Upper Heyford the simulator building, at Greenham Common the bowling alley and at Boscombe Down the MASH were all constructed using this principle.

The standby airfield at Boscombe Down had some modifications started in 1979, but nothing as substantial as those at Upper Heyford. Eighteen HAS were built in two clutches, each with its own stand-alone protected operations block. These were run from a small Hardened Control Centre approximately one-third the size of the Upper Heyford example. A number of bulk fuel installations were also constructed, as were a number of hardened generator houses. The HAS at Boscombe Down were all of the winged jet efflux type, but the generators housed below were never fitted.

EF-111 Raven

On 3 February 1984 Upper Heyford took delivery of an F-111 derivative, the EF-111A Raven, a heavily modified version of the successful bomber, the work being carried out by the Grumman Aerospace Corporation. The Raven carried a tactical

Upper Heyford. The Grumman Aerospace Corporation modified EF-111A was stationed at Upper Heyford from 1984, it saw active service during the bombing of Libya and the first Gulf War.

Upper Heyford. The Avionics test and interpretation site. Here reconnaissance information would be processed and passed to the squadron HQs for interpretation.

jamming system (ALQ-99E), which was designed to deny opposing control units the altitude, range and azimuth required for them to successfully intercept the target bombers. Twelve were based at Upper Heyford under 42nd Electronic Combat Squadron control. The complex avionics suite required a large specialist facility to service and repair the equipment and to this end a unique annex was built next to the existing avionics site. The Raven was used in anger in April 1986 when the aircraft supported the main F-111 bomber fleet during Operation El Dorado Canyon, the bombing of Libya. Ravens successfully disrupted a large piece of airspace, denying the Libyan air defence any possibility of destroying the incoming aircraft. The last of the Ravens left Upper Heyford in August 1992.

Winds of Change

At the beginning of the 1980s the world appeared far from safe. Two new Western leaders (Reagan and Thatcher) were resolute over the problem of the Soviet Union and considered a strong militaristic stance the only answer, whilst in the East the conflict in Afghanistan, coupled with the crisis brewing in Poland, pointed to an uncertain future. Few could predict how the decade would end, but when it did it left the world unrecognisable.

Of major concern to the Soviets had been NATO's decision to station the cruise missiles and Pershing IIs in Europe, a concern that was probably well founded as American spending on military projects saw a $32.6 billion increase just two weeks after President Ronald Reagan took office, but more was to come. From the outset Reagan, a virulent anti-communist, demanded an escalation in the arms race between East and West, gambling that America could afford the venture, even though the country was deep in debt, whilst the Soviet Union could not. It was a gamble that was to eventually pay off. By the twenty-sixth Party Congress in 1981 in Moscow the Soviet leadership, by now a shadow of its former belligerent self, hoped for dialogue with the West. Leonid Brezhnev was, by this time, a very ill man, mirroring Moscow's financial commitments around the world. Conflict in Afghanistan was entering its second year, whilst economic aid for Vietnam and Cuba was still in place. Technologically the USSR was falling way behind the West, severely limiting the ability of the Soviets to keep up any sort of pressure on the Americans. On the home front too it was impossible to keep up with consumer demand, such as it was, and waiting lists were implemented for everything from cars to kettles. The nation was in a state of decay from top to bottom. In June 1982 the beginnings of the Strategic Arms Reduction Talks (START) in Geneva were discussed, including the Intermediate Nuclear Force treaty (INF), which was to have far reaching effects. However, some in the West were not keen.

On 10 November 1982 Brezhnev died, starting a chain of events that would ultimately lead to the disintegration of the Soviet Union. The incoming Yuri Andropov, former head of the KGB, did not take up the fight with the capitalists as the West had feared; instead he started a dialogue of arms reduction. By 1983 he was talking openly of reducing the SS-20 deployments and even a non-aggression agreement between NATO and the Warsaw Pact; Moscow was clearly weak, something that was not overlooked in Washington. On 8 March 1983 Reagan issued his now famous 'Evil Empire' speech, just two weeks later increasing the spending stakes with the announcement of the Strategic Defence Initiative (SDI) or 'Star Wars'. If successful, SDI would quite literally render the Soviet Union's nuclear capability obsolete, achieved by using a space-based shield comprising rail-guns, laser and anti-missile missiles. When the first Cruise missiles were deployed at Greenham Common in 1983 any chance of the, already poorly supported, START and INF discussions succeeding were dashed as the Soviets walked out. Relations were now to take a major turn for the worse when, a few months later, the Soviet Air Force shot down Korean Air Lines flight KAL 007, killing all 269 passengers and crew. The Boeing 747, on route from New York to Seoul, had strayed off course, suspiciously close to Russian military installations. Washington responded by banning all Aeroflot flights into American air space. The rhetoric on both sides talked of 'terrorism' and 'spy planes', each citing the other as the initial aggressor in the incident. A month later NATO was placed on a nuclear footing as part of the exercise Able Archer 83. The situation now appeared grim to Moscow; East–West discussions had broken down and were at the lowest point since Cuba twenty years earlier. New missiles were stationed in Europe and a large number of troop movements in NATO member states now forced the USSR to place its vast military machine on full alert. Was the Western pre-emptive strike the Russians so feared on its way?

Crisis struck the Communist party once again when on 9 February 1984 Andropov, who had been suffering kidney failure, died and his successor, Konstantin Chernenko, was to last barely another year. It appeared the ageing Politburo would need a new post-revolution champion if it was to rise above mounting internal problems and take on the Reagan administration. Tit-for-tat issues again raised their head when the majority of Eastern Block countries refused to enter teams for the 1984 Los Angeles Olympics, citing the SDI and Cruise as the main reason. However, terrorism – there had been threats made against communist teams – and the fact that the US had not entered an official team in the 1980 Moscow Olympics probably had more to do with it. Privately both administrations were mindful of the direction they were heading and when Chernenko died the Politburo saw its chance to dispense with some of the old Soviet ideology – Mikhail Gorbachev was announced leader.

Reagan, meanwhile, changed the direction of his administration practically overnight, lining up a summit in October 1985. Gorbachev's appointment had an immediate effect on a wide range of issues, two major ones being reform of the by now completely rundown Communist system which was ultimately to see the break-up of the USSR, and the kick starting of the START and INF talks, which had been effectively abandoned by both sides. By the mini-summit at Reykjavik in 1986 both the US and the USSR were prepared to make massive cuts in their nuclear arsenals, but unfortunately SDI got in the way. Reagan still considered the system essential to national security and would not scrap the development programme. The political rhetoric now gathered pace as the Soviet's overwhelming conventional forces were cited as a major obstacle to any arms limitations. Secretly Britain breathed a sigh of relief; any agreement to remove America's missiles from the Continent would leave just the French and United Kingdom deterrents to keep the Russians out of Europe, but by 1987 the picture changed again. Gorbachev knew that he needed to push through an agreement to release military finances for internal reforms. Clearly Washington was not willing to give up SDI but it could be caught off guard. In February of that year Gorbachev announced in Moscow that all the brinkmanship of the last few years needed to be swept aside and an agreement reached for the 'survival of humanity'. In December the beleaguered INF treaty was signed, and all intermediate-range nuclear forces were to be scrapped from June 1988 when the treaty came into force. The days of many American bases in Britain, including Greenham Common and Upper Heyford, were now numbered.

The fate of Greenham Common was swift, under the terms of the INF treaty all intermediate-range nuclear weapons systems were to be deactivated and removed to the country of origin for destruction within three years. To ensure this process was under way a low-notice inspection regime was implemented, needing just sixteen hours' prior warning. The GLCM bases were first inspected in July 1988. The first Cruise missiles were removed from Molesworth in September that year and the first movements from Greenham were under way by July 1989. But it looks likely that the exercise on Salisbury Plain between March and April of that year was also used to remove some missiles away from the glare of the media. The transporters were parked up at Boscombe Down for that period and there was an increase of USAF air movements during their deployment at the Wiltshire airfield. The last flight of missiles left Greenham Common on 5 March 1991 and the 501st Tactical Missile Wing was stood down on 4 June that same year. Upper Heyford continued as an F-111 base through until December 1993, having being involved in the first Gulf War (1991), when the last aircraft of the 20th Fighter Wing departed. Both sites were disposed of by the Ministry of Defence in 1997, along with other USAF airbases at Elvington, Bentwaters, Kemble and Alconbury.

Protest

One major part of Britain's Cold War was the level of public opposition to both home-developed and American nuclear weapons. A number of groups sprung up through the 1950s and '60s, including the 'Spies for Peace' who revealed the Regional Seats of Government network, and the Direct Action Committee, a demonstration pressure group. The most famous of these was the Campaign for Nuclear Disarmament – CND.

Public opposition started in 1952 as Britain detonated its first atomic weapon, but it was the rapid changes in Government policy towards the end of the decade that finally forced many into action. Agreement had been reached in 1957 to base sixty American Thor IRBM across the east coast, whilst still being committed to developing Britain's own deterrent – the V-force. In February 1958 a launch meeting for CND was held at the Conway Hall in London and over the Easter holiday the first of many peace marches made its way from a rally in Trafalgar Square to AWRE Aldermaston where they were met by thousands of other protesters. The majority were educated middle-class individuals, far removed from the traditional political activists, leading Tony Benn, in 1963, to comment, 'They were a nice, keen crowd, though mainly middle-class – one of CND's greatest weaknesses.' The main ethos of CND was that if Britain denounced nuclear weapons, effectively taking the moral high ground, the rest of the world would follow suit.

Spies for Peace

Anti-nuclear protest was not solely the preserve of CND. Many smaller groups sprang up around the country, and some had a lasting effect; one such group being the 'Spies for Peace'. In April 1963 the group managed to force entry into the recently completed Regional Seat of Government (RSG-6) at Warren Row near Henley-on-Thames. What they found inside was a large number of sensitive documents listing the positions of other RSG sites and who would be living in them whilst the war raged above. In one single act the whole face of British Civil Defence was turned on its head and the public lost faith in the CDC as most considered the Government was only interested in self-preservation.

Aneurin Bevan, delivering a speech at the 1957 Labour Party Conference, warned against unilateral disarmament, suggesting Britain would lose its place on the world stage without nuclear weapons; the issue led to deep divisions within the party. By the early 1960s the great crusade was also in trouble, as some of the more notable figures, including actress Vanessa Redgrave, demanded wholesale disobedience to Parliament as Bertram Russell, one of the founding members, had initially suggested. The split caused the formation of the Committee of 100, whilst the political side, including Michael Foot and Barbara Castle, opposed the move. After the Cuban missile crisis membership of CND reduced dramatically as the focus of protest shifted to denouncing the war in Vietnam. However, pressure was still kept up at the Holy Loch submarine base, home of Polaris. With the announcement of Cruise came a renewed interest in CND and membership shot up as protests towards NATO's new nuclear framework spread across Europe; but it was events at Greenham Common that attracted the most media attention, interestingly not organised by CND.

Cruise Watch

The protest against Cruise was both static and mobile. GLCM were designed to be deployed well away from the parent site, giving a level of protection; the problem was CND had other ideas. As the launchers left Greenham Common on exercise they became prime targets for the protesters. To exploit this highly visible form of protest a network was set up called 'Cruise Watch', aimed at tracking the convoys and causing as many problems as possible. This was a major headache for the security services and made the convoys anything other than discreet. This forced deployments to be undertaken in the early hours and be surrounded by a massive police presence. Blockades were set up, occasionally causing accidents, and deployment sites such as Boscombe Down soon sprouted mini peace camps, but it was at Greenham Common that the large protests, so typifying the Cold War, were played out.

The peace camps started in late 1981 when a group comprising mainly women arrived on a march from Cardiff. The camps came to symbolise not only the struggle

Greenham Common. Cutting the wire during protests in 1984. (Courtesy David Hoffman)

against nuclear weapons but also the perceived view that nuclear war was a male-dominated environment. The Government took a dim view of the situation and it wasn't long before key members of the Greenham Women were under surveillance by the police and MI5. Periodically evictions were carried out, often ending in violence, damaging the Government's position and strengthening the disarmament argument. Even after the Intermediate-range Nuclear Force (INF) treaty in 1987, and subsequent removal of GLCM over the period 1988–1991, a small presence remained at Greenham Common until 2000 and a small 'peace' garden has been constructed close to the site.

eight

Intelligence

No account of the Cold War would be complete without a view of the intelligence war that raged unseen between East and West. This said, it would be all too easy to follow the standard route, describing the high-profile spies such as Anthony Blunt and Klaus Fuchs, and monolithic Government institutions such as MI5 and MI6. This chapter will concentrate on one department that is ultimately a product of the Cold War, the Government Communications Headquarters – GCHQ. Owing to the current security climate only sites and events connected with the Cold War will be discussed.

GCHQ

The origins of the Government Communications Headquarters (GCHQ) can be traced back to the Government Code & Cipher School (GC&CS) at Bletchley Park in Buckinghamshire, famous for cracking the enigma codes during the Second World War. By 1946 Bletchley Park had closed and after a short spell at Eastcote in West London the newly formed GCHQ moved to two sites in Cheltenham, beginning an association with the Spa town that continued throughout the Cold War. Over time GCHQ ran a number of sites around the United Kingdom and had an advanced network of listening posts around the world.

Control of GCHQ was transferred from MI6 to the Foreign Office in 1946, coinciding with an increased focus on Russian intelligence gathering. By 1948 the UK–USA Security Agreement had formalised an intelligence sharing scheme between GCHQ and the National Security Agency (NSA). The agreement also included organisations representing Australia, Canada and New Zealand.

The sites at Benhall and Oakley, Cheltenham, had originally been built during the first years of the Second World War to house Government departments relocating from the more vulnerable south-east. Both sites contained single-storey Temporary Office Blocks (TOB), a standard quick, cost-effective structure that appeared throughout the

GCHQ Oakley. Part of the original Second World War structures GCHQ staff used from 1950.

GCHQ Oakley. C-Block completed in 1954 marked a turning point in British intelligence sites.

GCHQ Oakley. Many different operations were undertaken by GCHQ. This ultimately led to varying levels of security and access was strictly policed.

British Isles. Similar types can be found surrounding the 1950s War Rooms at Reading and Flowers Hill in Bristol. After a short spell as US Army supply depots and, after D-Day, as home to teacher training and the Ministry pensions division, both sites were handed over to GCHQ during 1950 and fully occupied by 1952. Redevelopment of Benhall and Oakley was undertaken over several periods, usually in response to a growing intelligence community or the introduction of more complex equipment.

Oakley

At Oakley an impressive new office complex was completed by 1954, capable of accommodating over 800 staff. The brick-built structure, known as C-Block comprised two wings connected by a central connecting stairs and lift block. Other structures were modified or constructed during this time including a new staff canteen and motor transport yard. Secure transport is essential in intelligence situations and the ability to control access to vehicles had distinct advantages, especially if the revelations made by Peter Wright in his memoirs *Spy Catcher* are to be believed. Incidentally the Government tried to ban the publication reaching Britain in the mid–1980s, even petitioning the Australian government to do the same. They declined and the book (including this author's copy) was imported in large numbers.

Oakley contained many departments, all concerned with different aspects of national defence. These included the intelligence and linguistics analysts, mathematicians, engineers and IT specialists. The National Security Agency (NSA), National Criminal Intelligence Service (NCIS), Scotland Yard, Special Branch and the Armed Services all had their own offices within the site. And in keeping with other Ministry sites security clearance to one area does not entitle the holder access to all parts of the site. This is demonstrated at Oakley by the number of internal or secondary guard points constructed in the mid–1960s. Upgrades in security continued throughout the life of the site and in the early 1980s a robust security fence was constructed. This type mirrored closely those deployed around many Government sites towards the end of the Cold War, making use of razor wire and a secondary reel of wire placed at ground level to hinder anyone who did make it over the first fence. This arrangement was often complemented by sodium lamps, motion sensors, closed–circuit television cameras and patrolling security guards, often with dogs.

Entry to the site was on production of a pass inspected by a security guard who then raised a barrier; the main gate area contained six such entry points. Exit was also controlled and any car could be pulled over and searched before being allowed to leave; two purpose-built open-ended covers were provided for this. The site at Oakley was cleared at the end of 2004 in advance of housing and commercial development.

Blakehill Farm

The former Royal Air Force airfield at Blakehill Farm near Cricklade in north Wiltshire was transferred to GCHQ around 1965 for the purposes of research and development. The airfield, built during 1943, had been home to a Canadian glider squadron during the war and later performed minor air operations until its closure to flying around 1960. Blakehill Farm had many benefits over earlier sites, the main being the method

GCHQ Oakley. Entry/exit point. To the right cars entering the sites would be individually checked. Cars were also liable to be searched when leaving the site. This was done under the covered structures on the left.

Blakehill Farm. GCHQ undertook a number of radio trials from here between 1965–1997.

Blakehill Farm. A heavily guarded radio trials hut on the outskirts of the site.

of construction. The majority of the domestic buildings such as billets, mess halls and social buildings were constructed well away from the airfield. As the site did not have the 'clutter' of earlier wartime or expansion-period buildings it was soon cleared.

The site had at least five radio masts constructed on the extremities of the airfield and one circular antenna, comprising ninety-six monopoles around three equipment sheds. Contained within this array was a single relocated Chain Home tower, over 300ft in height. A number of trials were conducted on propagation and radio systems, including high-frequency radar systems studying weather conditions out in the north Atlantic. Clearly this array had other applications (see Chapter 5) as demonstrated by the types of soundproofing left on the P-dash site.

Irton Moor

The GCHQ site at Irton Moor near Scarborough originates from the First World War, then it was known as the Wireless Telegraphy Receiving Station, Scarborough. During the Second World War the site was instrumental in the tracking of U-boat transmissions and contributed to the success of the Atlantic convoys. After the Second World War the site, up until 1964, remained in Admiralty control, but then became a GCHQ station. Some assets on site are now used by private companies but still display their earlier military origins. For many years the site was signposted as CSOS Irton Moor and has only recently been fully associated with GCHQ. The Composite Signals Organisation Site (CSOS) remit was to intercept signals on one of the various arrays distributed around the 1 sq. km site.

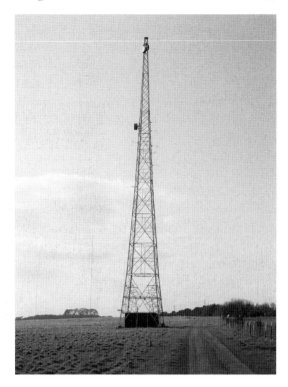

Opposite: Blakehill Farm. Anechoic sound absorption panels at P-dash. These foam shapes cut down the amount of background noise to a minimum.

Right: GCHQ Irton Moor. Irton Moor was originally used to triangulate U-boat transmissions. Later the site listened in to Soviet trawlers.

GCHQ were involved in some surprising operations throughout the Cold War, the majority of which will remain secret for a long time to come. Some information is now available, but is sketchy in some areas; this said, some exploits are worth mentioning here. In the early 1950s GCHQ monitored commercial traffic as part of a US–UK operation known as Scrum Half. The idea was to deny Warsaw Pact members essential goods and so damage the Soviet Army in both equipment and, more importantly in occupied countries, appearance. The list included aluminium, copper, diamonds and every form of electrical consumer goods. The operation had limited success.

From 1950 until the late 1970s members of the fishing communities in Aberdeen and Hull were recruited to monitor the Soviet North Atlantic Fleet. Known as Operation Hornbeam, recruits were trained to recognise specific ships and what to photograph when they saw them. Crews were sometimes complemented by radio and signals specialists, including members of staff from Irton Moor. This led to conspiracy theories, especially when the trawler *Gaul* was lost on 8 February 1974. The factory fishing vessel disappeared in the Barents Sea, one of the most sensitive military areas in the world, containing the major USSR base Murmansk. It was suggested that the crew were monitoring Russian naval activity and the ship was scuttled as the Soviet authorities discovered them. Up until recently some thought the crew were still captive in a prison in Russia. Others thought the ship may have snagged a submarine and been pulled underwater. The Government did not help, saying at the November 1974 inquest '…the *Gaul* capsized and foundered due to being overwhelmed by a succession of heavy seas'. The Government continued to deny recruiting trawler crews until at least 1996. A year later a television journalist, Norman Fenton, discovered the *Gaul* lying in 270m of water. Photographs undertaken by the Marine Accidents Investigation Branch show that the *Gaul* had sustained some damage in vital areas. A further inquest in 1999 upheld the position of the Government, noting that the *Gaul* was swamped by a succession of waves. However, the level of public interest forced the intelligence service to admit crews were recruited for spy duties during the Cold War.

The ability of GCHQ staff to monitor practically any transmission by the mid-1950s enabled the organisation, working with MI5 and MI6, to decipher the majority of traffic between Egypt and Russia during the Suez crisis in 1956. Whilst the Egyptian government belligerently proclaimed the Soviet Union would back them all the way to the Second World WarI, GCHQ were discovering the opposite. The Black Sea Fleet was maintained on a low level of security and it was clear that no ground troops would be committed; only lack of American support scuppered the venture.

By the end of the 1960s GCHQ was the primary source of intelligence data for all Government departments. Interceptions were now carried out around the globe using advanced radio technology and, increasingly, satellites. During the Vietnamese war GCHQ worked alongside the NSA intercepting transmissions at their outstation at Little Sai Wan in Hong Kong. And when the Conservatives took office in 1979 spending on defence issues, including new Government bunkers and GCHQ sites, outstripped what had gone before. New substantial office structures were built at Oakley and Benhall but there was to be a sting in the tail.

Union Blues

The British Government scored something of an own goal in early 1984 when new terms and conditions were announced for all GCHQ staff. Within this directive was the removal of statutory rights including membership of a trade union. To the Government this made perfect sense, as unionism within the Civil Service had caused major disruption over the last seven years and any effect on national security should be avoided at all costs. The staff thought otherwise, concerned that the Government considered union membership disloyal and that civil liberties were being eroded. This brought GCHQ firmly into the media spotlight, bringing not only adverse publicity but also acknowledging that GCHQ existed in the first place. Eventually the majority of staff gave up their union rights for a one-off payment, but fourteen staff were eventually dismissed by 1987 after a lengthy legal process through both the British and European courts. This led to a union rally in support of the staff every year in Cheltenham until 1997 when the returned Labour Government restored both union status and the fourteen who had lost their jobs ten years earlier.

The inevitable effects of 'Options for Change' and the relentless march of technology have seen a drastic decrease in GCHQ sites over the ten years since the end of the Cold War. The role of the intelligence services, especially GCHQ, have now taken on a renewed impetus and GCHQ is being remodelled for the twenty-first century. The Benhall site is to be the location for the new GCHQ centre, continuing the association of the organisation with Cheltenham.

Airborne Reconnaissance

A crucial part of the intelligence war was the ability to monitor Russian troop and equipment movements, the position of installations, especially missile silos, and intercept radio transmissions where possible. One of the most effective ways of doing this was from the air, preferably at extremely high altitudes. A number of 'classic' American aircraft were stationed in Britain during the latter stages of the Cold War, two, the TR-1 (U-2) and SR-71 Blackbird, are described here.

Lockheed U-2

The Lockheed U-2 was designed to fly higher than any Soviet missile batteries and fighters could reach. Introduced in 1956 after just eighteen months of development, the aircraft was essentially a powered glider. Losses were high, but not all of them were due to handling characteristics. In May 1960 a U-2 was shot down over the Soviet Union, causing an international incident and cancelling the Paris arms control conference before it had begun. And in October 1962 another was brought down as it tried to photograph missile complexes on the island of Cuba. The aircraft did make brief visits to the United Kingdom up until the late 1970s, but none were permanently stationed here.

In 1978 the USAF announced that a new suite of Tactical Reconnaissance aircraft were to be commissioned and a year later the Lockheed U-2 production line was

Lockheed U-2. The U-2 entered service in 1956 just eighteen months after the type was first discussed. Originally operated by the CIA, this reconnaissance aircraft was capable of flying at over 70,000ft. U-2s operated from RAF Alconbury from 1983.

Lockheed SR-71. The CIA took delivery of around fifteen aircraft in 1962. Capable of over three times the speed of sound at a height of 80,000ft detachments of Blackbirds operated from RAF Mildenhall throughout the 1980s.

re-opened. Thirty-five Battlefield Surveillance aircraft, designated TR-1(U-2), were built over a two-year period. From early 1983, operated by the 17th Reconnaissance Wing (SAC), the aircraft flew from RAF Alconbury in Cambridgeshire. Major works were undertaken on the airfield infrastructure to protect the aircraft. Initially five temporary protection shelters comprising steel corrugated sheet around a simple frame were constructed. These performed two functions: they kept the fragile aircraft from the worst of the weather and more importantly masked the aircraft from surveillance satellites. Similar sheds can be found at Upper Heyford that were used to cover the QRA F-111. From the mid-1980s at the end of the airfield-hardening programme, thirteen specifically designed HAS were built along with a protected avionics building, hardened HQ and standby generator houses.

SR-71 Blackbird

The CIA requested a replacement for the U-2 as early as 1958 and a contract for a faster, higher flying aircraft was awarded to Lockheed in August 1959. Subsequently up to fifteen early variant A-12 single-seat aircraft were delivered to the CIA in 1962. In March 1964 the USAF started to take delivery of an up-rated version, by now known as the SR-71. The technological difficulties of producing such an aircraft led to many new processes and materials being exploited within aeronautical engineering for the first time. Blackbird was required to operate at heights in excess of 24,300m and at speeds over mach 3. These excessive speeds subjected the airframe to large temperature variations and a titanium construction with a very advanced stealth shape was finally developed. SR-71 operated throughout the 1980s from RAF Mildenhall in Suffolk. KC-135Q tankers were also co-deployed to the base as Blackbird used a high-octane fuel called JP-7, unlike the wide-cut avtur most jet aircraft use. Blackbird could give detailed reconnaissance over an incredible 259,000 sq. km of territory per hour.

RAF Operations

The British Government worked closely with the Norwegian Royal Air Force in obtaining Russian fighter base information in the immediate post-war period. Strangely President Truman had cancelled all US intelligence flights over Soviet airspace at that time. This forced the Joint Chiefs of Staff to request that the British undertake the necessary spy flights. Churchill, known for his views on Stalin and Russia, quickly agreed. By 1951 three crews were training on the reconnaissance version of the B-45 and by 1952 flights from Sculthorpe had flown to Berlin and back via the air corridor. Just one year later crews, by now in American aircraft painted up to look like RAF ones, were flying right across the Soviet Union. Unfortunately these were not without incident and at least one aircraft was lost after departing RAF Brize Norton.

Royal Air Force reconnaissance took a radically different direction to that of the US government. The majority of intelligence gathering was performed by fast low-level aircraft carrying 'reccie. pods'. Most ground-attack aircraft from the 1950s onward carried camera pods including the Harrier, Hunter, Phantom, Jaguar, Javelin and Tornado. However, one specialist aircraft, the Canberra PR.9, is capable of high-level reconnaissance. First flown on 13 May 1949 the Canberra was the world's first jet bomber and surprisingly six are still in service with the RAF. Canberra did over-fly the Soviet Union on a number of occasions in the 1950s and often came under fire from Migs in the process.

Reliance on over-flights is now rare, as most reconnaissance is now covered by satellite technology, often allowing for real-time decisions to be made on the other side of the world.

Survive v.t. & i. Continue to live or exist (longer than); come alive through or continue to exist in spite of (danger, accident, etc.). *Oxford Dictionary*

nine

The Royal Observer Corps

The Royal Observer Corps (ROC) was a voluntary organisation with a long, proven and effective history that had been the 'eyes' of Fighter Command throughout the Second World War. In the Cold War the Corps was again called upon to watch the skies, but by the late 1960s the ROC had a totally different role, one that typified the type of warfare expected in the nuclear age. This chapter follows the history of the Royal Observer Corps from the reformation through to stand down.

At 1700 hrs on 12 May 1945, just four days after the surrender of Germany and the end of the war in Europe, the Royal Observer Corps was stood down. This was not to be a permanent arrangement. Radar was still in its infancy, it could easily be jammed physically or electronically, and many of the Chain Home stations were in desperate need of refurbishment. Immediately after the cease of hostilities the German air defence network was evaluated, demonstrating that effective countermeasures on the part of the Allies and the lack of radar range had left the Germans blind on many occasions. And whilst they did have a ground observation network, it had been in no way as effective as the Royal Observer Corps; clearly this wartime asset had potential in the post-war years.

Reformation

On 16 November 1946 the BBC broadcast an appeal for all interested members of the population to volunteer for service; letters had already been forwarded the day before to all members of the ROC who had expressed a wish to be recalled. Training was to restart on 1 April 1947; the ROC was back in business. By the end of 1948 1,420 posts were active around the country. Some areas had very sparse coverage, such as Northern Ireland and the Scottish Highlands, but the main framework was in place. Posts comprised mainly those that had been used throughout the war, but many were no longer suitable or had been removed, one example being those positioned on the roofs of buildings. Vandalism, post-stand-down, had also taken its toll; an upgrade was

Holme-on-Spalding-Moor. Orlit posts were built across the country in the 1950s. This particular one, a Type 'B' stands 1.5m above ground. Post crews would track bomber formations from here.

needed. Events in Berlin, throughout the summer of 1948, were to demonstrate the prudence of reactivating the ROC, meanwhile the Civil Defence Act was passed and organisations such as the Auxiliary Fire Service and Civil Defence Corps re-emerged in 1949. As the Berlin Airlift intensified that winter it was clear that Soviet aggression may well extend to the shores of Britain. The ROC would become, once again, an intrinsic part of the air defence network. Upgrades to the reporting centres, posts and communications were sanctioned, primarily in an attempt to standardise procedures across Europe under a new alliance, the North Atlantic Treaty Organisation (NATO), which had been signed in April 1949.

Orlit

By April 1951 the entire network of ROC posts had been assessed with recommendations to move 411 and place ninety-three new ones on the landscape. The existing posts were *ad hoc* affairs, ranging from no shelter through to elaborate brick-built structures. Standardisation was required and it came in the form of the 'Orlit Post'. Messrs Orlit Ltd of Colnbrook, Buckinghamshire, were asked in late 1951 to submit drawings of a prefabricated concrete post, the definitive two editions being accepted by the Air Ministry in 1952. Orlit already had substantial post-war experience in prefabricated construction, especially housing, replacing the bomb-damaged homes in many areas across the country.

Two posts were proposed; Type 'A' constructed at ground level; and Type 'B' standing on concrete legs 6ft (2m) above ground. The post itself comprised concrete panels bolted together creating a rectangle 10ft (3.05m) by 6ft 8in (2.03m). The post was accessed through a door into a small storeroom that contained equipment and the telephone; the observation platform was accessed through another small door. The platform was surrounded by the concrete (or occasionally wood) walls of the post that was protected from the elements by a removable cover. In the centre of the platform was a plywood pedestal on which the tracking instruments were mounted. Access to the Type B post was via a set of steps that were usually made of steel. The construction programme took until 1955 to complete, by which time 413 sites had been updated.

'Rats and Terriers'

The visual reporting of aircraft was, in the early 1950s, to undergo a radical change due to one major factor, the advent of the jet-powered aircraft. Britain had been operating the Gloucester Meteor since 1944 and the de Haviland Vampire had entered service by 1946, but the majority were still piston-engine propeller driven aircraft; but jet technology was also available to the Soviet Air Force. The repositioning and upgrading of existing posts was now critical, jet aircraft were proving that the old wartime network was effectively obsolete. Posts now needed to be more evenly spread throughout the countryside if the 'new' threat was to be tracked.

The code word 'Rats' had first been sanctioned for use in 1941 as a quick way of denoting fast, low-level aircraft; naturally 'Terrier' was the name of the intercepting fighter. With the speed of aircraft generally increasing this was one of the few codes that saw reuse. A pair of fighters, in the early 1950s the Meteor, would operate at two flight levels, usually 275 and 100m, but this had major drawbacks. Firstly the presence of a Rat was indicated to the high-flying aircraft by firing a Very pistol and flares were often difficult to see from a distance during the day. Secondly the Meteors' range was drastically reduced at low level, even extra tanks could not push the endurance much beyond forty minutes; thankfully airborne tactics did not go fully low level until the 1960s.

Delivery of the English Electric Canberra to the RAF in 1951 highlighted a growing problem for the ROC. Aircraft were now starting to operate much higher and faster than ever before and whilst the Canberra was the first of the jet bombers to see service it certainly wasn't going to be the last. The Soviet Air Force already had 'rivet for rivet' copies of the Boeing B-29, giving them the endurance to reach American and British targets. Now a new series of jet-powered bombers were under construction which give them extra height and speed.

The RAF had been advancing on all fronts with the Rotor plan air defence system that had included the reorganisation of Fighter Command sectors. The programme called for the building of protected command centres and eventually saw the Chain Home stations with the new Type 80 radar system. By 1953 the changes were at an advanced stage and the ROC aligned its area map to correspond to that of Fighter Command. With this reorganisation nine out of the thirty-nine group headquarters were disbanded, but fifty-eight new posts around Britain and one new headquarters building were opened in Northern Ireland.

Through July 1954 the Royal Observer Corps took part in a large exercise called 'Dividend', designed to test out the new Fighter Command structure along with that of the ROC. By now the aircraft available to both East and West were far too fast for the antiquated tracking systems the ROC operated; the exercise demonstrated that the days of visual and audio spotting were over.

Fallout

The international stakes were upped considerably in the early 1950s as first the United States (1952) and then the Soviet Union (1953) tested thermonuclear devices. The ramifications were immense. The American test device was stored in a two-story refrigerated building and weighed over eighty tonnes; meanwhile the Russian bomb was a deliverable unit that had been tested by means of an air drop. Clearly the Soviet Union had the upper hand and, coupled with the new long-range bombers, was in a good position to carry out a pre-emptive strike. As if that wasn't enough a new and lasting spectre was becoming apparent. Radiation poisoning had claimed victims in Japan in 1945 but the fallout was nothing compared to that of a thermonuclear device. As tests were conducted throughout the 1950s by America and the Soviet Union and finally at Christmas Island by the United Kingdom team in 1957, it became apparent that the force of a ground-burst fusion weapon introduced massive amounts of fallout into the atmosphere. This new menace had the ability to debilitate defending forces and large areas of food producing land for weeks, not to mention the millions who would die from poisoning. Suddenly the flash and blast of a nuclear explosion didn't seem that bad.

The test information on fallout was quickly passed throughout NATO members and the Home Office started to consider how the monitoring of such a situation could be undertaken. Estimates of fallout patterns during a nuclear exercise in 1954 appeared in contemporary Home Defence leaflets such as 'Home Defence and the Farmer'. In this 1958 pamphlet a diagram noted that a bomb blast on the north-west coast would, with the prevailing wind, spread fallout as far as the east coast, beyond London. But what if the wind changed? Government estimates put the movement of a radioactive plume from Birmingham to the east coast at nine hours, which was far too quick to effect a civilian evacuation in its path. The military also needed an effective warning system, primarily to disperse troops, vehicles or aircraft away from the plume footprint. For any monitoring to be effective the organisation concerned would have to cover the whole of the United Kingdom and the Royal Observer Corps was the natural choice. By May 1955 the Air Council had agreed to the use of the ROC in a monitoring capacity, albeit as a secondary duty to aircraft tracking.

The United Kingdom Warning and Monitoring Organisation

The detonation of the first hydrogen bombs brought a realisation that large civilian casualties could be expected through the effects of radioactive fallout. However, if the population had time to shelter then the effects of that fallout could be drastically reduced, so by 1955 the Home Office had devised a system called the United Kingdom Warning and Monitoring Organisation (UKWMO) that covered the whole of the British Isles. Once activated the UKWMO was to perform a number of functions, both internally and with other NATO members. By the mid-1970s a large complex infrastructure existed ensuring that the maximum time between detection and detonation was given.

Warning Against Air Attack

The detection of an air attack would be possible from a number of sources; conventional bomber fleets would be picked up as they crossed Europe by the bases positioned along the east coast. And by 1963 the Ballistic Missile Early Warning System (BMEWS) also monitored for missile attack. All information would be passed to Home Office staff stationed at the UK Regional Air Operations Centre (UK RAOC), High Wycombe, who would decide whether, on military advice, to set the national warning network in motion.

The Network

Britain was divided into 250 warning districts following the existing telephone charging boundaries; each district had one carrier control point (CCP) and a standby in case of failure. Initiation of the system was by the turning of one key at UK RAOC that would alert all CCPs simultaneously, the majority of which were positioned in main police stations, one such site is under the police station at Swindon in Wiltshire. The network was know as HANDEL and used the speaking clock line from Strike Command to the CCPs; from the CCP a designated line was provided out to two specific warning devices. The first was the WB600 powered siren point, almost 7,000 of which were strategically placed around urban areas on masts or public buildings. One major problem with the siren was the lack of protection against EMP, and as they were often situated on large metal poles or on tall buildings they often received lightning strikes, knocking them out. During the system upgrade in the early 1980s the electronics were replaced to cover such eventualities. The WB600 siren also contained two copper heater coils to stop the fans freezing up in the winter.

The second device was known as the WB400 Carrier Warning Point (CWP), distributed in rural areas where the sirens would not be heard. The unit comprised no more than a speaker box operated by battery and could be found anywhere from police or fire stations to pubs or private houses. Once the alert was issued it was up to the recipient to warn people in the immediate vicinity using some rather antiquated means, hand sirens, whistles, maroons and gongs were all suggested. Again there were problems, batteries often went flat and test signals were often ignored, usually necessitating a visit from an engineer investigating a non-existent fault. Again the 1980s saw this equipment replaced by the more up to date WB1400 complete with trickle charger, disposing of the battery problem, and protection against EMP. The warning itself would be given by a verbal message or rising and falling tone, backed up by broadcasts on television and radio, hopefully allowing at least some of the population time to seek refuge. The UKWMO was promoted in 1979 with the release of a Government information booklet covering all aspects of the organisation during an attack scenario. The final statement is rather worrying in a country populated by over forty million people:

06:00: Life goes on.... Through the existence, readiness and prompt response of UKWMO, ten million lives may have been saved – to see the dawn of another day.

'UKWMO – Protecting by Warning' (1979).

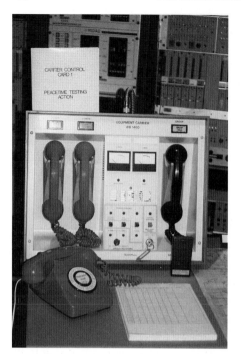 

Above left: Carrier Control Point. Situated mostly in police stations, from here local air-raid sirens would be operated.

Above right: Warning Siren. Sirens were positioned around major population areas to warn of imminent air attack. The majority were removed in the early 1990s, however areas that are prone to flooding have retained the network.

Command Structure

A three-tier structure existed within the UKWMO by the mid-1970s concerned with the monitoring of nuclear explosions and prediction and assessment of fallout patterns. The primary field level was operated by the ROC who fed information to the Group Control; from here the information was collated and fallout warnings issued where necessary. The Group Control then passed the information onto a Sector Control, which would feed NATO and other organisations with an overall picture of the situation.

Meteorological Monitoring

If the prediction of fallout patterns were to be accurate then a full picture of the meteorological condition over the British Isles was required. Each Sector Control had three trained meteorologists stationed as part of the staff who would interpret information supplied by the Meteorological Office at Bracknell. If Bracknell was damaged or destroyed information could be drawn from two other sources, the Radio Sonde network or Upper Air Stations. Complementing this were eighty-seven of the ROC posts who could also monitor basic weather conditions, primarily pressure and wind direction, again for the assessment of fallout patterns.

The UKWMO was promoted as a civil protection service but the reality was that it played an important part of the United Kingdom deterrent. Once a nuclear weapon had been detonated on or over British soil some form of comparable strike would have been inevitable. By using UKWMO the Government would have information on the yield of weapon used, position of burst and type of target. Once this information had been confirmed through the Home Office representatives at UK RAOC, both the deterrent force and public warning system would have been activated simultaneously.

The ROC Go Underground

To actively record any effects of fallout the monitoring team would have to be protected from blast and radiation; with the steadily diminishing task of aircraft reporting the natural move was towards protected underground posts and command centres. The Air Ministry was already committed to other major projects and did not consider the financing of yet more reorganisation to be its responsibility. The UKWMO and ROC upgrades were eventually financed from the Home Office budget. The Home Office had, by 1956, decided on a standard protected post design, one that became the most numerous of the Cold War structures. Along with new and improved sites came the advent of a series of new instruments to record flash, blast and fallout, a situation that found the ROC far removed from its previous wartime role.

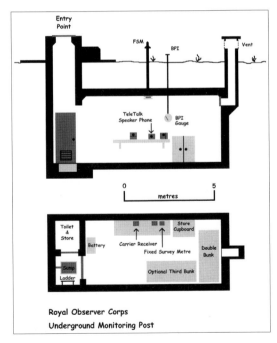

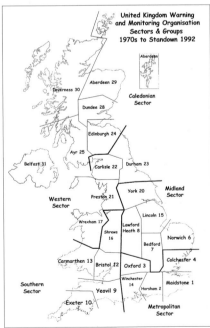

Above left: ROC underground monitoring post.

Above right: UKWMO site distribution from the 1970s. (After Cocroft et al. 2003)

The construction of the first of 1,563 underground posts began in 1957 and by mid-1958 nearly 100 posts had been handed back to the ROC. Problems beset the construction programme from the outset. Landowners were often reluctant to release land and in some areas the geology proved to be difficult. Areas containing an igneous parent rock had, in many cases, to be blasted out whilst others were often waterlogged causing delays and in some cases the eventual abandonment of newly constructed posts. Looking at just one post it is easy to see how much of a logistical nightmare positioning could be.

Wootton Bassett

Wootton Bassett is a small Wiltshire market town just a few miles to the west of the railway town, Swindon. The original post was established at Wootton Bassett in January 1938, designated 23/A3 in the Western Headquarters Group situated at Bristol. In November 1953 the post received an Orlit observation platform and came under the command of the Oxford Group, now following the RAF sector 'Southern' and designated 3/M3. In April 1956 the post was moved 5km to Toothill on the outskirts of Swindon, where another Orlit platform was erected, still reporting to Oxford. As part of the Home Office UKWMO upgrades an underground post was constructed in July 1961 that was subsequently abandoned in 1967 due to the constant ingress of water. A new post was built on the airfield at Wroughton in June 1968, designated 3/K3 and was in use until the stand down of 1991. So what archaeology remains? The original site is now occupied by a school, no trace of the post remains. The Toothill site has an extremely large housing estate around it, although part of the surrounding fence remains, presumably the underground section is still extant. The post on Wroughton airfield forms part of the Science Museum collection and is open to visitors.

A 'Typical' Monitoring Post

The underground post at Amesbury, built in July 1964, is a classic monument to its type. Few features are visible above ground. The post is situated in the middle of a field about 100m from a track and is surrounded by a three-strand wire fence on concrete posts with a metal gate in one corner. Buried underground is a reinforced concrete box 6 x 2.5 x 2.3m. Here a crew of three would have monitored the blast on a Bomb Power Indicator (BPI) gauge, and recorded radioactive signatures through a Fixed Survey Meter Probe (FMSP). Contact would be maintained with the other two posts in the Amesbury group at Gratley in Hampshire and Wylye in Wiltshire, along with the group HQ at Winchester by landline.

Above ground is an access block with a counterbalanced steel trap door covering a 4.5m shaft that gave access to the post via a steel rung ladder. The access block also, as a later addition, contained a louvered ventilation duct and the fixed point for a Ground Zero Indicator (GZI). This was an instrument that worked like a pinhole camera, recording the initial flash of a nuclear detonation onto a gradated sheet of paper, allowing a fallout assessment to be reached. At the other end of the site is another small louvered ventilation shaft; master posts (one out of the group of three)

Underground Post. The underground monitoring post at Amesbury is one of 1,563 built between 1957–1968 across the British Isles. Over 800 still survive.

often had the radio aerial fitted to this. Three tubes of varying diameter also run from the surface down into the bunker for instruments and communications. One carried the baffle plates for the BPI. Another more prominent tube 50cm high and 6cm in diameter would, in times of emergency, be fitted with the FMSP under a hard rubber cap. A small tube is also present to allow the post office (as it was at the time of construction) to pass a landline down into the post.

Conditions were fairly rudimentary; the Government required a post which could support four crew for a week, although this number was later reduced to three. Tests at the prototype post, built at Farnham in 1956, proved that a crew could survive the ordeal but the lighting was poor, carbon dioxide build-up threatened the crew and the concrete structure was hard to keep warm. Improvements were slight but did help, the floors were insulated with rubber matting and the 12-volt light was eventually replaced by a strip light, but overall poor conditions prevailed throughout the use of the monitoring posts.

Field Force

As the United Kingdom Warning and Monitoring Organisation (UKWMO) grew the ROC moved further away from aircraft reporting. A low-level area survived along the east coast where observers in the recognition role were still considered of worth. The rest of the sectors were steadily disappearing below ground and by 1960 Fighter Command had the reporting of nuclear bursts as the ROC main priority.

Throughout the 1950s the chances of aircraft delivering an atomic weapon to the designated target had rapidly diminished, the weapon of choice was now the ballistic missile. During 1960 the United States started construction of the Ballistic Missile Early Warning System (BMEWS) on the North Yorkshire Moors at Fylingdales, close to Scarborough and Whitby. This site was linked, along with Thule in Greenland and Clear in Alaska, to NORAD at Cheyenne Mountain in the United States. Britain now had the notorious 'four-minute warning' in place. Any information needed to be passed as quickly as possible, especially to monitoring posts, which were, by their very nature, often in remote rural areas. All posts by the early 1960s had received new designations and were grouped into threes; one from each group was selected as a master post and was fitted with a VHF radio allowing the crew to contact the group HQ. A carrier receiver unit was also now situated at or near most master posts; this crew would then alert the other two posts. It was also hoped that enough landlines would survive between the groups of three to allow for the post-explosion monitoring task to be effective. By 1964 nearly all underground posts had been constructed and all protected group headquarters had been commissioned. With the warning and monitoring system in place most thought that would be it, but the next five years proved it is never worth being complacent in a government department, especially when it comes to budgets.

Group Headquarters

By the end of the Second World War most Royal Observer Corps groups were located in purpose-built centres. By 1947 these centres had been reoccupied and formed the command structure of the ROC posts until the UKWMO protected centres were introduced in the 1960s.

The 1942/3 pattern centres were built around a two-story operations room containing, on the lower floor, the plotting table and a long-range map. From a three-sided balcony above staff were able to monitor the situation as it developed. The standard design had three single-story wings, which included accommodation for both male and female staff, a mess hall, controller's office and a room for the GPO Officer. The centre also contained a generator house with heating provided via a boiler, fuel storage and stand-by lighting circuit. Thirty-nine sites were reoccupied in 1947 and were realigned with the six new Fighter Command sectors during the 1953 reorganisation.

As the role of the ROC gradually moved towards warning and monitoring it was recognised that the wartime control centres did not provide adequate protection against nuclear blast, radiation and fallout, and upgrades were required. Just as the monitoring posts were to be moved underground so the control centres were to be redesigned; two types were suggested, the surface and semi-sunken. In the event both types were adopted and were built in almost equal numbers, along with the refurbishment of four previous sites owned by the RAF and AAOR. By 1965 the last of thirty-one group headquarters, No. 3 Oxford at Cowley, was opened.

The new headquarters were designed to operate under emergency conditions for up to thirty days, having independent water, fuel, sewage, air-conditioning, kitchen, generators and food storage. A complement of between forty and sixty crew, both male and female, would operate the centre, running in three shifts. To release valuable

York. This building served as the Twenty Group HQ from 1942 to 1961.

The Royal Observer Corps Group Headquarters at York. Twenty Group HQ from 1961 to 1991. This building is now owned by English Heritage and is open to the public.

space only twenty bunks were provided so a system of 'hot bedding' was implemented for the off-duty personnel. Representatives from the Home Office also formed part of the crew, advising on scientific and weather matters. The centres were equipped with the same instruments as those at the monitoring posts but a number carried other devices to allow for the position and power of a blast to be accurately recorded.

Bhangmeters, AWDREY and DIADEM

The bhangmeter was fitted to the six sector UKWMO headquarters. It was a proven detection system developed by Sandia National Laboratories in the late 1950s, principally for use in test detonations by both the American and British test teams. The instrument contained an optical sensor that would record when a flash exceeded a pre-set level, as in the case of a nuclear explosion. Between 1963 and 1970, twelve satellites, the Vela project, were launched, each carrying an array of detection devices including the bhangmeter. An up-rated version of the instrument, the Atomic Weapon Detection Recognition and Estimation of Yield (AWDREY), was fitted to twelve group headquarters in the 1960s. A detector head was permanently fitted to the exterior, usually the generator exhaust, which was the highest point, of the group control. The instrument comprised photoelectric cells with 360-degree vision that would react to the initial flash of a detonation. This instrument differed from the bhangmeter in that it could detect the double pulse of a thermonuclear device as well as EMP. The information was passed to a four-figure display unit situated on the upper gallery of the operations room, producing a print-out that gave the precise time and potential yield of the weapon detonated. A further upgrade to the system in 1974 saw the introduction of the Direction Indicator of Atomic Detonation by Electronic Means (DIADEM) that allowed for triangulation, giving a more accurate plot.

Détente

In the summer of 1965 the Royal Observer Corps assumed a purely monitoring and warning role as the RAF put its weight behind the Radar Air Defence network. Communications were, again, upgraded during 1966 and the layout of the group headquarters changed with the introduction of data transmission and post states. Information on fallout was plotted as before but now use was made of a telex system to move the information around both internally and externally. The position of monitoring posts was assessed yet again, including the possibility of matching them up with the Local Authority areas (discussed later). In the end the position of the group HQs were centralised with monitoring posts all around, cutting down on the all-important communication vulnerability.

1968 was a watershed for British voluntary services. International relations were better than they had been for nearly a decade, the world had been to the brink of nuclear disaster in 1961–62 and despite the Vietnam War there was a distinct thawing of the Cold War. The Labour Government, under Harold Wilson, took the opportunity to make major savings in all aspects of public spending, not least in defence. A contract for fifty American F-111 bombers was cancelled, saving, even after a compensation payment of £400 million, £250 million. This decision was all the more difficult to swallow as the TSR2 had been cancelled in favour of the swing-wing American aircraft. Bases in Malaysia and Singapore were to close, cutting not only the cost of overseas bases but also the air transport fleet as well. But it was the voluntary defence sectors that were to suffer the most. The Civil Defence Corps, Auxiliary Fire Service and a host of other groups were to be cut, saving an estimated £14 million in 1968–69 and £20 million through 1969–70. That famous phrase 'care and maintenance' was used, but the harsh reality was one of complete disbandment, flooding the market with large amounts of stockpiled equipment. The ROC did not escape unscathed. Warm words were uttered in Parliament but the harsh reality was that 686 monitoring posts and two group HQs were to close with the loss of at least 5,000 staff.

Calm Before the Storm

After the upheaval of the 1968 review both the UKWMO and ROC settled down to a period of relative calm. Operations and procedures were expanded and tested through exercises at group and national level, including working with the Government on the Concord noise project in 1970. DIADEM was tested and fitted to the group HQs that carried AWDREY, considerably upgrading the UKWMO estimation capability. Communications were also refurbished, all lines between monitoring posts and group headquarters were given designated landlines and in the early 1980s the National Carrier Receiver units were replaced with new equipment, including those at the posts.

At group level the teleprinter systems were replaced in 1984 with Message Switch Equipment (MSX), and by 1988 this had been upgraded again with System Exchange 2000, in line with all United Kingdom telephone exchanges. Communications were further augmented by the latest microwave technology along with some satellite interfaces. The computer age had arrived, but so had another review into the UKWMO; changes were inevitable, but these were intended to improve the system rather than streamline it, and unfortunately they never reached fruition.

No one could have predicted the changes that would occur through 1988–91, international politics struggled to keep pace; the end result was to be stand down for both the UKWMO and ROC. In 1988 Gorbachev announced to the United Nations that troops would be withdrawn from Afghanistan within one year; it was also his intention to remove 50,000 Soviet troops from Europe along with all offensive weapons. Against this backdrop the Government was considering an update to existing equipment for the ROC. AWDREY was to be replaced with more sensitive optical equipment, along with seismic and electromagnetic detectors. The long-running discussion on a common HQ for both the ROC and UKWMO had nearly been settled, three sites around Oxford being favourite, and new generators had been supplied to monitoring posts. But some things had to go. The warning siren network was to be removed, and the public were to be warned through television and radio broadcasts from now on.

During 1989 Eastern block countries started to remove symbols of Soviet power forming Communist free governments. Citizens in East Germany could now escape to the West through the Hungarian border. Eventually the Berlin Wall was opened and the process of reunification began, with Moscow's blessing. A reduced threat from the Warsaw Pact countries led to NATO announcing that no European states were now considered enemies, the Soviet Union was steadily shrinking away from the 'Iron Curtain'. Throughout the period exercises continued, during 1990 three were instigated, 'INTEX' over 17–18 March and 'POSTHORN 1/90 and 2/90' on 20 May and 14 October, respectively. These involved the full complement of operations controls and monitoring posts and were to be the last undertaken. On 10 July 1991 the decision was taken to restructure warning and monitoring on a more cost-effective footing and the Royal Observer Corps, along with the UKWMO, was stood down. Some 250 observers were retained by the MOD, manning the Nuclear Reporting Cells (NRC), but these too have now been stood down. Monitoring, however, lives on in the Radioactive Incident Monitoring Network (RIMNET) system.

ten

'Civil Defence is Common Sense'

From 1948 tensions in Europe drove the Government to resurrect the Civil Defence Corps, and by the early 1950s this had grown into a large organisation primarily concerned with rescue after a major conventional or nuclear attack. From the mid-1950s the H-bomb began to change that concept and by 1960 it was accepted that there was no defence from a ballistic missile attack, and more alarmingly there would also be little rescue. Many elaborate plans were developed in an attempt to minimise the effects of a National Emergency – how effective they might be was, luckily, never discovered. Today as part of the 'peace dividend' many structures are being sold off or demolished, but was the cost justified? Just how would the Government look after a population traumatised by nuclear war and how would the 'machinery of Government' survive? This chapter will look at the Civil Defence Corps and later civil protection ideas, whilst the next will investigate some of the varied Government shelters designed to ensure their (not our) survival.

Backdrop

Civil Defence was not a new idea; it had held legal status throughout the Second World War, proving to be both an effective voluntary morale-boosting network and rescue organisation. The system was disbanded at the end of the conflict only to be resurrected three years later against a backdrop of deteriorating East–West relations. Britain continued to play host to American aircraft throughout the immediate post-war period, but this was neither permanent nor in most cases planned, often being just 'through' flights to Europe. On 18 June 1948 relations between the former allies took a turn for the worse as a new currency was introduced for West Germany, including parts of occupied Berlin. The same day the Soviets sealed off the frontiers and by 24 June Berlin, and 2.3 million people were isolated from the outside world. Pressure mounted on Western governments to act and by July sixty B-29 Superfortress bombers were stationed at RAF Scampton and RAF Waddington, quickly becoming known as the 'atomic bombers'. The deployment had been arranged by the British Government, primarily to bolster their own position, but Washington was in charge of any nuclear drops through the National Security Council report NSC-30. An important precedent had been set, one that was to see United States forces stationed in Britain for the rest of the Cold War. Britain moved onto the front line.

In January 1949 President Truman announced military aid for his European allies, formally creating the North Atlantic Treaty Organisation (NATO) in April of that year. All NATO members were now obligated to come to each other's aid in times of Soviet aggression. By 29 August 1948 that aggression moved from a conventional to a nuclear one as the USSR exploded its first fission device. It was against this backdrop of international tension that the Civil Defence Act (1948) was passed, leading to the formation of a voluntary Civil Defence Corps (CDC) in April 1949.

The Act

The announcement of the Civil Defence Bill at the opening of Parliament in October 1948 paved the way for the Home Office to make provision for the protection of the public against attack from overseas. The Act was comprehensive, requesting that the designated Minister deal with the following:

(a)   the organisation, formation, maintenance, equipment and training of civil defence forces and services;

(b)   the organisation, equipment and training for civil defence purposes of police forces, fire brigades and employees of local or police authorities employed primarily for purposes other than civil defence purposes;

(c)   the instruction of members of the public in civil defence and their equipment for the purposes of civil defence;

(d)   the provision, storage and maintenance of commodities and things required for civil defence; and

(e)   the provision, construction, maintenance or alteration of premises, structures or excavations required for civil defence and the doing of any other work required for civil defence.

Civil Defence Act (1948)

The Civil Defence Structure

The Civil Defence Corps (CDC) was a voluntary national body ultimately controlled for Central Government by the Home Secretary, who was responsible for training throughout the country. The organisation was based on a regional network broadly following the county and county boroughs (in London), and in Scotland counties and large burghs. From division level the responsibilities for recruitment, training and organisational control fell to the County Councils. This was again broken down to a sub-divisional level in large counties such as Yorkshire. Below this the local authorities ran a division comprising HQ, Warden, Ambulance, Rescue and Welfare. The London and Metropolitan Boroughs organised the HQ, Warden and Welfare Sections whilst

Bully Fen Training Ground. CDC training grounds were designed to present a wide array of rescue situations. The 'ruined' buildings were specifically designed for the task.

the London County Council administered the Rescue, First Aid and Ambulance sections. Other voluntary services were also considered part of the Civil Defence framework, although they were autonomous at the group level. These included the Auxiliary Fire Service (AFS), Women's Royal Voluntary Service (WRVS), St John and St Andrews Ambulance Brigades, and the National Hospital Service Reserve.

Training

Training was carried out at a number of levels and locations. Staff training was held at Sunningdale in Berkshire, whilst three national Civil Defence Schools ran at Easingwold in Yorkshire, Taymouth Castle in Perthshire and Falfield in Gloucestershire. These sites had, from the late 1930s, been Anti-Gas Training Schools and were ideally suited to the 'new' CDC training requirements. At a local level most County Councils had their own training grounds comprising a variety of locations; bomb sites left over from the war and brick or other derelict factories were all pressed into service. One such site at Bully Fen, in the Hackney Marsh area, is typical of the regional centres. It was the first purpose-built Advanced Training Ground for the London area CDC, opened in April 1953 by the then Home Secretary, Sir David Maxwell Fyfe. The centre comprised lecture halls, domestic accommodation and a collection of 'new' ruined buildings intended to present a wide array of situations for practical training. Local training centres, usually in buildings already owned by the authority, were also set up around the country, where weekly meetings were held. These performed as much a social function as anything else, fostering camaraderie clearly had its recruitment value whilst team building at the same time.

Industrial Civil Defence Service (ICDS)

By 1951 it was realised that the CDC had one major drawback: being essentially a voluntary organisation with few full-time salaried members, it was only at 'full strength' at evenings and weekends. Obviously it would be brought to readiness during times of increasing tension, but an unannounced attack would leave the CDC woefully unprepared. More importantly for the Government's credibility, recruitment targets were not being met; clearly something had to be done. To solve these issues the Home Office introduced, in 1951, the Industrial Civil Defence Service (ICDS). The ICDS was to run parallel to the Civil Defence Corps and contained a similar framework comprising all the relevant sections except Welfare. Any company with over 200 employees was encouraged to set up their own ICDS section, run by the company's management. Whilst the title contained the word 'industrial', giving the impression that it was aimed at heavy industry and manufacturing, it also covered offices and even department stores, as well as aircraft factories, transport divisions and the utilities.

> *It is hoped that personnel engaged in the transport undertaking will take full advantage of the training facilities available in order that they may be equipped to play their part in maintaining the services which are so vital to the life of this nation.*

British Transport, Civil Defence Training Booklet (September 1951).

By 1961 the Industrial Civil Defence Service had 4,000 units across the country, effectively covering some areas for twenty-four hours a day seven days a week. The benefits to industry were obvious, whilst the defence of the nation was suggested as reason enough, the opportunity to have a substantial number of employees trained in first aid and fire fighting did not go unnoticed. Even after the abolition of the Civil Defence Corps the training was still seen as beneficial and continues to have a positive effect on working life today; companies still train employees in emergency situations as part of Health & Safety requirements, yet another Cold War legacy.

Atomic Operations

Prior to the advent of the H-bomb, rescue operations worked on the point attack principle, expecting devastation and residual radiation around ground zero, with the possibility of rescuing casualties from within 800m of the centre. Beyond that damage was expected to be severe for another 800m, but only 2 per cent deaths and 10 per cent injuries were expected from moderately protected families. An airburst similar to that at Nagasaki was used to produce the rescue framework. After a point attack a three-tier rescue attempt would be launched. The first 'echelon' involving local forces stationed within the target area would be expected to administer first aid, remove casualties from the immediate area and co-ordinate refugee movements. In the event of a heavy attack the second 'echelon' would be activated, these mobile units equipped with extra lifting gear and first aid equipment were designed to reinforce the rescue effort. The third 'echelon' comprised military units to be used if the emergency reached critical levels. In such an event they came under the general direction of the Civil Defence HQ but ultimately remained under military command.

'Millions Would Survive the H-bomb'

Recruitment was slow and causing concern by 1952. The object had been to create a force nucleus approximately one-third the size of expected wartime requirements, and in the event of war, be able to build up strength using those already recruited as training staff. One reason suggested for the lack of volunteers (only 44 per cent of the target in 1952) was the reluctance of the population to consider more civil defence after the long war period. A measure of the problems faced within some organisations can be gauged from recruitment posters for the National Hospital Service Reserve. Nursing, the traditional preserve of the female members of the population, specifically targeted men offering 'good pay, good prospects, full training with pay, good conditions' and most interestingly deferred 'call up'. National Service had never been popular and by the early 1950s it would appear that the possibility of missing this was considered incentive enough for some to join the CDC. Unfortunately no figures are yet available for how successful this was. It was also proposed that the CDC be promoted as a 'permanent fourth arm of defence' and have its status elevated accordingly. By late 1953 the CDC received another blow when the USSR demonstrated its thermonuclear capability; many now started to question the validity of trying to instil a Blitz mentality against a weapon of such destructive power. Even so the enrolment figures for the CDC and allied services topped the half million mark over the period 1953–54.

Protection

The early 1950s saw an explosion of protected sites being built across the country including Anti-aircraft Operation Rooms, War Rooms, and the 'R' series bunkers for the east coast Rotor sites. Civil Defence (CD) was no different and a small number of specialist structures were built near possible targets, but the majority of controls comprised refurbished wartime structures and cellars. Guidelines were laid down by Home Office CD circular 3/52 suggesting a tie between population and the number of controls and sub-controls needed.

- Up to 100,000
    One Control Centre Headquarters
- Over 100,000
    One Control Centre HQ + One Sub-Control
- 250,000 to 300,000
    One Control Centre HQ + Two Sub-Controls
- Over 400,000
    One Control Centre HQ + One Sub-Control per 100,000

A few purpose-built sites were constructed, such as at Bassett Green Road, Southampton and Gravesend, Kent, but in the main Civil Defence Control was directed from the new War Rooms (described in the next chapter) wherever possible. In areas where this was not possible existing controls, often in the basements of old houses in outlying areas, were used. Sub-Control sites were again a mixture of new and old. In Bristol a network of four Sub-Controls surrounded the city, all co-ordinated from the Civil Defence Control underneath the Council House in the centre of the city. Belfast saw the construction of six purpose-built structures between 1954–56 all reporting to the Mount Eden Park War Room. Cardiff followed suit in 1956, but a number of older structures were also reused. Large urban areas, on the advice of the Home Office, retained and reactivated parts of the old Air Raid Precautions (ARP) infrastructure now used as sector Warden posts.

H-bomb Changes

In 1955 a new command structure was devised to counter the enormous destructive capability of the H-bomb threat. The original sections remained, although at a reduced capacity, and more emphasis was placed on mobile columns. This essentially military division was intended to fight its way back into the devastated area, although how effective this would have been in the face of a 10-megaton explosion has to be questioned. The columns included the Auxiliary Fire Service and appliances from the National Fire Service as well as a bewildering array of communications, rescue and welfare vehicles. Some estimates put this at over 500 items of transportation in any one column.

The H-bomb Sections

The rescue attempt would be co-ordinated from the HQ using both mobile and fixed controls and signals officers. These staff oversaw the repair and maintenance of the network including line laying, in areas where the predominantly overhead telephone wires had been damaged, and the utilisation of despatch riders. This was complemented by scientific and reconnaissance officers who would survey the level of radiation within the emergency area, using radiac equipment, and determine the safe time for rescue crews to spend in the devastated area. The lynchpin of the whole operation was the Warden, who assessed the amount of damage within his area and directed the ambulance and rescue crews 'on the ground'. The Warden was also the link between the CDC and civilian population and was expected to organise 'domestic self-help' parties from the survivors.

Rescue teams carrying personal equipment including a saw, wrecking bar, lashings, wire cutters and first-aid kit, would be the first on the scene. They could be backed up with heavier rescue gear brought forward from the countryside assembly points, including cranes and bulldozers. Purpose-built vehicles also formed part of the mobile column; known as the Column Rescue Vehicle (CRV) they carried enough equipment to cover all rescue situations. Crewed by eight men, Leader, Deputy Leader, Driver/Storekeeper and five Rescue staff, they carried everything from wheelbarrows to oxy-acetylene cutting equipment. The rescue crew would be expected to deal

Column Rescue Vehicle. By the mid-1950s the rescue sections within the CDC were well equipped. Whether they would have been effective after a nuclear strike was, thankfully, never discovered.

with all situations from light surface casualties through to debris clearance and some unpleasantness could be expected:

Carefully strip the site of debris until all bodies or parts of bodies are accounted for.

Light Rescue, Civil Defence Handbook No. 5, (1957).

Ambulance and First Aid Sections would be built up using existing county ambulance services complemented by vehicles supplied by the Home Office. First-aid crews were to render the casualties safe to move, place them on stretchers and organise their movement to designated ambulance loading points. From here they would be taken to the Forward Medical Aid Unit (FMAU) where the casualties would be categorised. The staff at a FMAU would ideally comprise four doctors, four trained nurses and thirty-six nursing auxiliaries, complemented by administrative staff. This was primarily to act as a buffer for the hospitals that would, by this time, be at breaking point. And as the number of survivors built up the Welfare Section would swing into action.

Of all the sections in the Civil Defence Corps Welfare was probably the most optimistic. Whilst other areas of CD readily acknowledged the post-nuclear strike problems, welfare appears to have languished in its apparent success throughout the Second World War. As late as 1952 the concepts were much the same as they had been a decade earlier, and the prospects of a long, drawn-out war were still considered most likely. It appears that evacuation was to be the main task of this section and most training issues centred around this. Welfare sections would be responsible for the organisation of reception and billeting along with care for the homeless, either migrant or from bombed-out areas and emergency feeding. Of special consideration was the plight of children and expectant mothers; pages of contemporary training manuals were given over to this. On considering what to do with evacuated groups of children, out of school hours, came the following advice:

> *Members of the Welfare Section working as billeting officers may also be ready to organise country walks and picnics as a way not only of relieving householders but of getting to know the children better.*

Welfare Section, 'Manual of Basic Training', Vol. 1, (1952).

The homeless would also put a considerable strain on the army of trained housewives and WRVS members, once war did break out. The following excerpt demonstrates that the concept of nuclear warfare was still far from the minds of the CDC Welfare Section.

> *At first some may be dazed, exhausted and inert; others excited, noisy or tearful. Many will want a kindly listener to their particular bomb story and most people will recover fairly quickly if their immediate needs are met and they feel reassured. Some, however, may continue to be dispirited and others respond to the sense of being in a group and appreciate community singing and so forth.*

Welfare Section, 'Manual of Basic Training', Vol. 1, (1952).

The H-Bomb changed most CDC tactics, but the Welfare Section continued to view the full destructive force of such weapons with a Blitz mentality, probably best summed up in the following extract from a recruitment leaflet of 1959.

> *The welfare section would help with evacuation, and after an H-Bomb attack would have the job of taking care of the very large numbers of people made homeless. These people would be dazed and bewildered; they would want food and water and clothing; shelter and news of their families; they would have to be kept warm, kept healthy, kept going – until they could look after themselves again.*

'The H-Bomb: What about the millions of survivors?' (1959).

That same year the Government accepted that nuclear war would probably be an unmanageable event and the mobile column system was mothballed, leaving a very denuded framework to soldier on through the 1960s.

The Fire Service

The fire service, both Local Authority run and the Auxiliary Fire Service, would be one of the most important aspects of Civil Defence, post-nuclear attack. The effects of the heat pulse from a detonation causes what are known as 'primary' fires and if these are left unchecked 'secondary' fires would quickly engulf large urban and industrial areas. All members of the Industrial Civil Defence Service and Civil Defence Corps received elementary fire training, including the use of the well-proven stirrup pump, but the scale of devastation needed a greatly increased pumping capacity, probably beyond the capability of the Local Authority Brigades. This led to the reformation of the Auxiliary Fire Service.

The origins of the Auxiliary Fire Service (AFS) can be traced back beyond the outbreak of the Second World War; at the time it provided a backup service to the local authority fire brigades, much the same as its Cold War successor. By 1941 all fire-related services were amalgamated into the National Fire Service which continued until 1948 when responsibility reverted back to the Local Authorities. Less than six months later the Civil Defence Act (1948) called for the provision of a fire fighting service autonomous from the Local Authority brigades and by November 1949 the AFS had been reformed. The AFS had been very effective throughout the Second World War, especially within the urban districts, but now it faced new challenges on a massive scale. Initially the AFS was equipped with war surplus pumps and appliances, but this was in no way effective enough to deal with the mass fires expected in modern warfare. This led to the design of one of the most enduring symbols of the Cold War, the Green Goddess.

Green Goddess

In 1952 a prototype self-propelled pump was designed on a Bedford seven-ton 4x2 SHZ chassis; tests proved it was capable of negotiating a 45-degree incline and could reach 50mph on the road. A modified version, the RLHZ self-propelled pump 8.4 ton, went into production in 1953. Bedford produced the chassis on their standard army lorry framework with a Bedford six-cylinder, 110hp petrol engine, whilst bodywork

The Green Goddess. It was painted green to identify Auxiliary Fire Service appliances from their local authority counterparts. Over 5,100 were built.

was produced by a number of firms around the United Kingdom including the well-established coach builder Plaxton, based at Scarborough.

The main equipment was a fixed pump, Sigmund FN4 single stage, feeding four hoses at 100 psi giving a volume of 900 gallons per minute. This was complemented by a portable pump, in case the way to the incident was blocked to the vehicle. A 35ft extendable ladder was carried externally and later additions included a foam-laying capacity for possible chemical hazards, especially in industrial areas. Normally a crew of six, one officer and five fire fighters, operated the pump that was painted AFS dark green so as to identify it from the Local Authority red appliance; the Green Goddess was born.

The Green Goddess was not the only equipment in the Auxiliary Fire Service's arsenal. For fire fighting after a major nuclear attack to be effective it had to be autonomous. A Mobile Control Unit, again on a Bedford chassis, co-ordinated the efforts of the fire fighters deployed out in the field. A mobile kitchen, pipe carriers, motorcycles, wireless cars, Commer Q4 water tankers, telephone cable layers, field telephone unit and, later, foam tenders were also deployed, basically a complete fire station set up in the field. A total of 5,150 Green Goddess appliances were built between 1953 and 1956. When, in 1968, it was decided to stand down the Civil Defence Corps, including the AFS, some of the equipment was retained, stored at Home Office Depots such as Bruntingthorp and Steventon in Oxon under the control of the Office of the Deputy Prime Minister.

A typical Buffer Depot store. This example is situated at the Home Office site at Steventon, south of Oxford. Equipment sheds were positioned around the country, containing temporary shelters, first-aid stations and rescue gear.

Romney Huts, Steventon. This site housed the Central Region Green Goddess fleet until the mid-1990s. A total of ninety-one vehicle huts are on this site.

Deployment

The Home Office considered the Local Authority Fire Services (LAFS) enhanced by AFS appliances would probably be enough, albeit in a reduced capacity, to meet the demands of a conventional war. However, nuclear attack would require a completely different stance. Most LAFS were stationed well within urban areas which, if targeted, would make the possibility of fire fighting and rescue impossible. Plans were laid in the 1950s for a Mobile Fire Column (MFC) to counter the threat of urban losses. During the build-up to conflict the majority of LAFS appliances would be removed to a safe area designated by the Home Office or Local Authority along with the equipment released from Home Office stores around the country. Once an attack had passed and the local radiological conditions allowed the MFC, ideally comprising around 150 vehicles, would advance into the devastated areas in an attempt to suppress mass fires.

The Green Goddess is probably one of the most familiar pieces of Cold War equipment, seeing service in the major fire strikes of 1977 and 2002. Nearly 900 appliances remain from the original AFS stock and continue to be ready if needed. Concerns about the level of cover the fifty-year-old Green Goddess can give are often raised, but it has to be remembered that it is a mobile pump and not a fully equipped rescue vehicle. A contract with TNT Express (UK) Ltd to store and maintain the emergency fire service stockpile for a period of five years commenced on 1 July 1991. The Home Office had an option to extend the period of the contract to a maximum of ten years and it is already beyond that date. That said, the Government announced in 1998 that it has no plans to replace the Green Goddess so this Cold War icon is likely to continue for some years to come.

Civil Defence in the '60s

A Problem Decade

Throughout the 1960s the Cold War started to heat up, and in 1962 the world had moved to the edge of the nuclear abyss. When Khrushchev offered his support for the left-wing Cuban government headed by Fidel Castro, he had also had one eye on being able to threaten Washington from the Caribbean. By 1962 the Americans had set up a naval blockade and were threatening an invasion of the island. As tensions grew between the two superpowers Britain put the Royal Observer Corps on alert and dispersed nuclear weapons out to the 'V' bomber fleet. As the situation grew steadily worse, many in the Western World considered war inevitable; thankfully agreement was reached and direct conflict was avoided. Cuba introduced a new Cold War phrase into Western vocabulary – the 'Hot Line'; if nothing else the crisis had demonstrated a lack of communication between Moscow and Washington, now there was a direct link. This decade also saw the 'nuclear club' expand with both the Chinese and French testing atomic devices, and the decision by France to withdraw from NATO. 'Flexible response' became the new NATO strategy that if viewed objectively meant that communism would be contained by any means possible, be that economic or militaristic. Further afield Washington was involved in an increasingly costly struggle against communist expansion in Vietnam, whilst Moscow took decisive steps to quell the wave of popular dissent in Czechoslovakia. Then in 1967 the Arab–Israeli Six-

The Oxford City and County Control was built in 1962, only to be abandoned in 1968 when the CDC was stood down. This bunker is now the site of a commercial broadcasting station.

Day War erupted forcing both superpowers to once again raise alert states. Protests against war abroad and nuclear weapons began to gather speed throughout the 1960s, effecting policy, especially in Britain. Increasingly world events had had little scope for British involvement; at a time when Moscow and Washington were increasingly fighting the Cold War by proxy British policy had been one of reductionism. Military bases in Malta, Cyprus, Guyana, Aden, Singapore, Persian Gulf and Malaysia were all reduced or closed. The Wilson Government also announced in 1968 that Britain, with the exception of Hong Kong, would only maintain military bases in Europe and the Mediterranean from 1971.

The policy of reductionism also had a detrimental effect on Civil Defence and the other voluntary services including the axing of 686 monitoring posts run by the Royal Observer Corps. Increasingly, Whitehall moved away from the 'community effort', proposing that the survival of the Government 'machine' was inextricably linked with the survival of the nation, and throughout the 1960s it embarked on a number of bunker-building programmes. The credibility of the Civil Defence Corps was damaged and membership slowly dwindled from there on in. The situation wasn't helped by constant discussions in Government over the cost of supporting an increasingly ineffective organisation; furthermore, the public were not convinced of the wisdom of evacuation. Millions of people would ideally have to be moved to reception areas and supposed safety. As Britain was such a small landmass any concerted use of the H-bomb would mean nowhere would be safe from the effects of fallout. Also, pressure groups such as CND and 'Spies for Peace' ensured that Government plans for self-preservation were kept firmly in public view. Apathy grew and by 1967 less than half the CDC members were still in uniform. Whitehall saw its opportunity, cutting the CDC would save between £14 and £20 million in the first two years, and in April 1968 the Corps was disbanded. One training college, Easingwold, limped on critically under-funded, but the public would now have to look after themselves.

A Decade of Détente

The concept of civil defence now slowly melted away as sites were demolished or turned over to other uses, usually storage, the communications systems decayed and most of the Auxiliary Fire Service equipment was sold off. Internationally the scene was changing too, after almost two years of negotiation the Strategic Arms Limitation Talks (SALT) reached agreement and was signed in 1972. President Nixon and General Secretary Brezhnev agreed to reduce anti-ballistic missile systems, bombers and stockpiles of IRBMs; it looked like the journey down the long road to nuclear-free peace had started. The fact that all the equipment removed from service on both sides was mostly obsolete and due for the scrap heap didn't really matter at the time. The British Deterrent was also upgraded as the first of the Polaris submarines came on line in the early 1970s. So the official standpoint by 1975 was one of a more peaceful world and a stronger Britain, no real need for civil defence. The reality could not have been more different.

Home Defence policy received a review in 1971 creating the Emergency Services Division, ominously under the direct control of the police, whilst aspects of civil protection became the domain of the local authority. Meanwhile Central Government concentrated on building a network of Sub and Regional Headquarters primarily concerned with the preservation of some sort of structure after an attack. The local authority took responsibility for burying the dead, mass feeding centres (although they had no control over food stocks), road clearance and transport access, public advice, and dealing with refugees. The Home Office now had little involvement in civil protection other than to issue Emergency Planning Circulars covering Government advice. One message above all else now underpinned what was left of civil protection – 'stay at home'. Clearly in times of a national emergency a population staying put had far more benefits than one on the move. Government advice now changed to suit this new doctrine, the best-known being 'Protect and Survive', first published in 1976 (discussed later).

By this time, internationally, things were taking a turn for the worse. 1976 saw Jimmy Carter voted into the Whitehouse with a personal agenda to improve human rights in Eastern Europe. But Carter went further, establishing full diplomatic relations with China, a process started by Richard Nixon; Brezhnev was not pleased. Throughout the 1970s the United States Air Force had been upgrading its fleet in the United Kingdom, primarily as part of the 'Flexible Response' doctrine, and this now reached full operational status. The Americans now had F-111 bombers, Phantom interceptors and A-10 ground attack aircraft complementing their already comprehensive air armada in Europe. By 1979 these were housed in Hardened Aircraft Shelters (HAS) as part of the NATO-financed improvements, but it was the stationing of Russian SS-20 missiles in Europe that started the destabilisation of détente. Even against this backdrop both sides managed to reach a workable agreement on arms reductions signing the SALT II document in June 1979, but unfortunately the treaty was not ratified by either side as superpower relationships took a further nosedive. To counter the SS-20 threat NATO decided in early December 1979 to station Pershing II and Ground Launched Cruise Missiles in Europe; it looked like a new arms build-up was on the horizon. Then as the year drew to a close the USSR invaded Afghanistan, on 29 December, in an attempt to prop up the Soviet-installed government. During this turbulent year two new leaders now came into the fold, both of whom would have a major impact on the last decade of the Cold War – Margaret Thatcher and Ronald Reagan.

Reconstruction and Revision

The new Conservative Government, lead by Margaret Thatcher, came to office in May 1979 during a period of intense international stress. Soon after, the new Home Secretary, William Whitelaw, announced that a review of all home defence procedures was to take place, and by August 1980 the review was published and spending on home defence now increased from £13 to £45 million, taking effect from 1983–84. This had not been the only study in progress; James Cotterill had been investigating, since 1977, the Government's public shelter policies. This concluded in 1980, estimating that to provide shelters of adequate strength and durability would cost the country around £70 billion, far outside the national purse. The idea of evacuation was also revisited during this period, but evacuation to where? The civilian population would have to stay at home for Armageddon. Steps were taken to increase the efficiency of some aspects, the Green Goddess pumps received an overhaul, readiness was to be trimmed from four weeks to one and large grants were made available for local councils to employ designated Emergency Planning Officers. Unfortunately, rebuilding the Civil Defence Corps was not financially viable, especially since the country was still suffering the effects of a decade of economic mismanagement. Local authorities would continue as the civil 'protector' whilst the Government decided on a public information campaign.

Civil Defence – Why We Need It

A process designed to stimulate public thinking now got under way, and naturally it had its opponents. The first-term Conservative Government received severe criticism for considering Civil Protection part of Britain's deterrent; this was unfortunate as the idea had first been tabled back in the 1950s with the Civil Defence Corps. But the bottom line was that no real preparations had been made for over a decade and the Government realised that once the Ground Launched Cruise Missiles were stationed at Molesworth and Greenham Common the Island would become a prime first-strike target. A two-tiered campaign was formulated, one aimed at justifying the British deterrent, the other suggesting the old civil defence concept was waiting in the wings but the public would have a certain amount of responsibility for themselves. The problem was, a far better informed public wanted neither, and to make matters worse some local authorities started to take a defiant line, declaring themselves 'nuclear free zones'. The Home Office set out its stall in November 1981 with the publication of *Civil Defence – Why we need it*. Covering a number of points it attempted to match the disarmament lobby with a civil defence posture, citing:

> *Even the strongest supporter of unilateral disarmament can consistently give equal support to civil defence, since its purpose and effects are essentially humane.*

'Civil Defence – Why we need it' (1981).

One popular misconception was that the Government would bolt for cover at the first sign of war and be protected against all effects for weeks on end. The Home Office made attempts to quell the suggestion:

> *Most senior ministers, government officials, and service chiefs would have to remain at their desks if war threatened, and they would have to take their chance like anybody else if the UK were attacked, but there are plans for government to be delegated to civil defence regions. Some ministers would, with small staffs, occupy emergency headquarters to be ready to carry on basic government after an attack. These war headquarters, although reinforced, are certainly not invulnerable. Most civil defence operations in a war emergency would be directed by local officials, working in the basements of town halls and similar premises.*

'Civil Defence – Why we need it' (1981).

In reality major problems were emerging. Many local authorities were less than enthusiastic at becoming the civil defence front line. However, financial grants from Central Government were available to help shoulder the burden and to cover the post of emergency planning officer, something previously done by the town clerk in many areas.

The Deterrent

In June 1980 Whitehall announced its intention to replace Polaris/Chevaline with the Trident system, inciting a new round of opposition from Members of Parliament, CND and other public bodies, clearly some form of justification was needed. A number of government departments set about producing literature intended to convince a sceptical Britain that an independent deterrent was needed, with limited success. The Ministry of Defence (MOD) had a straightforward message:

> *Either side of the Urals – It's still target Europe.*

'A Nuclear Free Europe: Why it wouldn't work' (1981).

The MOD argued that the world would be far from a safe place if Europe became 'nuclear free'. First the range of the Soviet SS-20s meant that any proposed withdrawals would be pointless. If NATO removed its weapons they would have to be taken to America, whilst the USSR could still strike from behind the Ural Mountains outside Europe. And if NATO dismantled the deterrent then Europe would become weaker and more vulnerable, as had happened in the run up to the Second World War. Balanced reductions on both sides were the only answer.

The Arms Control and Disarmament Research Unit (ACDRU), part of the Foreign and Commonwealth Office, took a less dramatic tone, setting out eighteen points supporting the use of nuclear weapons in arms controls. However, it still issued the same message:

> *Any one-sided reduction by the West would weaken its ability to deter aggression – and therefore make war more likely, rather than less. You can't opt out of a fight with a bully by shutting your eyes and hoping he will go away. Nor would Britain be safer without nuclear weapons: and our key role within the Alliance would still make us a certain target in any war.*

'The Balanced View: Nuclear Weapons and Arms Control' (1981).

As expected, CND, and others, had a field day.

Final Plans

During the mid-1980s Civil Defence planning saw its final Cold War reorganisation. The Government recognised that the extensive skill base that had been developed over the previous decade could be utilised for emergencies other than those caused by an aggressor country. In line with this realisation the Civil Protection in Peacetime

EITHER SIDE OF THE URALS – IT'S STILL TARGET EUROPE

ESTIMATED RANGE (about 3,000 miles) of Soviet SS-20 nuclear missiles if based behind the Urals.

Government justification, 1981. (© Crown Copyright)

Act was passed in 1986. The act enabled local authorities to use civil defence resources in connection with events other than war; Civil Defence had effectively ceased to be a stand-alone framework. Any use of equipment could now be used outside the original 1948 Civil Defence Act, clearly a cost-cutting exercise, but Central Government would underwrite any resources used.

The possibility of an attack coming 'out of the blue' was considered to be almost non-existent. Any aggression would surely come after a period of international tension, allowing a civil defence posture to be prepared well in advance. However, the 1986 act still required the whole framework to be up and running within one week, whilst the more important aspects such as medical and food would have a forty-eight-hour readiness.

Government Functions

As tensions grew towards an armed conflict it was seen that the role of Central Government would become increasingly difficult to perform. Lines of communication could be compromised and in the event of a conventional exchange be quite easily disrupted. With this backdrop civil protection would be devolved to Regional Emergency Committees (REC) dispersed to eleven regions around the United Kingdom. But the REC would have no powers until a situation warranted it; Central Government would still run the country.

Regional Emergency Committees

The Regional Emergency Committees comprised, on activation, representatives from police, military, utilities, communications and local government, all under the chairmanship of a Department of the Environment (DOE) or Department of Transport (DOT) representative. The beauty of the RECs was that they could be activated to meet the needs of a singular event, co-ordinating all emergency services whilst Central Government monitored the situation, having only a financial input. In times of war the RECs would answer to a Minister or Ministers who would act as Commissioner for that regional area. Following an attack the Commissioner would be given full authority to govern in place of Central Government.

As the Berlin Wall was dismantled and many East European Countries removed their Communist governments, the threat of attack dramatically reduced. Equipment housed at buffer depots was disposed of during the early 1990s, as were many of the by now ancient vehicles; but some were retained. The Home Office still maintain a fleet of Green Goddess pumps, some of which saw action in Operation Fresco in 2002 covering the fire service dispute. But more importantly some of the lessons learnt throughout the years of the Cold War have helped form the new defence line against terrorist attacks, especially those involving strikes against highly populated areas with chemical weapons, such as the Underground. Only time will tell if these measures are, indeed, effective.

eleven

Bunker

One structure above all others typifies the nation's view of the Cold War: the so-called 'nuclear bunker'. This much-maligned generic term is often used to portray a Government 'bolt hole' where hand-picked officials, both Royalty and Ministers, would hide whilst the rest of the population was exposed to the full force of nuclear war. However, bunkers are neither simple holes in the ground, nor are they easy to track down and interpret. Over the period of the Cold War structures built for one purpose or organisation were modified or taken over by another, also Government policy drove many changes in protected-site usage, further adding to the often confused network of regional, sub-regional and local controls. This chapter is intended to demonstrate the variety of structures that fall into this category.

War Rooms

By 1951 plans had been drawn up for structures that were intended to protect the 'machinery of Government' in the event of nuclear attack. It was clear that London would be a prime target, just as it had been in the Second World War. Accordingly protected structures were built in each of the twelve Home Defence Regions. These large areas of the United Kingdom originated from the Second World War, where Britain was segregated into a number of specific regions, each with a Regional Commissioner and supporting staff. If Central Government was incapacitated or the Island had been invaded, the Commissioner would have assumed control of his area, governing until such time as unified control was reinstated. By 1956 the last site, Shirley in Birmingham, had been constructed, but the days of the War Rooms were already numbered.

Each War Room cost around £100,000 and most were constructed on existing Government sites. The structures were intended to give a protection factor (PF) of at least 400, provided by a concrete outer shell 1.5m thick. Internally the majority of the walls were also reinforced concrete adding to the PF within the central map room whilst supporting the often 2m + thick roof. Built as an annex to the main

structure was a plant room that housed a diesel generator with standby batteries and air filtration equipment supplied by intakes on the roof. Interestingly the concept of fallout was secondary to the fears of a gas attack when the War Rooms were being built, but luckily the filters could cope with both. The structures were intended to gather information from the devastated area using police, military and civil defence sources, then co-ordinate rescue and welfare attempts. Around fifty staff were in place to assist the Commissioner in the immediate post-attack period, including members from the fire, police and health services, scientific advisors, and military staff along with Civil Defence Corps officials. Ominously, at Bristol, the cemetery superintendent was also provided with an office. If Central Government was lost then the Regional Commissioner would also become responsible for all aspects of life within his home defence area including food, law and order, and working parties. Those staff already in the War Room would support this regional government, had the need arisen.

War Rooms were broadly similar in layout. Single and double-storey structures were built, and the double-storey structures were either semi-sunken or above ground. The layout of a typical two-storey War Room comprised a central map room overlooked by control cabins, then around that was a series of offices and communications rooms. Water was stored in a tank room on the lower floor, although at Reading (Region No. 6) a large tank is situated above both stairwells giving additional supply. The London regional War Rooms had no real facilities for long stays and comprised four single-storey above-ground structures; clearly by 1952/3 the capital was considered a prime target, and regional government was thus well provided for. However, by the mid-1950s the War Rooms were considered too restrictive for 'long haul' situations, one that had become a reality since the detonation of the first Soviet H-bomb. Government, if it were

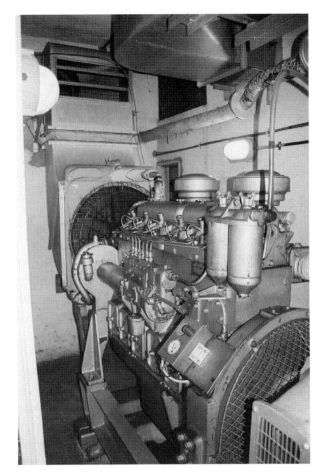

Opposite: Reading War Room.
A double-storey semi-sunken
protected site, completed in 1953.
(Courtesy University of Reading)

Right: The diesel engine used to
run the standby generators at the
1950s War Room at Reading.
(Courtesy University of Reading)

Below: Reading War Room.

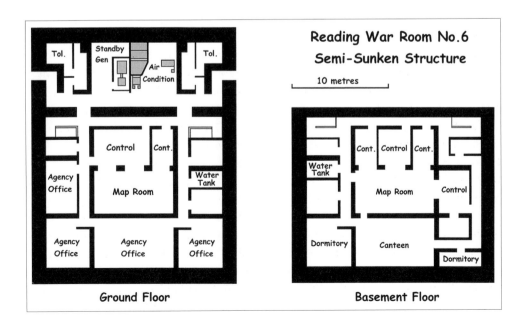

Reading War Room No.6
Semi-Sunken Structure

10 metres

Ground Floor

Basement Floor

to continue, would need added protection, and planning for a new series of bunkers was initiated by the late 1950s. As with so many structures built for the Cold War the role of the War Rooms changed, but until very recently all survived virtually intact.

Regional Seats of Government

By 1956 a reshuffle of responsibilities occurred reinforcing the Regional Commissioners' role. This involved the creation of a series of Regional Seats of Government (RSG); the possibility of autonomous area rule after a nuclear attack was now expected. The Regional Commissioner would now be given total responsibility for his designated area, and to assist this yet another series of protected structures was proposed. The network of War Rooms was largely abandoned; only those at Nottingham, Cambridge and Kirknewton were retained, although these were heavily modified and extended. By the early 1960s thirteen RSG existed, including the three mentioned above. Now a series of other structures and locations were used. Catterick, York, Brecon, Armagh, Dover Castle and Preston were all situated on army barracks sites. Warren Row and Drakelow were the sites of former underground aircraft factories whilst Edinburgh and Bolt Head had both originated as semi-sunken Rotor bunkers. The newly organised RSG were still placed within the existing Home Defence framework, but Region 5 sites for London were downgraded to Civil Defence Controls, the capital would now be run from outside. Work on the protected structures for the RSG was, in the most part, complete by 1963.

The Regional Commissioner was now supported by a staff of up to 400, covering every aspect of government including armed services, police, public health, food, fire, fuel and communications, including those representing the BBC who maintained and operated a small studio capable of live and pre-recorded transmissions. One interesting factor was the reduced thickness of the protected sites; they still provided a PF of over 250, but there was now no ability to withstand a close or direct strike from a nuclear weapon, only the radiation.

Sub-Regional Headquarters

The problem with redefining the Regional Seats of Government network was that it effectively removed the Regional Commissioner from direct contact with the Local Authority and thus Civil Defence. The old War Room network had primarily been concerned with the rescue effort in devastated areas, but with new responsibilities now vested in the Commissioner this had been severely reduced, and was further hampered with the repositioning of many protected sites. In response to this the Home Office proposed a further twenty-five Sub-Regional Headquarters, housing around 200 staff each. Building commenced around 1964, although some sites such as Kelvedon Hatch, previously an R4 Sector Operations Centre in the Rotor system, were converted a few years earlier. Other redundant sites were also pressed back into service, such as the Anti-aircraft Operations Room at Ullenwood in Gloucestershire and the Bristol War Room at Flowers Hill. Both these protected structures came under the control of the Regional Seat of Government (Region 7–West) protected at Bolt Head utilising another Rotor structure, this time an R6 semi-sunken operations room. New protected sites were also planned to coincide with the building of government office blocks. However, one of the only structures from this is situated at Hertford, as the plan was again re-evaluated in 1966, primarily due to the reduction of civil defence commitments.

Sub-Regional Controls

A new Home Office directive now proposed a flexible plan for the survival of Government, which became known as the Sub-Regional Control (S-RC) network. Now each Home Defence region was to contain at least two S-RCs, giving much more flexibility to the scheme. The principle was simple, all S-RCs would operate simultaneously in times of tension, each headed by a junior minister; if a control was incapacitated or destroyed the other would continue to run. The majority of the existing protected sites were again used, undergoing refurbishment on a fairly *ad hoc* basis, although some unusual structures were now included. the Second World War food cold stores were utilised at Loughborough and Hexham, whilst underground storage areas originally used for explosives were modified at Swynnerton and Bridgend.

Bridgend 8.2

During the Second World War Bridgend, South Wales, was chosen as a satellite site for the Royal Ordnance Factory at Woolwich, subsequently designated ROF 53. The factory was split into two sites, either side of Brackla Hill. Waterton on the east side machined the various shells and casings, whilst the Brackla site, on the west side, manufactured and loaded the shells. At its height over 40,000 people were employed at the factory. On the Brackla site seven magazines were built into the hillside using a mixture of cut and shut, and boring techniques. These were used to store filled shells and high explosives prior to delivery, each one serviced by a rail link. The loading platform for each pair of tunnels was also covered by a bomb-proof roof and it was possible to close a shutter door across the entrance. At the end of the war the factory closed, but the tunnels remained.

In 1961 the Home Office acquired two of the shell storage magazines and converted them into a Sub-Regional Control (S-RC). The reuse of earlier structures in this way was nothing new, and Swynnerton had also seen the conversion of two magazines for the earlier SRHQ network; but the architecture of the Brackla site is unique, owing mainly to the type of buildings used. The original magazine design was quite restrictive in terms of modification, leading to only the cavernous railway loading bays being utilised. This still allowed for a two-storey unit over 80m long to be built inside the original structure, with an additional 10m extension being built on the front of the platform, housing entrances, generating equipment and filtration systems. The two magazines were broadly similar in refurbishment, containing the same filtration, generation and communications systems. The two sites were then linked by a concrete tunnel running from the back corner of the northern protected site to the front corner of the southern one. Replication in both units allowed for each to operate independently of the other if the walkway was breached. This was not the case at Swynnerton.

 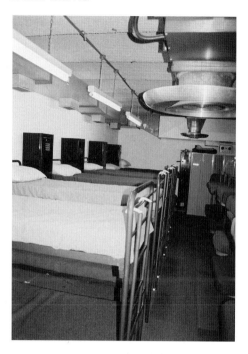

Above left: One part of the Sub-Regional, and later Regional Government Headquarters 8.2 at Brackla, Bridgend. From this site the whole of Wales would be controlled after a nuclear attack.

Above right: Kelvedon Hatch RGHQ 4.2 dormitories; staff ran a 'hot-bed' system as there was nowhere near enough sleeping space for 600 staff. (Courtesy J.A. Parrish & Sons)

Kelvedon Hatch RGHQ 4.2. Communications and visual display unit room, part of the post-rotor refurbishment. (Courtesy J.A. Parrish & Sons)

Bridgend 8.2 replaced the earlier Regional Seat of Government, originally sited at the Brecon Barracks, and was to have been one of a pair in line with the S-RC system of dual running. However, the closest Wales got to this was a hardened basement under the University of Bangor. A large number of redundant Rotor structures were also refurbished during the reorganisation, including Kelvedon Hatch, which now became S-RC 4.2.

Kelvedon Hatch 4.2

Kelvedon Hatch started life as an R4 Sector Operations Control as part of the 1950s Rotor system, the construction and location of which was to prove ideal in later years. The structure was recessed into the side of a small hill and constructed over a 7m raft of gravel, acting as both soak-away and shock absorber against any ground bursts. Above this a three-storey structure over 3m thick and strengthened by tungsten rods was constructed using reinforced concrete. Around this a brick skin was built, which in turn was covered with wire meshing covered in pitch. The pitch helped seal the bunker from water penetration and it was hoped the mesh would protect against electromagnetic pulse (EMP). Finally the whole structure was re-covered giving further protection and restoring the hillside. Access to the bunker was, in line with other Rotor sites, via a bungalow guardhouse and then down a 110m tunnel that entered, in this case, the bunker at the lowest level.

In the early 1960s Kelvedon Hatch underwent a major refurbishment to bring it in line with Home Office requirements, now being designated S-RC 5.5. Structurally the layout of the bunker saw considerable change. The three-storey operations well was covered over at each level giving nearly a third more floor space. Most of the original Rotor period plant was retained, but the two generators, originally housed in a separate structure nearly a kilometre away, were brought to the bunker site. These two Rolls-Royce 125 kVA units were repositioned at the entrance of the original access tunnel from the guardhouse, necessitating an alternative entrance being knocked through the back of the guardroom. The bottom level now accommodated the uniformed services, who would liase with Government officials, and a suite of communications systems. This included a BBC studio, which by the 1980s could broadcast television as well as radio, a GPO (later BT) exchange, and both the military and Home Office also ran separate radio rooms.

The second floor housed the Government Department, including an office for the Regional Commissioner, and later the Prime Minister had a designated room on the same floor. Representatives of many of the major departments were also represented including MAFF, housing, police, energy, health and transport, all with a view to maintaining the machinery of Government within the Metropolitan area (London). The top floor was given over to dormitories, a small medical room (originally the emergency battery room), canteen kitchens and a common room, all required to cater for up to 600 staff for over four weeks. Kelvedon Hatch went on to become Regional Government Headquarters 5.1 in the 1980s and was finally disposed of in 1994. It now houses an excellent museum dedicated to the Cold War.

The Labour Government finally disbanded the Civil Defence Corp in 1968, ultimately leading to a reduction in the number of S-RCs required. Some slight alterations were made to the Home Defence areas towards the end of the decade to counter the CDC loss, including the reorganisation of London that became, once again, Region 5. Kelvedon Hatch was redesignated 5.1, now having overall control of the Capital in an emergency situation. Below Kelvedon Hatch were five groups dividing up the city, four reused the original 1950s War Rooms whilst at Southhall a redundant the Second World War Civil Defence site was reused. From the mid- 1970s the Sub-Regional Control system suffered, as did most of the country, from poor politics and discontent, but a dramatic change was on the horizon and in 1979 a new view on Government protection and civil defence was voted into office – the Conservatives.

Regional Government Headquarters

By 1980 a review of Home Defence had started the biggest and final change to the network of protected sites, currently running under the S-RC system. Now the concept of devolved Government shifted back to the single site per Home Defence Area, similar to the Regional Seats of Government seen in the early 1960s. This lead or Regional Government Headquarters (RGHQ) would be in total control, although a standby protected site was maintained in case the HQ was destroyed or incapacitated.

Hack Green 10.2

One of the major capital works of the early 1980s was the conversion of the former R6 semi-sunken structure at Hack Green, becoming RGHQ 10.2, covering Greater Manchester, Merseyside and Cheshire. The origins of the site, like so many other protected structures, can be found in the Rotor programme from the early 1950s, being a Ground Control Intercept station. From there it had become part of the United Kingdom Air Traffic System but was abandoned by the mid-1960s. By the mid-1970s it had been identified as a possible S-RC by the Home Office. English Heritage surveyed this site in 1998 and demonstrated that plans for conversion were in an advanced stage by 1976, but work did not start until 1980. The project was radical, the entire structure was gutted, including the removal of floors, partitioning walls and the roof. Along with this was the addition of a new plant room, built on the side of the bunker and the reorganisation of the entrances.

New flooring allowed for a third level in the structure and the internal layout now mirrored the requirements of the Home Office RGHQ. This included more emphasis on the ability to survive gas and fallout conditions, ensuring the HQ could still function in the 'locked down' condition. Upwards of 200 staff were needed when the bunker was fully operational and dormitories were provided for both males and females along with a common room and large canteen area. As with most HQs, space was at a premium, and the staff were organised into three shifts, allowing for hot-bed conditions in the cramped environment. If the RGHQ was to function correctly it needed a vast array of communications systems and the lower floor of the site was redesigned to provide this. Provision was made for radio, both civil and military, telecom landline and microwave systems, fitted with surge suppressors in case of EMP, along with a BBC studio for live

Above: Hack Green RGHQ 10.2.
The former Rotor R6 semi-sunken
structure was converted in the
early 1980s to become a Regional
Government Headquarters. (Courtesy
Hack Green Secret Nuclear Bunker)

Right: Hack Green RGHQ 10.2.
Personnel decontamination station;
here staff could shower and change
before entering the bunker, reducing
the risk of fallout contamination.
(Courtesy Hack Green Secret Nuclear
Bunker)

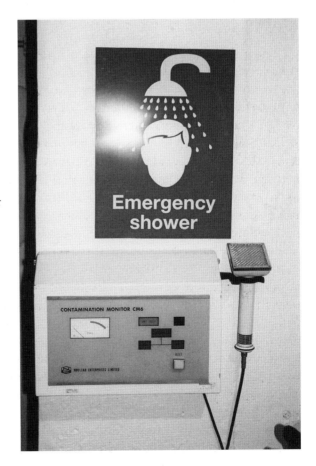

Hack Green RGHQ 10.2. This small BBC studio could broadcast pre-recorded messages and in the
months after a nuclear attack would be the Commissioner's only link with the majority of survivors.
(Courtesy Hack Green Secret Nuclear Bunker)

and pre-recorded broadcasts. From the lower level the Regional Commissioner would
co-ordinate the restructuring of his designated Home Defence Area, working with the
surviving local government-protected sites (discussed later) and other RGHQs in an
attempt to bring some level of order to the civilian population.

Final Plans

In the mid-1980s the Government embarked on the final round of bunker building,
driven in part by the arrival of the Ground Launched Cruise Missiles at Greenham
Common. Now a series of Regional Emergency Committees would oversee Britain's
transition to a war footing, dealing with aspects of civil protection and essential service
preparations, these would then report to the RGHQ site within its designated area.

In the mid-1980s three final new bunkers were built at Chilmark in Wiltshire,
Crowborough in Sussex and Cultybraggan on an army site near Sterling. These were
the last purpose-built structures to be built for Government protection before the end
of the Cold War. But the concept of protection did not disappear with the dissolution
of the USSR in December 1991, and some sites limped on for a further year. In 1992
thirteen RGHQs, including the newly commissioned and highly expensive site at
Chilmark, were sold off, but Crowborough was retained, going on to form part of a
police training centre.

Central Government also made plans for its own survival; one of the most famous
has to be the underground tunnels at Corsham in Wiltshire. The site, formally a stone

Chilmark RGHQ. This protected site was the final statement of Government 'self-preservation'. The structures visible are ventilation stacks for the air conditioning and generators. The complex was completed in 1988 and disposed of just four years later.

The Central Government war headquarters, constructed in the Corsham Quarries complex. This is just one of five lift and escalator entrances to the protected site.

quarry and then an aircraft factory, was earmarked in the early 1950s as a seat of Central Government. By 1957 plans had been drawn up for a 7,000-strong staffed centre covering in excess of a million square feet of usable space. Passenger and goods lifts were built, as were new ventilation systems, and rather bizarrely a bar was installed. The site received, in line with other sites, a major refurbishment in the early 1980s, including a downsize in the number of staff needed to run it. By 1992 the site was effectively placed into care and maintenance.

County and Local Authority Sites

If the changes in regional government are confusing, especially when considering the reuse of so many protected sites, the role of local government is even more complex. Throughout the period of the Civil Defence Corps the Home Office funded, on a very loose basis, the construction of protected controls in areas considered vulnerable to attack. Once the CDC had been disbanded many protected sites were placed into 'care and maintenance', however this, for most, was to be short lived as changes to Home Office policy prompted the reuse of many from the early 1970s.

Running parallel with the CDC sites, certainly from the time of the S-RC reorganisation, was the government's requirement for local authorities to define their responsibilities. This included providing an emergency centre for each county, known as the county main. By the 1980s there were nearly fifty such sites. Whilst most were laid out in a similar pattern, often a central operations room surrounded by offices, communications rooms and dormitories, where they were situated varied enormously. The conversion of town hall basements made up the majority of the sites, as for Buckinghamshire at Aylesbury, Kent at Maidstone, and the county halls at Northallerton for North Yorkshire and Trowbridge for Wiltshire. However, other sites were reused, such as the Anti-aircraft Operations Rooms in Cheshire, the East Riding of Yorkshire, and West Glamorgan. The War Room at Flowers Hill in Bristol was also pressed into use, as was the now redundant CDC control in Gwynedd. Some unusual sites were chosen, including beneath fire stations at Mold in Clwyd and Framwellgate in Durham. The basements of County Courts were also utilised at Caernarfon in Gwynedd and in Hereford. The Oxfordshire Emergency Control was constructed in the grounds of a school at Woodeaton 7km outside the city, whilst at Winchester a purpose-built protected site was built in the centre of the city underneath the castle.

Each county council was also obliged to maintain a standby protected site in case the main was destroyed or incapacitated for long periods. Again these structures were at a mixture of locations and often contained within a variety of buildings. These included town hall basements like Scarborough, civic centres such as Dartford, redundant Civil Defence controls like that at Christchurch and, for a time, the surface blockhouse on Woodstock Road in Oxford. District councils also provided an array of protected sites, again some using old Civil Defence controls, such as at Salisbury in South Wiltshire, whilst others were purpose built, such as the West Oxfordshire site at Whitney. The Wiltshire county standby is located under the library in the market town of Devizes on Sheep Street. This structure is worthy of description, if only to demonstrate some of the thinking that went into their design.

Above: Woodeaton, Oxford Emergency Control. Built in the 1960s this site is still used as an emergency planning cell by the county council. (Courtesy Oxford City Council)

Right: West Oxfordshire Control. Situated at the council offices in Whitney. The cover has beneath it the escape exit whilst the stack behind draws in air for the filtration system. (Courtesy West Oxfordshire District Council)

Wiltshire County Standby. Situated underneath Devizes Library, the above ground structure is designed not to crush the bunker below if it collapsed. (Courtesy Wiltshire County Council)

Wiltshire County Standby

The Wiltshire County Standby comprised a central control room with offices and domestic accommodation arranged on three sides, situated in the basement of Devizes Library. The original structure dates from the late 1960s–early 1970s, but appears to have been upgraded in the mid-1980s. Above ground the structure is two storeys high. The major part of the layout comprises external walls only, the rest being left open. This has advantages in that if the building collapsed the weight of the debris would pose little threat to the bunker below. The standby was accessed through an internal door just inside the building and then down a flight of stairs. An emergency exit, via a set of ladders, allowed the occupants to leave if the main entrance was blocked.

Ventilation was provided by four Microflow air-supply units, produced by MDH of Andover, Hampshire. The company still provides specialist Nuclear, Biological and Chemical (NBC) filtration systems for both the MOD and civil sector. Each of the four units had a separate supply from outside, containing an inline filter as it entered the building. Air could be pumped using a 12-volt DC electric motor fitted centrally to the unit or, in the case of power failure, be hand cranked. Only one outflow existed to expel foul air, which, incidentally, is the only external sign of the bunker below.

Water was stored in seven 1,000-gallon tanks, five in series in a specific room with a hand pump, while two others stood in the control room and were used to top up the main tanks. In peacetime and during any build up to war water came from the library mains circuit piped from above. If the mains supply to the building was lost,

Above left: Wiltshire County Standby. Ventilation was provided by Microflow air supply units that were capable of filtering fallout and, to a certain degree, chemical agents. (Courtesy Wiltshire County Council)

Above right: Wiltshire County Standby. The small kitchen would cater for up to fifty people in an emergency. (Courtesy Wiltshire County Council)

water could be hand pumped to a small header tank in the kitchen. The kitchen area comprised a small room with a Belling oven and wall-mounted water heater, sink and some storage units. The kitchen had two doorways, one leading from the corridor, the other leading into a separate room, which had yet another door leading back into the corridor. This served as the canteen and rest room, two doors being fitted so that staff did not have to go back through the kitchen after eating.

A small unisex toilet facility contained three units, flushed by a hand pump, separated by hardboard partitions. A hand-wash unit was operated by a push button on the wall. Next to the toilet unit was a large storage room which, in times of emergency, would have been converted into sleeping quarters, with bunks and, presumably, a 'hot bed' arrangement.

Communications were handled in two separate rooms, a radio room covering incoming messages from emergency services and radio hams (Raynet), and a telephone block, where eight operators used landline connections. Operators in this area had direct connection with other county centres including the Regional Government Headquarters (RGHQ) at Chilmark. Landline connections were vital. To ensure they were not damaged during a nuclear detonation they had a lightening suppresser fitted, which, it was hoped, would dampen the effects of the Electromagnetic Pulse (EMP).

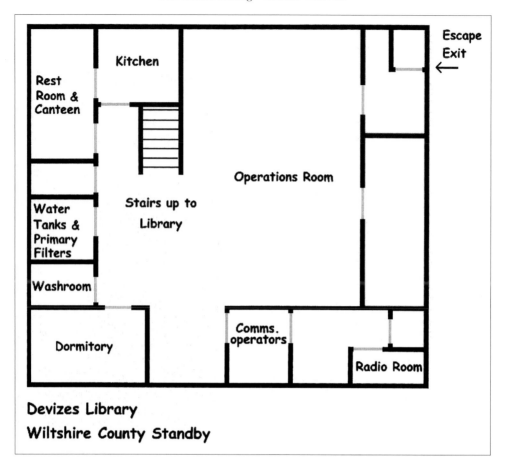

Devizes Library
Wiltshire County Standby

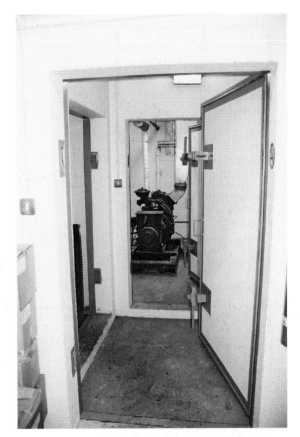

Opposite above: Wiltshire county standby.

Opposite below: Thornbury. The Offices of South Gloucestershire District Council. At the rear of the building is a small control bunker financed during the final stages of the Cold War. (Courtesy South Gloucestershire District Council)

Right: Thornbury. View from the main protected site through the blast doors to the emergency generator. (Courtesy South Gloucestershire District Council)

Below: SX2000. The SX2000 was introduced into many bunkers during the early 1980s.

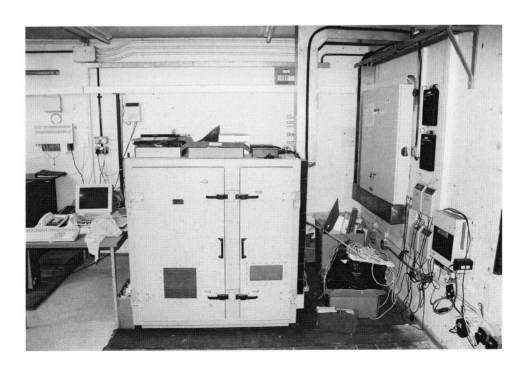

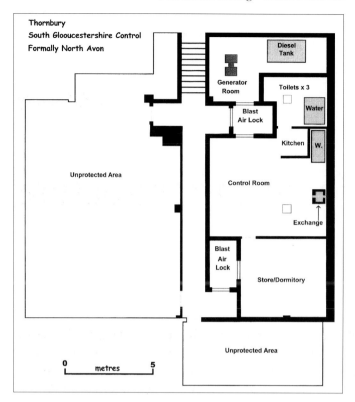

Thornbury
South Glooucestershire Control
Formally North Avon

Diesel Tank

Generator Room

Toilets x 3

Water

Blast Air Lock

Kitchen

W.

Unprotected Area

Control Room

Exchange

Blast Air Lock

Store/Dormitory

Unprotected Area

0   metres   5

South Gloucestershire control.

A large office was also provided, presumably for senior staff members. This had two hatched windows, one on either side, which connected through to smaller office rooms. As information came in it would be passed through to this room. The office opened on to the central control room where all the rescue operations, food distribution, public order, fallout and all other aspects of civil dependency were co-ordinated.

The Home Defence review of 1980 spawned yet another round of protected sites, which by the mid-1980s attracted 100 per cent Central Government funding. New structures, often including above-ground offices appeared at a number of locations, including Shire Hall at Reading and County Hall at Truro. The offices of the South Gloucestershire District Council were also a direct result of this initiative. A small bunker was constructed in 1986 when the new office complex was built. The site is a substantially smaller construction than the majority of older sites and on activation would have protected up to fifteen officials. Other sites received major refurbishments in accommodation, filtration and communications, including the introduction of SX2000 units, whilst lower order equipment was installed in the county standbys and district centres. By 1992, like their larger RGHQ components, they were decommissioned, but some sites still function as emergency planning centres, such as at Scarborough, where part of the original control is maintained whilst the rest is used to store planning documents. The majority of county, district and local bunkers survive to this day, primarily because of their locations under town halls or other civic buildings.

twelve

The National Infrastructure

The role of the utilities after any nuclear attack is difficult to ascertain; clearly massive disruption would be caused to all we take for granted. Water supplies would be cut off and gas and electricity supplies would be disrupted far beyond any target, due to the effects of Electromagnetic Pulse (EMP). Some areas of the transport system could well be out of action permanently; rail and roads might survive in outlying areas but the air and sea ports, with their obvious military applications, would probably be beyond repair. So was there any point in protecting any of the main assets such as reservoirs, railway stations and electricity supplies? This section will investigate some of the problems facing anyone maintaining the National Infrastructure after a major nuclear exchange.

Water

Clean, safe water is a necessity for life and any disruption or contamination of the supply would have serious health implications. To this end a number of precautionary measures were taken in an attempt to continue some level of supply following an attack. The Government required regional water boards to maintain and finance the upkeep of Home Defence emergency water supply equipment. This included pumping equipment to lift water from wells, streams and rivers, purification and treatment equipment and the means to deliver it through standpipes and water bowsers. The bowsers originated from a number of sources including Auxiliary Fire Service (AFS) tankers. When the AFS was disbanded in 1968 a number were retained for this purpose. Senior officers from water authorities were posted to Regional Government Headquarters (RGHQ) to co-ordinate the overall re-supply attempt, appointed by the then Department of the Environment, whilst the water boards would appoint liaison staff to work in the Local Authority Emergency Centres (LAEC). Each water authority was encouraged to survey old and disused sources to establish whether they could be utilised in a national emergency, making the plans available to the county Emergency Planning Officer. It was also considered that areas of the country where water was gravity fed would be of major significance, post-attack. Interestingly the majority of protected control rooms appear to be close to such reservoirs, suggesting that the north and west of the country may well have been called upon to supply other areas of Britain.

Protected Sites

Initially the re-supply of water was a fairly *ad hoc* affair with the onus being placed on the individual, supported where possible by the Welfare Section of the Civil Defence Corps (CDC). Water companies held emergency equipment, as did the CDC, but the infrastructure of supply still considered point target attacks by fusion weapons the most likely threat. After the Civil Defence network was stood down in 1968 the situation steadily deteriorated, although some plans were made for the distribution of water. Throughout the 1970s the concept of Home Defence began to build with a series of Government circulars explaining new policy guidelines. This took its final form in the 1980s with renewed Government interest in the protection of the water supply, following the Conservative bunker-building programme in other areas. Accordingly, to encourage water companies to construct protected centres a 100 per cent grant from the Home Office was made available. Not all companies took this offer up, although those that did built some very large structures, often gaining new office accommodation in the process. Other control centres were placed out at reservoir sites, such as those by Thames Water at Blunsdon and Donnington, near Stow-on-the-Wold.

Thames Water Control. The control bunker at Donnington, near Stow-on-the-Wold, forms part of a group of eight around the Thames Water area. (Courtesy Colin Stares)

Blunsdon Emergency Control Centre

The policy of locating control bunkers at sites of major strategic importance is graphically demonstrated at the Thames Water site at Blunsdon reservoir, a few miles north of Swindon. Two large covered reservoirs stand 40m above the average height in the town, delivering via gravity rather than pump. The site clearly had significance in the Civil Protection planning of the 1980s as the reservoirs have a large protected control bunker situated between them. Filtered breathers fitted to the tops of both reservoirs are presumably to keep out contaminants. The bunker was constructed in 1987 as part of the Government upgrade of control of emergency water supplies. The building is a standard design intended to give thirty days protection for twelve staff with or without power or water supply.

The Emergency Control Centre is a semi-sunken, 15 sq. m structure, standing just over 1.5m above ground, covered by 10cm of topsoil. Effectively it is a concrete box with 300mm thick walls capable of withstanding a blast over a pressure of $52kN/m^2$ entered via a pair of steel doors at ground level in the north-west corner; the doors are wide enough to allow large equipment into the bunker. Behind this a flight of concrete steps descend 2m down to a 200mm thick concrete blast door. All entrances and contaminated areas are separated from the occupied areas by further 200mm blast doors manufactured by Johnson Marine and Military Doors Ltd, Driffield. Behind the first blast door is an airlock and off from this are two further concrete doors, one to the decontamination room, the other to the generator room. The decontamination

Thames Water Control. The site at Blunsdon is identical to that at Donnington. Built in the 1980s it has a protection factor of 100 and is designed to accommodate twelve staff for two weeks. (Courtesy Colin Stares)

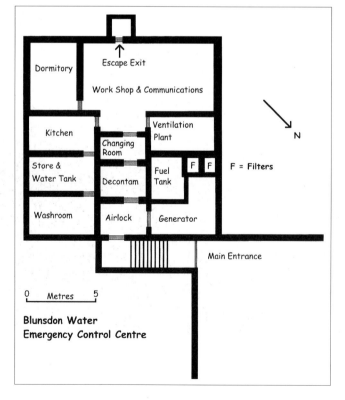

Escape Exit

Dormitory

Work Shop & Communications

Ventilation
Plant

Kitchen

Changing
Room

N

Store &
Water Tank

Decontam

Fuel
Tank

F F   F = Filters

Washroom

Airlock

Generator

Main Entrance

0   Metres   5

**Blunsdon Water
Emergency Control Centre**

Above: Thames Water Control.
Internal view of the site at
Blunsdon, near Swindon.
(Courtesy Colin Stares)

Left: Blunsdon emergency
water control.

Thames Water Control. The ventilation of the Blunsdon bunker was via two filtration units drawing air in from a large concrete stack outside. (Courtesy Colin Stares)

room contains a shower to be used before proceeding into the changing room, where uncontaminated clothing would be stored.

Entry to the living and working areas is via a 100mm steel pressure door. The work area is a large single room measuring 5m by 8.5m designed for up to twelve people to repair equipment and use communications systems. Domestic arrangements include a dormitory, capable of accommodating four triple bunks and a few lockers. A washroom accessed from the work area comprises a hand-basin, urinal, chemical toilet and waste-water tank that could be emptied outside via a hand pump. A rudimentary kitchen comprises a sink, worktop and shelving; no cooking facility is apparent but such may have been fitted during transition to war. A large humidifier, situated above the sink demonstrates the problems many protected sites had with moisture. Two taps run into the sink, one connected to the mains supply and the other to a 4,032-litre standby tank in an adjacent room.

Access to the ventilation room is through a connecting door in the work area. Here, two fans, which can be electrically or manually operated, draw air in through a bank of filters and then into the air conditioning piping that runs around the building. The most visible part of the structure is the external intake for the air-conditioning system that stands 3m high and is 1m square. The centre works on the positive pressure principle, keeping the internal pressure above that outside. This principle, via an outflow valve in the wall of the changing room, keeps contamination outside the work and domestic sections of the centre.

The plant room contains a diesel generator that draws air through a louvered intake next to the entrance and exhausts through a vertical pipe visible on top of the bunker mound. A further pipe near the exhaust is a breather for the fuel tank, which was replenished next to the entrance. The tank provided enough fuel for the generator to run for thirty days. As the air intake for the plant room is external it was treated as a contaminated room accessed via an airlock, necessitating full decontamination procedures before re-entering the bunker. A square escape hatch is externally visible at the southern extremity of the bunker, accessed internally by a steel ladder off the work area. The site can be clearly seen from the A419 Swindon to Cirencester road.

If an attack did occur disruption to the water and sewage system would have been inevitable. A ground burst thermonuclear device would render most of a major city's pipework unrepairable, and if this was not bad enough other problems would also manifest themselves. Fuel and electricity for pumps and treatment plants would inevitably be in short supply or non-existent. Demand on the surviving infrastructure would increase as stockpiles were created or fire fighting escalated. Maintenance staff would find it difficult to travel due to blocked roads, poor communications and the constant threat of fallout, if staff actually stayed at work at all. The constant demand on overstretched equipment would mean a steadily dwindling capability to pump water as spare parts for maintenance ran out. And water, especially that in open reservoirs, could be easily contaminated by fallout debris. It is worth pointing out that the particulates suspended in the water would be the problem in this situation, not the fluid itself.

Help Yourself

The majority of public information was concerned with individuals stocking up water to cover a prolonged period. Directions in the mid-1950s note that whatever you kept water in it must be covered and went on to say that a domestic water softener would remove some harmful chemicals such as strontium and barium. By the early 1980s more specific guidelines were set down. It was considered that each shelter occupant should have enough water for fourteen days at a rate of 1 litre per day, and this was just for drinking. It was further recommended that a further fourteen days' supply would be needed for cooking and washing. There are lots of storage opportunities in the average household and so long as it is not demolished during the attack, it would be possible to store up to 700 litres in various places. These could include the sinks, bath and toilet cistern. 'Protect and Survive' also recommends covering these with polythene and wooden planks to cut down on fallout contaminating the supply. Not forgetting to tie up the toilet handle so it could not be flushed is also mentioned. Contemporary public information films invested a lot of time demonstrating how to use water over and over again before discarding it. For example, water used to wash your face with could then be put in a pan to steam the contents of a tin, when that was finished you could wash the utensils in the boiling water, effectively using the same resource three times.

Sand Filters

The principle of the sand filter was sound enough but just how effective it would be at an Emergency Feeding Centre is quite another matter. The type of filter adopted by the Government came from a civil defence idea dating back to the early 1960s which could remove contaminants and clear cloudy water. To remove radioactive material a 25-litre can had 5cm of washed gravel covered by course linen placed in the bottom, this was covered by 25cm of washed sand and clay of equal proportions, with another layer of course linen covering that. The rest of the can was filled with the contaminated water and allowed to filter, passing out through holes in the bottom of the can. This process would produce around 5 litres an hour and every 75 litres the filter material, by now fairly radioactive had to be changed. The local government officials would clearly have had major problems supplying safe water at the proposed 1,000 meal kitchens, never mind to the population at large.

Sewage

As with water supplies a nuclear strike would cause havoc to the sewage system, much of which dated from the Victorian era and was already at breaking point in some areas. As treatment plants ground to a halt due to lack of power, and pipes started to back up, the danger to public health would greatly increase. A number of ways were suggested to combat this biological problem; first and foremost any water not known to be treated had to be boiled, failing that sterilisation tablets could be used or in the case of neither being available the sand filter could be used.

A variety of methods were suggested to dispose of sewage, all dependent on the situation you found yourself in. At the RGHQ Kelvedon Hatch the sewage was blown out of the bunker, under pressure, onto neighbouring fields, whilst at the Wiltshire county standby in Devizes the waste was hand pumped out into a nearby sewer from either the three toilets or water interceptor. However, the advice to the public was somewhat basic. 'Protect and Survive' suggested a chair with the seat removed with a bucket, preferably lined with a bag, situated below. Once full the bag was to be placed in a designated dustbin in a room next to the shelter. It would be at this point that most people realised just how much they relied on the Water Board.

Sanitation for the Masses

By the 1980s a number of sanitation methods had been devised for areas where large numbers of people had gathered, loosely based on Army and World Health Organisation guidelines. Latrines and urinals would be placed downwind of the main site and away from any potential water sources. Some basic screening should be provided for privacy, paper must be supplied, as should soapy water for hand washing. And as a basic requirement one latrine should be provided for every ten people. Clearly toilet facilities on the outskirts of major towns and cities would be a major undertaking. It was also proposed that someone was detailed to wash down the seats once a day, to cut down on infection, as if the horror of nuclear war wasn't bad enough.

Normal Service Will Be Resumed?

The water authorities' target was to provide 5 litres per person per day as soon as possible after an attack, but this would not start immediately as it would be assumed that the majority of the population would have their fourteen-day supply to hand. In this time the RGHQ representatives would liase with the LAEC staff, communications willing, to build up a picture of usable water sources and distribution points. Unfortunately by this point water, like food, would have become a rapidly dwindling commodity and areas with high mortality rates, primarily through radiation, would be unlikely to see water deliveries for a very long time indeed.

Electricity

Electricity has become, over the last hundred years, as important as food or water; our society depends on it for practically everything and, since the mid-1980s, the rise of the computer has increased this dependency ten fold. The National Grid is a complex network stretching the length and breadth of Britain, moving power generated in one part of the country to areas of peak demand, almost instantaneously. However, the system is fragile, as was graphically demonstrated in London in 2003 when power failures left people wandering the streets, normality tends to cease the moment the lights go out. So how would the country cope immediately after a major nuclear attack and what consideration was given to restoring a rudimentary supply afterwards?

Emergency National Grid Control Centre. This large structure at the back of Becca Hall on the outskirts of Leeds would have been responsible for re-routing power and setting up a rudimentary grid after a nuclear strike. (Courtesy Country & Metropolitan)

Standby National Grid Control Centre. If the main control centre at Becca Hall was knocked out then staff would relocate to this small bunker at Rothwell to the south of Leeds.

Between 1950–56 a series of emergency control centres was constructed, to serve as regional operations buildings. These performed both peace and wartime functions and worked in conjunction with the Emergency National Grid Control Centre based at Becca Hall on the eastern outskirts of Leeds. From here the attempt to direct power to those areas most needing it would be co-ordinated. Becca Hall, like most main bunkers, had a standby in case the primary site was damaged or destroyed. Strangely the standby control was located at Rothwell Haigh on the edge of Leeds, a lot closer to a potential target than the main site. The Rothwell bunker was located next to a GPO protected repeater station suggesting the decision to build there was financially driven rather than tactical.

Regional emergency controls were also constructed throughout the late 1950s and early '60s on the outskirts of Manchester, Birmingham, Bristol and London; representatives of the generating boards would also be located at the county 'mains'. The majority of these structures take on the appearance of a normal office block. As with the water centres, the attraction of a new office building at little or no cost to the company probably swayed the generating boards' decision to build. Some other structures were planned, such as protected standby switching centres, but few were built before the end of the Cold War. But from the early 1960s equipment had been stockpiled around the country at National Grid Strategic Reserve Depots (NGSRD), with at least one in every Civil Defence region.

One of the biggest threats to electrical supplies would be the effect of Electromagnetic Pulse (EMP) (discussed later). The immense power surge would quickly overload power cables and at the very least trip out large parts of the grid. Also a high percentage of the grid, especially in rural areas, is carried around the

Regional National Grid Control Centre. The site at Keynsham, east of Bristol, was responsible for the control of electrical supplies to the south-west during a national emergency.

National Grid Strategic Reserve Depot. This large building, to the north of Cirencester, was built in the 1960s. Equipment and spares were stored here and would be used to repair local services – if possible.

country by overhead cables, and large sections of these would be damaged by any attack. Power stations would not fare much better as they would be likely targets, especially in the run up to a nuclear confrontation. The disruption would have been so great and over such a wide area that the likelihood was the National Grid would collapse and take many years to repair, even if it could be repaired at all.

Most protected sites had their own means of providing power. Bunkers such as the RGHQs, ROC Group HQs, protected exchanges and county mains had their own generator plants to supply electrical power for lighting and ventilation. Hospitals, fire stations and water treatment plants also carried generators to cover power failures in peacetime as well as war. Civil defence equipment stockpiles contained generators which could be set up in priority areas, but none of these examples was linked to the grid, generating power for just the task in hand. The amount of equipment stored in the NGSRD would cover repairing short runs of cables but nothing like the amount needing attention after a national emergency. Some Government sites would, however, fare little better than the majority of the population. The Royal Observer Corps monitoring posts' power supply was taken from a rechargeable battery, not having generators. A programme of re-equipment announced in the late 1980s was intended to address this, but only a few posts received the equipment before the organisation was stood down in 1991.

Home Shelter Power

To this problem there was no real answer. The public were encouraged to take spare batteries for radios and torches, beyond that there was not much you could do. Even if the power cables and sub-stations were not damaged in your area it was highly likely that the power would be routed elsewhere leaving you in darkness. One helpful suggestion came in the 1980 publication *The Nuclear Survival Handbook*, a private publication by Barry Popkess. He suggests:

> Rechargeable batteries. Both nickel cadmium and wet batteries or accumulators are in this category. A peddle bicycle upon a stand, with a dynamo attached to the hub will produce the necessary current. Although it provides exercise in cramped conditions, those pedalling will require a higher caloried diet than would otherwise be the case in a shelter situation. They may also need more water than is available.

Clearly post-nuclear attack Britain would be a very dark place to live.

Communications

If war was to break out the country's ability to respond to aggression, co-ordinate civil defence and perform Government functions relied on the ability to communicate around the British Isles. Events during the Second World War had demonstrated that lines of communication could be severely disrupted by heavy bombing, especially since most were routed through towns and populated areas. Whilst this was considered to be a major potential problem in the Cold War it was compounded by a new menace, Electromagnetic Pulse (EMP).

EMP

When a nuclear device detonates a large electrical field is generated, much the same as in a flash of lightning. However, EMP is far more powerful and causes widespread damage to electrical circuitry and power lines. The existence of the phenomenon was noted during the development and testing of weapons in the 1940s, and through the 1950s it became apparent that EMP posed a major problem. A series of high-altitude detonations code named Operation Fishbowl, carried out by the Americans in the Pacific in 1962, graphically illustrated EMP's destructive capability. One test, 'Starfish Prime', caused widespread disruption of communication and electrical systems in the region, especially Hawaii. The information from these tests allowed scientists to build up an accurate picture of the effects of the phenomenon. Optimum EMP was achieved by air burst at an altitude of 30,000m. Obviously this had a tactical application; unfortunately it is also indiscriminate, all sides were at risk from the effects. Defence scientists at Aldermaston calculated that an air burst of around 1 megaton over the North Sea would effectively disrupt most of Northern Europe, rendering communication between military, government and rescue organisations nigh on impossible in the short term.

The British Government must have been aware of the problem in the 1950s as Rotor Sector Operational Centres, such as Kelvedon Hatch, have a wire mesh cage built around them, which acts like a Faraday cage. Later essential equipment was constructed with suppressors, filters and cages to try to counter the effects. At Devizes, the standby county main's landline connections were routed through a lightning suppresser that, it was hoped, would dampen the effects. On larger sites such as the by now refurbished Kelvedon Hatch (now designated RGHQ 5.1) Rainford protection systems were fitted to the communications links, stopping any surges entering the large communications network.

'Protect and Survive', published in the early 1980s, makes a guarded reference to EMP effects, but it was not well explained, stating only to 'Keep any aerial pushed in'. This simple advice would have given some protection, unless, of course, the radio was switched on at the time of detonation, and then that would have been the end of that! The Army went a little further in 'Nuclear Survival in the UK – Aide Memoire', published in 1980, suggesting 'Switch off radio and disconnect antenna and battery. Disconnect landline from telephone.' The Army were given this advice in information covering two sides of A4, 'Protect and Survive' covered sixteen pages, mostly containing illustrations, and clearly had the space for a line or two. Whether it was intended to inform the public on EMP is hard to substantiate. However, once large parts of Britain had been reduced to smouldering ruins one gets the feeling that the population at large would really not have mattered.

Telecommunications

Protection of communications from EMP, conventional bombing and sabotage came in many forms. One physical way to protect landlines was to bury them as deep as possible; this had been on-going since 1925 especially as cities such as London were growing at an alarming rate. During the 1950s the General Post Office (GPO) embarked on a plan to protect main trunk routes through major cities, building three underground Telephone Trunk Exchanges at Birmingham, Manchester and London, the latter by the 1970s comprised over 22km of tunnels. These were supported by eight protected Carrier Repeater Stations placed around England. Along with these large civil engineering projects came the rerouting of many cable positions, taking them out of and around the most vulnerable targets and populated areas. The scheme was completed in 1958 and like so many other projects from the 1950s was obsolete almost as soon as it was finished.

Telephone Trunk Exchanges

The Telephone Trunk Exchange (TTE) network formed part of the post-war Government requirement to provide a secure, protected trunk cable network which linked major defence, industrial and administrative centres. Five major TTE structures were planned at Birmingham, Manchester, London, Glasgow and Bristol, but by 1950 the latter two sites were removed from the plan. Work started on the buildings in 1951 and the last site was up and running by late 1958, although it would have been earlier if the GPO had not been involved with the Rotor programme that absorbed most of the cable-laying capacity at the time. The sites were staffed continuously until the late 1970s as the exchanges increasingly performed normal telecommunications duties.

London (Kingsway)

The TTE site in London, code name Kingsway, was built within an existing structure, the deep-level shelter below Chancery Lane tube station. The site was acquired by the then GPO as part of the Emergency Powers Act in 1949 and just under two years later work started on converting the existing two tunnels into the exchange building. Four more tunnels to house the exchange equipment were excavated, along with four lifts allowing staff and equipment to enter the building from various sites on the surface. Entrances to the site included passenger lifts in Took's Court and High Holborn, whilst goods and equipment were moved via a lift in Furnival Street.

Accommodation was for 200 staff and supplies of fuel and food were provided for an estimated six-week stay. Water from an artesian well provided a clean supply for the occupants and was also used in the air-conditioning system to keep the temperature at a steady 59–62 degrees. The complex also contained a kitchen and dining room, welfare, sleeping quarters, sick bay and, most essential during any nuclear conflict, a fully stocked bar. The site was commissioned by October 1954. In the mid-1980s two sections of the by now downgraded exchange were refurbished to accommodate a Government bunker.

Manchester (Guardian)

The TTE site in Manchester, code name Guardian, was built to new specifications, including a 140m two-storey tunnel and another 600m of associated linked passageways, shafts and offices. The whole project cost an estimated £4 million and was commissioned in December 1958. The main entrance to the site is located at the Rutherford Exchange building via a lift. Two emergency exits via the cable tunnels were provided if the main entrance became blocked, which would be highly likely in an attack as this was situated inside the exchange. These were over a mile apart, located in Salford and Ardwick. A separate lift entrance provided access for goods and any heavy machinery that was required. As with Kingsway areas were given over to staff accommodation, including dormitories along with a canteen and rest room.

Birmingham (Anchor)

The third of the TTE sites, code name Anchor, was located underneath the exchange building on Colmore Row; this also contained the main access via a lift. The bunker was built to a similar specification to that seen at Manchester, as no previous structures were present. Construction started in 1953 and was completed four years later, officially opening on 9 November 1957. The cost of the original structure topped £4.5 million with at least half of that covering the equipment that needed to be installed. The site consisted of two large tunnels lined with reinforced concrete sections along with a number of smaller excavations to contain accommodation, offices, sleeping quarters, and a kitchen and restaurant. The equipment was air-cooled via a large ventilation plant that, in line with other sites, kept a positive pressure within the structure, keeping out contaminants. The site is now in an advanced state of decay due to a rise in the water table, primarily caused by the lack of industry now in the area.

Repeater Stations

Along with the three TTE sites, eight semi-sunken protected repeater stations were built at points around the main re-routed cable networks. When a telephone call is sent down a cable it needs to be amplified at regular intervals or it cannot be heard at the receiver point; these buildings performed this vital service. They had, however, a much greater amplification power than the normal civilian use stations. The project was managed by the GPO to Ministry of Works specifications, starting in 1952 and not completed until well into 1958. The structures were 67m long by 26m wide, but two, which handled traffic from Corsham and Shipton, were an extra 7m longer. The upper structure was constructed of reinforced concrete half a metre thick with a single-storey annex to house an office and rest room for staff; critically this was not blast proof.

Contained within the reinforced upper floor was the air-conditioning plant room that contained the fans, filters and extractor fans to keep the atmosphere inside constant. This would have less to do with staff survivability and more to do with making sure the equipment was in working order. A positive pressure could be maintained as the fans ran, ensuring dust and contaminants did not enter the structure. The lower floor contained a further plant room with two diesel-driven generators. Each fan performed separate tasks but were able to assume a lead role in an emergency. On the failure of the mains supply the generator responsible for ensuring the communications systems continued working would start up automatically. The diesel was supplied by two buried tanks containing 6,000 gallons of fuel, and if the

Protected Repeater Station. Eight such sites were built around Britain in the late 1950s, primarily to support Rotor programme traffic; however, they also handled other official loads. This site is at Rothwell.

generators failed a series of batteries could provide power for a few days. As the Repeater Stations performed the role of an ordinary exchange they were kept in working order up until the 1980s, by which time the new microwave and fibre-optic systems had made them obsolete.

Backbone

The vulnerability of sections of the trunk network, even with the building of the TTE and repeater stations, led to the development of a microwave transmission system that became known as 'Backbone'. The use and origin of this network has been the focus of much discussion and would appear to be an amalgamation of structures from the GPO, Home Office and other services rather than a specific purpose-built network. However, it is an intrinsic part of our Cold War legacy and no matter what the origin some sections are worthy of discussion here.

The concept of Backbone was first introduced in the 1955 Defence White Paper which proposed a chain of radio stations within a national framework, intended to continue running after the landline network had been damaged or destroyed by enemy action. This was expanded a year later by the Official Committee for Civil Defence who gave a number of reasons why a communications network was vital for the security of the nation. The Rotor GCI sites around the country needed to be in constant contact with the Sector Operations Centres; currently they were linked by landline, something that had taken the GPO nearly two years to complete. A secure network would also be needed to co-ordinate any retaliatory strike, naval action and

Above left: Post Office Radio Link. This site at Birdlip in Gloucestershire was designed to link military sites into the Backbone network, this one most probably carried GCHQ traffic.

Above right: Microwave Relay Station. Many masts such as this at Birdlip are still in use today. They are often very prominent due to microwave transmitters and receivers needing to be inter-visible.

direct any forces overseas. On the home front any rescue effort into major populated areas would need a reliable communications network, as would the administration of the country through the Regional Government Headquarters. A lot rested on any network surviving a national emergency; to ensure that it did, three distinct systems were proposed.

The Skeleton Network

The rerouting of main trunk cables was to be extended beyond that started in the early 1950s, including a main ring around London between 45 and 90km from the centre. In less vulnerable areas rooms were to be set aside below exchange buildings for operators in the event of an attack, much the same as had already been completed in many provincial towns.

Radio Links

The problem with moving even more cables was the GPO's already insurmountable commitments in other defence areas, coupled with telephones and television becoming increasingly popular with the public. To counter this it was proposed that a series of transmitters and relays could be used to supplement the system; it would use the up-and-coming microwave system making landlines over large distances virtually obsolete. The key invention for the microwave power generation was the cavity magnetron, developed by Randall and Boot at the University of Birmingham during the Second World War, primarily as a requirement of radar development. By the early 1950s the use of microwave in data transmission was in an advanced stage of development.

Each of the fourteen originally proposed radio stations were to be at least ten miles from any considered target. The site would have a single-storey protected structure, very similar to the above-ground section of the GPO repeater stations. In the event this did not happen; most sites received Ministry of Works timber buildings to house equipment or brick and breeze-block structures. Between the stations stood a number of relay masts that were able to receive and transmit information, often being unmanned.

Radio Standby-to-Line

A series of low capacity radio stations separate from the Backbone system was also devised, essentially to carry purely defensive traffic. The idea was to reduce the reliance on repeater stations, often situated on cable lines every three or four miles (these are the small brick structures often seen on the roadside leading into villages and towns). The radio links covered ground between a specific military site and the Backbone radio transmitter station.

Network Development

What makes the concept of Backbone so difficult to pin down is the fact that it contained so many different facets. It also involved, as did many projects through the 1950s and '60s, a number of major changes primarily due to technological advances. No original towers appear to survive, but the steel-stepped structures are still visible in some areas. One criterion for positioning was that each tower needed to be visible from the next and so they are often in extremely prominent positions. The familiar round receiver/transmitter arrays seen today superseded a horn-shaped structure of which some are still visible, the Birmingham Tower being one good example. Not all masts were built using angled sections, and from the 1960s a number of concrete towers appeared, often placed in areas of conservation sensitivity, and the public record is full of lengthy debates as to appearance and siting in such areas. Purdown on the outskirts of Bristol and Wotton-under-Edge were two such sites where these structures can still be viewed.

Interestingly, more towers were constructed in the 1960s in the centre of major populated areas, suggesting that a thermonuclear strike was accepted by this time as probably final. One such structure has taken on iconic status – The Post Office Tower – in the centre of London.

Post Office Tower

The Post Office Tower, later to become the BT Tower, was designed by Eric Bedford, Chief Architect at the Ministry of Works in the late 1950s. Construction started in June 1961 and the main structure was 'topped out' three years later on 15 July 1964.

Above left: Microwave Relay Station. The tower at Purdown in Bristol was built in 1970. It was approved by the Royal Fine Arts Commission for its design.

Above right: The 'Backbone' tower at Wotton-under-Edge. This massive concrete structure was designed to withstand a blast wave of up to 160km per hour.

The building cost around £9 million, is 175m high (188m including the top aerial) and weighs 13,000 tonnes. Specifications required the tower to be able to move less that 20cm in a 160km per hour wind and its primary purpose was to carry microwave aerials to transmit both speech and television media. The site became operational on 8 October 1965 and was listed a Grade II structure in 2003. Whilst the tower is clearly a civilian-built structure it still had some military and governmental applications; four floors were given over to equipment to power the transmission of data. Interestingly, the circular aspect of the tower offered low wind resistance, which could just as easily come from a nuclear blast as foul weather. This was a requirement of other similar towers at Purdown and Pye Green, Staffordshire. The towers' connection to the early days of microwave communication is demonstrated by the surviving horn aerials still visible within the later arrays.

Essential Service Routes

Roads

Since the end of the Second World War the rail network around Britain has been steadily reduced, most famously by the cuts proposed by Dr Beeching in March 1963, and so the reliance on the road network has increased. Clearly the road network is important in peacetime, but in the build-up to war, it would be seen as essential. Control of the road network would, along with food, be one of the first visible signs of the emergency to come, especially whilst the Government and military were dispersing to predisposed control centres and bases.

Control of main highways during transition to war and restrictions on travel remained similar to those that had been in place during the Second World War, especially throughout the period of the Civil Defence Corps. However, this changed dramatically after the Corps' demise in 1968. By the mid-1970s an advanced network of motorways had been constructed which had major advantages over the old 'A' road system; a high percentage bypassed major population areas and comprised, on most sections, six lanes. These wide expanses were less susceptible to damage than their single-track predecessors, whilst allowing more direct routes from one area of the country to another. Motorways were incorporated into the designated Essential Service Routes (ESR) which, developed over a twenty-year period, contained the routes identified by the Government as priority routes during the build-up to war.

If the movement of equipment and supplies was to be effective then the public would need to be kept off these designated routes, and emergency planning considered this. Home Office Defence Circular 4/71 explained they would be '…controlled by the police, possibly assisted by the armed services…'. It is likely that the ESRs would be closed very early on and be controlled by members of the Territorial Army with a small police presence to give local advice. Of course this would cause problems, as tension grew across Europe; large sections of the population, especially those in urban areas or close to industrial and military sites, would feel the urge to move to less vulnerable locations. Traffic chaos would be almost immediate, and inevitably the 'stay at home' policy became entrenched within Government and local planning. Advice encouraging the general population to stay put became one of the cornerstones of civil protection. 'Protect and Survive' advised:

> *Your own Local Authority will be best able to help you in war. If you move away –*
> *unless you have a place of your own to go to or intend to live with relatives – the authority in*
> *your new area will not help you with accommodation or food or other essentials. If you leave, your*
> *Local Authority may need to take your empty house for others to use. So stay at home.*

'Protect and Survive' (1976, reprinted 1980).

Obviously it was hoped that if the threat of starvation didn't deter the traveller, the invasion of his home by refugees probably would. What was clear was that roads not designated Essential Service Routes would quickly become impassable. Duncan Campbell in 'War Plan UK', quoting a Home Defence conference held in Cambridge in 1981, explained it would probably be best to '…allow escapees to seal off minor roads themselves through traffic jams, fuel shortages and breakdowns'. The transition to war would present some very difficult situations for the authorities. Of course some priorities were larger than others, none more so than the stretch of the M4 motorway between Reading and Swindon in the mid-1980s. Motorists travelling eastbound today pass two large signs proclaiming 'Works Depot' with red borders. Nothing would appear to be unusual with that, but these signs actually indicate the route to the large munitions store at RAF Welford, using a private spur off the motorway. Interestingly Welford received a major upgrade in the early 1980s along with RAF Greenham Common a few miles down the road; it remains to be seen what type of munitions were actually stored at Welford since it has far superior road access, especially for large multi-wheeled vehicles.

How the roads were used after a nuclear attack would depend heavily on the amount of destruction they suffered. Early civil defence literature notes the obstacles faced by the rescue services throughout devastated areas.

> *Movement of vehicular traffic would be seriously restricted or prevented over very wide areas, perhaps just at a time urgent rescue work would have to be done and fires would have to be put out. Blockage of roads by debris will vary with:*
>
> (a)   *distance from ground zero;*
> (b)   *width of street;*
> (c)   *the direction of the street in relation to ground zero, e.g. whether it is radial to ground zero or at right angles to the direction of the blast;*
> (d)   *height and nature of construction of buildings fronting the street.*

'Manual of Civil Defence', Vol. 1, (1956).

All these factors considered, considerable effort would be needed to ingress the inner areas of an affected town or city. British Transport Civil Defence (1951) suggested it 'may require mechanical equipment to clear a path for their heavy vehicles'. After the demise of the Civil Defence Corps in 1968 the concept of rescue was replaced by one of survival; roads that did not connect important assets (military sites, ports, depots etc.) would be left blocked for the foreseeable future. However, the issue of motorised transport would probably become academic as the last of the petrol and oil ran out.

Rail

Rail up until the mid-1960s had been the primary mode of transport, especially regarding goods and equipment, but through the 1970s and '80s the emphasis moved to road transport. The rail network, however, even in a reduced capacity, continued to feature in emergency planning and was considered a primary transport system during the build-up to a national emergency. Early plans relied on a network of hardened assets, primarily control rooms and signal boxes, dating from the Second World War; however, as part of the restructuring of the civil defence network in the early 1950s a number of purpose-built control shelters were proposed, possibly to manage the evacuation of large numbers of the population. In the event only four were built, demonstrating the programme, like the Gun Defended Areas and Rotor sites, was an early victim of the H–bomb 'problem'.

Even with all thoughts of evacuation abandoned the rail network was still considered an essential part of the national infrastructure and provision for its control still deemed a necessity. To counter this problem a number of Mobile Emergency Controls (MEC) were developed, giving the rail chiefs the flexibility to locate where needed. This naturally relied on the track remaining intact and unblocked, so large population and industrial areas would be fairly inaccessible. However, outlying and country areas would survive a nuclear exchange, unless of course there had been a build-up using conventional weapons when the rail network would have been a major target. The MEC trains were dispersed around the country in sidings and sheds up until their disposal in 1979–80. Rail transport also suffers from one major problem – power. By the end of the Cold War over 3,000 units were diesel powered whilst the rest relied on vulnerable overhead electrical supplies. After a large nuclear attack oil-based fuels would be in extreme shortage and the power cables would take years to repair, even if a major electricity supply was re-established.

Oil and Gas Supplies

Oil-based fuels are probably the most important tradable commodities in the Western world, demonstrated on a global scale by the eagerness of the West to liberate Kuwait in 1991. At a more local level the week-long petrol crisis caused chaos in Britain in mid-September 2000, almost bringing the army onto the streets. But oil is far more important than just a fuel provider, the process of refinement produces lubricants, plastics and a whole host of other by-products which the British manufacturing industry uses. If it were to be removed from the economic system the country would, quite literally, grind to a halt. Clearly this was taken into consideration over the whole period of the Cold War. Pipelines, some dating from the Second World War, have been laid around the country, landing oil from the North Sea platforms and tankers importing fuel at different grades of refinement, and also connecting both military and civil airfields. To put some figures to this pipe network, 67 million tonnes of crude oil were transported by pipelines in 1991, the year the Cold War ended, of which over 50 per cent was for national consumption. A measure of the importance was demonstrated by:

They (the police) *would work in close liaison with local authorities and would be responsible for the security of essential surviving resources such as food and fuel...*

Civil Protection, Community Advisors Training Notes (1986).

Presumably any hostile force would view oil refineries as extremely viable targets; cutting the ability to produce fuels, especially for aviation and road transport, would seriously hamper the country's ability to prepare for war. A large number of power stations were also oil fired up until the end of the Cold War and any drop in supply to these would have had an effect on both the industrial and social infrastructure of Britain.

As with other essential resources the oil industry made its own provision for a national emergency. Each of the eleven Home Defence Regions had a designated control centre that would oversee the production and supply within that area. Officials would also work at Regional Government HQ level alongside representatives from the Department of Environment, co-ordinating supply efforts and resource identification. At a lower level the local authorities would appoint a fuel officer, who, after identifying surviving stocks, would allocate it to the essential services on a very limited scale.

One of the first actions of any emergency planning legislation was to 'freeze' the supply of petrol. Two reasons drove this; an adequate picture can be built up of existing stocks that would be held by the local officer appointed to co-ordinate distribution, but more importantly, the restriction of supplies greatly enhanced the Government's 'stay at home' policy. After a major attack petrol stocks would become the most important commodity in Britain after water and food. The ability to drill and pipe North Sea oil to the coast would presumably be one of the first casualties, closely followed by the ability to refine crude into something more usable. Re-supply, in the short term, would be impossible and, even if it did happen, it would have to be petrol or diesel. Basically all forms of combustion engine transport, especially those used by civilian agencies, would disappear in a very short time indeed. It is not clear how Britain planned to recover from such a major disaster, as very little official material is in the public domain.

Money and the Arts

Two rather grey areas in the planning covering the National Infrastructure are those relating to the preservation of the nation's art treasures and the role of the financial system after a complete breakdown of social structure. One has to remember at this point that even if the Cold War did 'heat up' it would not necessarily mean a nuclear strike was imminent; the whole episode could conceivably be decided conventionally. This has been graphically illustrated recently with the discovery of maps depicting British towns and cities, transcribed in Russian and stockpiled in East Germany; clearly not all had an eye on nuclear annihilation.

Financial Considerations

In a purely conventional war money and the financial institutes would continue to operate, albeit at a rudimentary level. It is tempting to see a Britain on the edge of financial collapse and to a certain degree this would happen, but money as we understand it would continue, just as it did in the Second World War. Nuclear war, however, would change the financial landscape forever. By the early 1980s the reliance on electronic networks was becoming a major part of any financial transaction, and by the late 1980s this reliance was total. Clearly any form of disruption to the network would cause chaos. Companies now have a series of repositories which 'back up' data from their mainframes, ironically some stores are Cold War structures including the former Command Centre at Greenham Common. The policy of data 'back-up' on a large scale is a fairly new concept and whilst companies did keep electronic data during the Cold War it was nowhere near the scale of the late 1990s. The point is it probably would not have mattered anyway.

A concerted effort to totally disrupt the national infrastructure would undoubtedly rely on the effects of the Electromagnetic Pulse, and whilst this may not have had a major detrimental effect in the 1950s and 60s, the later periods would have seen an almost total breakdown. Financial centres such as London and Frankfurt would undoubtedly be targets and it is tempting to suggest that the West's reliance on the capitalistic system would be its ultimate downfall, a theory backed up by the surviving maps. Money would cease to have any intrinsic value and it is highly likely that it would be replaced with commodities with rising values such as food, water and shelter.

National Art Treasures

The place of the arts and, indeed, heritage in general, is questionable in post-nuclear strike Britain, but it would be prudent to protect the collection in the case of conventional warfare. The main Government art store was situated at Manod Quarry, Blaenau Ffestiniog. This site dates back to the early days of the Second World War when damage from invasion and air attack were real prospects and an underground solution was sought. Manod was considered suitable because of its isolated location and existing tunnels, the result of 100 years of slate mining and quarrying. The Government installed an air-conditioning plant to maintain a stable environment for the works of art, along with a narrow-gauge railway using specially made wagons, on a two-foot gauge. The site reverted to the original landowner in the early 1980s. Other art stores are difficult to track down, but one large purpose-built structure at West Camp, RAF St Athan near Cardiff, was used as a store for the National Museum of Wales from the early 1980s. Further sites included Westwood Quarry near Bradford-on-Avon where the Victoria and Albert Museum stored its exhibits during the war; this site closed in 1983.

thirteen

'You and Your Family'

Throughout the Second World War the British civilian population was subject to a number of devastating attacks. The Blitz in London and the destruction of Coventry are but two of the hundreds of raids during the six years of the conflict. Underground stations doubled as refuges and public shelters were built, whilst many constructed Anderson shelters in their gardens. The loss of life was considerable but not total and after a night in the shelter many emerged to find quite arbitrary destruction of property. In a row of terraced houses, so typical of Britain's urban areas, only a few buildings in the street may have been destroyed, the rest losing window glass and roof tiles. Physical and psychological injuries were terrible but not overwhelming, and most survived with little or no long-term effects.

The Cold War was a completely different concept; the destructive force of nuclear weapons already aimed at this country by the late 1950s would have caused horrific loss of life and destruction on a hitherto unimaginable scale. This chapter will look at the dangers the ordinary family faced and how the Government suggested they protected themselves if the unthinkable did happen.

Nuclear War

Of the three major effects produced when an atomic bomb explodes, two – blast and flash-burn are not new although they have their own special characteristics. The third – radiological effects – is novel in character and in its results.

British Transport, Civil Defence Training Booklet (September 1951).

The effects of a nuclear attack on Britain would totally overwhelm all the emergency services immediately and have major long-term implications for the survival of all in the British Isles. Heat, blast and radiation poisoning would expose millions to an excruciating death, one that could not be eased by the equally devastated medical services. By the late 1950s a population who had just got used to the concept of 'atomic warfare' were suddenly faced with a weapon – the H-bomb. Possessing a much greater destructive capacity, and an increased threat from nuclear fallout, the H-bomb was to influence all preparations made and protective advice issued for the rest of the Cold War.

The Effects of the Bomb

It is important to understand the extremes the British population would be exposed to during a nuclear exchange if the depth of Government advice is to be recognised. When a nuclear warhead detonates an unstoppable process is unleashed that has three main characteristics, and all have very adverse effects on the human body. However:

> *Everything within a certain distance of a nuclear explosion will be totally destroyed.*

'Protect and Survive' (1976 reprinted 1980).

Light

On detonation a nuclear device emits an extreme burst of light, many times brighter than the sun and possibly lasting up to thirty seconds. Coupled with the burst is intense heat capable of causing fires up to 10km away from the explosion. Using a 10-megaton weapon as a guide, anything within a 3.5km radius of an airburst or 2.4km of a ground burst would be vaporised by the heat. Combustible material is liable to catch fire up to 10km from ground zero.

Anyone caught out in the open at the time of detonation would be exposed to this physically debilitating effect. Looking in the direction of the explosion would cause major eye trauma. Up to 10km from ground zero the exposed eyeball would probably melt, beyond that the retina would be damaged beyond recovery.

Heat

Heat generated by the release of energy creates a fireball, which in the case of a 10-megaton bomb can reach up to 5km across in less than a second, reaching over one million degrees Celsius. The effects of this are dependent on atmospheric conditions and the position of the detonation in relation to the ground. An airburst would produce around 25 per cent more radiated heat than a ground detonation, also foggy or hazy conditions would mask the heat intensity the further out from ground zero it was felt.

> *The effects are severe on unprotected persons. Severe burns would result up to one mile from Ground Zero and less severe up to 2½ miles from G.Z.*

British Transport, Civil Defence Training Booklet (September 1951).

The information available in the late 1940s early '50s used data collected in the aftermath of Hiroshima and Nagasaki, where a high percentage of the initial deaths were caused by the effects of heat on lightly clothed civilians. With the development of thermonuclear devices many more casualties were expected.

Radii of Heat Effects

	Radius from G.Z. in miles	
	Nuclear Bomb	(500 N)
	Air burst	Ground Burst
On people exposed in open		
Lethal burns	½	4
Third-degree burns (charring), exposed skin	1	8
Second-degree burns (blistering), exposed skin	1½ – 2	12 – 16
First-degree burns (reddening), exposed skin	2½	20

(Note 1 mile = 1.6 kilometres; 500 N = 10 megatons)

'Manual of Civil Defence', Vol. 1, Nuclear Weapons, (1956).

Burns victims would need immediate treatment if they were to have any chance of recovery; the reality of obtaining this treatment was hinted at in Ministry of Health information leaflets from the mid-1960s:

> *(j) Under emergency conditions and where there is likely to be a considerable delay in the patient receiving hospital treatment, fluid lost from the body oozing from large burnt areas must be replaced.*

> *(k) Give aspirin to relieve pain; for an adult 2 tablets every 6 hours.*

'Emergency Home Care', Ministry of Health (1967).

The lack of medical care, post attack, was graphically underpinned in a paper entitled 'The Medical Effects of Nuclear War' published by the British Medical Council in 1983. The Council considered that anyone suffering third-degree burns covering more than 30 per cent of the body would not survive. But this can be extended to second-degree burns if on the trunk and face, where serious nerve damage would still occur. Clearly survival from the effects of heat if caught out in the open would depend on some sound advice:

> *The clothing of exposed people, though it may itself catch fire, affords some degree of protection to the skin at ranges greater than ½ mile, particularly if the clothing is not in close contact with the body, and providing that the burning clothing can quickly be removed or the flames extinguished.*

'Manual of Civil Defence', Vol. 1, Nuclear Weapons, (1956).

Heat flash would also start many fires in the surrounding areas, dependent on the materials available. The main fire zone from a 10-megaton bomb could extend up to 16km from ground zero, with isolated ones as far out as 35km. Many houses were therefore under threat well beyond the destruction zone and some guidance was clearly necessary. 'Protect and Survive' had some thoughts on the subject:

> *Coat windows inside with diluted emulsion paint of a light colour so that they will reflect away much of the heat flash, even if the blast which will follow is to shatter them.*

'Protect and Survive' (1976 reprinted 1980).

Bizarre as this sounds it is probably good advice. The many atmospheric test shots had demonstrated that the heat, whilst extreme, did not cause all combustible material within the affected area to burn. Plastics, such as window surrounds, would deform but because the heat was not sustained they would not burn. Light materials such as a newspaper or net curtains, and the clothes and hair of anyone caught by the heat flash, even through a window, would, however, ignite.

> *Go round the house and put out any small fires using mains water if you can. If anyone's clothing catches fire, lay them on the floor and roll them in a blanket, rug or thick coat.*

'Protect and Survive' (1976 reprinted 1980).

But fires would be starting everywhere by this time, overstretching the emergency services immediately:

> *…in wartime the attendance of the local fire brigade might be delayed or the weight of its attendance reduced, and in the immediate period following nuclear attack it might be unable to attend at all. In such circumstances the community may be cut off. Left to its own resources, its survival would partly depend upon an awareness of the risk from fire.*

Civil Protection, Community Advisers Training Course (1986).

Any form of nuclear attack would cause major uncontrollable fire damage, primarily due to the lack of fire-fighting equipment available and fallout conditions making some areas too dangerous to enter for weeks. The coverage of full-time appliances during the late 1970s–early '80s would have had difficulty dealing with a Hiroshima-sized explosion, as a single event, never mind something on the scale the Government planned for. The North Yorkshire Fire and Rescue Service, through the 1980s, had sixty appliances and twelve standby pumps to cover an area of 8,321 sq. km, containing mostly isolated rural communities. The Home Office retained around 900 Green Goddess pumps to complement local authority appliances, but it has to be remembered that this figure was the national distribution, so additional coverage would be thin. When the Government said appliances 'might be unable to attend at all', they clearly meant it.

Blast

Blast is probably the most destructive component of the nuclear explosion and can flatten or damage large areas around the target. Expansion of hot gasses in the fireball causes a pressure wave to travel out from ground zero. At the centre of the explosion the pressure may reach fifty times the normal atmospheric reading, but this drops as the wave moves outward. Initially the pressure wave travels above the speed of sound (1,200km per hour); behind this the speed drops, but the resultant wind can still be above 500km per hour and is extremely destructive. As the fireball rises into the atmosphere, air is drawn back into the centre, and whilst not travelling as fast as the expanding shockwave, still has destructive capabilities especially on structures already weakened by the initial shockwave. The effects on civilians, using information gathered from Japanese sites, suggested that few fatalities would be expected to result directly from the blast.

Serious internal injury from the direct effects of blast from high airburst bombs is rare.

British Transport, Civil Defence Training Booklet (September 1951).

That said, there would be casualties from the secondary effects, again dependent on the individual's location and relation to ground zero.

Most of the blast casualties in this country would be caused by the indirect or secondary effects of the blast such as falling masonry, flying debris and glass.

'Manual of Civil Defence', Vol. 1, Nuclear Weapons (1956).

In outlying areas the effects of blast and the casualties resulting from it could be expected to be lighter, but the sheer destructive force of the megaton-range weapons suggested that this could be a long way from ground zero. By 1980 it was considered that a 1-megaton airburst would cause 'severe/moderate damage' out as far as 11km, and presumably flying glass would be out a lot further than that. The British Medical Council considered that any major orthopaedic, abdominal or crush injuries would be fatal. Again the possibility of treatment would be academic as the time delay in reaching most areas, especially after the stand-down of the Civil Defence Corps, meant most would be dead well before rescue arrived.

People would also be trapped by the collapse of buildings and might become casualties for this reason or even be suffocated without receiving other physical injuries.

'Manual of Civil Defence', Vol. 1, Nuclear Weapons (1956).

The effects, therefore were very significant and, along with burns victims, would quickly swamp any form of medical help still available, not to mention the rescue services. The Home Office, in its usual 'matter of fact' way sums up the situation.

The dynamic effects of these strong winds are a potent and distinctive feature of nuclear weapons and would give rise to a very significant proportion of the casualties resulting from such explosions.

Civil Protection, Community Advisers Training Course (1986).

Protection against the effects of blast was wholly dependent on the type of shelter or structure you were in at the time. The majority of the population would have been sheltering in their homes, which, if closer than 11km to ground zero, would presumably now have no roofs. Any closer than that and:

When the blast wave passes over a building the sudden increase of pressure and the following wind may cause the building either to explode or collapse.

'Domestic Nuclear Shelters' (1980).

The idea of protecting the civilian population had been investigated over the years but was finally laid to rest when the Government stated:

The risk of war is at present considered so slight that the enormous expense of providing shelters to every family in the land could not be justified. It would cost billions of pounds. As it is, more is being spent on civil defence than previously – about £45 million a year by 1983/84. This is an insurance premium against the remote risk that NATO's continuing deterrent policy might fail. For more than 30 years it has kept war away from Europe.

'Civil Defence – Why We Need It' (1981).

Of course this was in stark contrast to other European countries, and came at a time when NATO was rearming with Pershing II IRBMs and Ground Launched Cruise Missiles were being based in Britain, increasing the nuclear threat to this country. Switzerland was, throughout the Cold War, one of Europe's most prolific shelter builders, and by 1980 nine out of ten of the population had some form of purpose-built refuge. This was complemented by the biggest shelter in Europe, the Sonnenberg Tunnel, with space for around 20,000 people supported by a hospital, food stockpiles and emergency power generation.

It was possible to construct your own shelter in Britain. Tests carried out by the Civil Defence college at Easingwold had determined four types which could be employed in case there was a rise in international tensions. There were two types of home-built garden shelters, each taking two people an estimated twenty-four hours to construct. The materials included carpets and blankets for making earth roles, pillowcases to double as sandbags, and rain proofing from such things as vinyl flooring or shower curtains. These would be destroyed if closer than 11km from ground zero and had natural ventilation so radiation poisoning would also be a major concern. For those wishing for a more permanent arrangement there were two substantial constructions, one in kit form so it could be carried through the house to the back garden, the other requiring major building work and costing an estimated £6,000 – £10,000 in 1980. These could survive up to 3.5km from ground zero and had forced-air ventilation, and whilst the choice would appear to be obvious, as with most Government advice there was a catch:

> *If you wish to install a permanent shelter you may need planning permission. You should check before submitting plans or beginning work. Your local District Council will tell you about planning permission and the building regulations. A permanent shelter may affect the rateable value of your home, and this is a matter for your local District Valuer and Valuation Officer.*

'Domestic Nuclear Shelters' (1980).

Unfortunately this is not the end of the story, whilst injuries from flash, heat and blast would easily reach the millions across the country a more sinister, invisible effect would also be at work, compounding the demand on medical care and drugs – fallout.

Radioactivity

Fallout and radiological poisoning are phenomena unique to nuclear weapons, comprising the initial release of radiation as the reaction occurs and from debris resulting from the effects of the explosion known as fallout. Initial nuclear radiation is the release of particles at the point of explosion. These are very penetrative and extremely harmful, but have only a short range and brief duration. The lethality of heat and blast have far more range than these particles and so they pose no real threat to the individual as they would already be dead within the effective range.

Fallout

Fallout is altogether more dangerous and could, in the event of a large-scale attack on the British Isles, cause millions of deaths in the long term. Fallout is dependent on the type of burst employed to destroy the target. An airburst uses the reflection of the blast wave to the ground to cause damage and heat is also intense over further distances; however, the fireball does not touch the ground so vaporised material is not mixed with the radioactive particles found within it. Fallout in this case is much reduced and short lived, although initial protection is required. Conversely, a ground burst produces massive amounts of fallout and can contaminate large areas downwind of the initial detonation. As the highly radioactive fireball raises into the atmosphere it takes with it both vaporised and solid material. The larger solid particles fall back to earth in the immediate area, but lighter ones can travel hundreds of kilometres downwind causing major hazards for millions.

The Early Days

Fallout was a little-understood phenomenon until the early 1950s when most radioactive contamination was thought to be confined to the immediate area of the blast. The best protection therefore was to stay out of the area until the radiation had decayed to a safe level. Civil defence rescue teams would have to work in the peripheral zones where there was a possibility of survivors still in the wreckage.

> *On the other hand, the area heavily contaminated from a low airburst bomb will almost certainly be pulverised by the blast, and there might be no need for Civil Defence workers to enter it unless there were people trapped in shelters* (presumably Government Officials, Author).

British Transport, Civil Defence Training Booklet (September 1951).

Clearly rescue teams would come into contact with individuals suffering the effects of radiation poisoning, this had happened in Japan, but advice covered this, pointing out:

> *As contamination by radioactive particles is not penetrating, clothing worn can be ordinary porous type (close woven overall suit very suitable) so long as it is closed up at the normal openings at neck, sleeves and trouser legs. It is desirable that the hair should be covered (e.g. by handkerchief knotted at corners).*

British Transport, Civil Defence Training Booklet (September 1951).

By the mid-1950s the situation had dramatically changed when it was realised that radioactive fallout would probably account for as many victims as the explosions themselves. On the Government side a series of protected structures known as War Rooms were designed and built, as were many Civil Defence Controls, whilst the military proceeded underground with the Rotor project and Anti-aircraft Operations Rooms. On the public side the story was very different; outside London (which still had some deep-level shelters) there was no provision. The Civil Defence Act (1948) did leave the way open to requisition and build civil shelters if need be, however most people would be left to their own devices.

Fallout emits two types of radiation, short-range Alpha and Beta particles and long-range Gamma rays. Short-range particles are only dangerous when ingested. However, they will burn the skin if allowed to come into contact with it. Gamma rays are similar to X-rays and can penetrate most materials making them a much greater threat. Gamma radiation damages the bone marrow and other sensitive areas of the body including the central nervous system, stomach and intestines, and will burn the skin. Depending on the dose, the victim of radiation poisoning could recover within a few days or die anywhere between three to four days and eight weeks after the attack. Luckily advice was at hand:

Q 'Is there any treatment for radiation sickness?'
A 'For animals, no. But for humans, rest, good food and good nursing are the best treatment.'

'Home Defence and the Farmer' (1958 reprinted 1959).

Whilst the general population were requested to undertake the following:

Persons exposed to radiation from a nuclear explosion or radioactive fallout may suffer from radiation sickness, the symptoms of which are extreme lassitude, vomiting and diarrhoea, sore mouth, a tendency to sepsis (infection) anaemia (blood disease) and loss of weight. Radiation sickness is not infectious.

(a)   Ensure rest.
(b)   Prevent bedsores.
(c)   Care for the mouth.
(d)   Tempt the appetite.
(e)   Maintain and if possible improve the patient's morale.

'Emergency Home Care', Ministry of Health (1967).

Population Protection

The measurement of radioactive dose rate has changed over the years, previously expressed as Roentgen Equivalent Man (REM) and Radiation Absorbed Dose (RAD); however, the current measurement is the centiGrey (cGy) and will be used here. Mammals are capable of repairing damage from radiation poisoning, the human body being able to replace cells damaged by around 15 cGy-in-air per day. Measuring equipment detects radiation in the atmosphere (hence 'in-air') which is then used to calculate dosage, expressed as cGy/h. Radiation passing through the body damages both blood cells and bone marrow; doses of 400 cGy-in-air would be fatal to around 5 per cent of the population over just a few minutes' exposure, whilst 800 cGy-in-air over just a few minutes would be fatal to 95 per cent of those exposed. The possibility of predicting the amount of radiation due to fallout was impossible before an attack as the factors involved were varied. However, the Government set an ideal public exposure figure of 15 cGy/h-in-air per day.

Fallout, travelling downwind, will eventually settle out, contaminating large areas of the landscape; danger to those sheltering comes from radioactive material settling on roofs as well as around the shelter. Remaining under cover reduces the effects, but the more material between fallout and the individual, the lower the dose rate. Through a process of radioactive decay the dose rate will decay. In the case of fallout, activity is reduced by a factor of ten when the time is multiplied by a factor of seven; this is known as the 'seven-tenths rule'. Structures act as a barrier to radiation, proportional to the type of material and thickness used in the construction. This is expressed as the Protection Factor (PF). Protection factors rely on the density of a given material and its ability to absorb gamma rays. A structure that reduces an external radiation rate of 250 cGy/h to

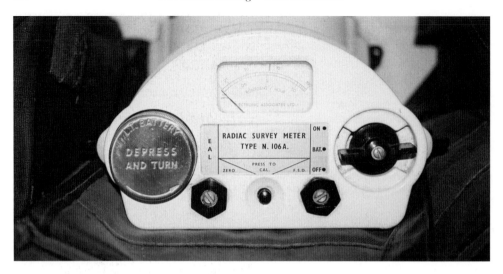

Radiac Meter. Standard equipment at Home Office sites in the early 1960s. (Courtesy J.A. Parrish & Sons)

an internal rate of 25 cGy/h is said to have a PF of ten. The Emergency Control Centre built in the late 1980s at Blunsdon was designed to have a PF of 100, whilst a modern detached two-storey house had a PF of seven; the problems are obvious.

The Fallout Room

Protection against the effects of radiation, especially fallout induced, was totally dependant on the type of structure used as a shelter. Just a few years after the Second World War many of the shelters constructed still survived and modification of these was suggested.

> *Shelters of the last war type would provide a very substantial degree of protection, which could be made complete with extra thickening.*

British Transport, Civil Defence Training Booklet (September 1951).

By the mid-1950s the number of shelters surviving was negligible and protection in many cases moved into the house itself. Slit trenches with an earth covering were suggested but nothing could compare to a structure with a cellar, however since the Second World War this once essential element of building construction had been largely ignored, but not to worry:

> *Where the ground floor of the house consists of boards and timber joists carried on sleeper walls it may be possible to combine the high protection of the slit trench with some of the comforts of the refuge room by constructing a trench under the floor. Once a trap door had been cut in the floorboards and joists and the trench had been dug, there would be no further interference with the peacetime use of the room.*

'Manual of Civil Defence', Vol. 1, Nuclear Weapons (1956).

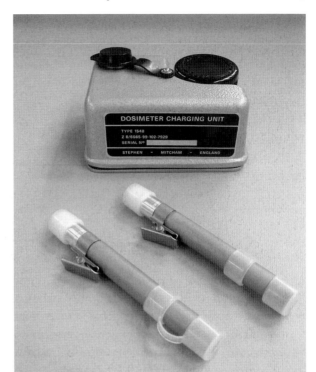

Right: Quartz Fibre Dosimeters. This simple design was used throughout the Cold War. Personnel carried the pen-like reader when outside the protected site. It was zeroed by pushing it into the charging unit.

Below: PDRM 82. The Plessey PDRM 82 was standard issue throughout the 1980s reading in cGy/h-in-air.

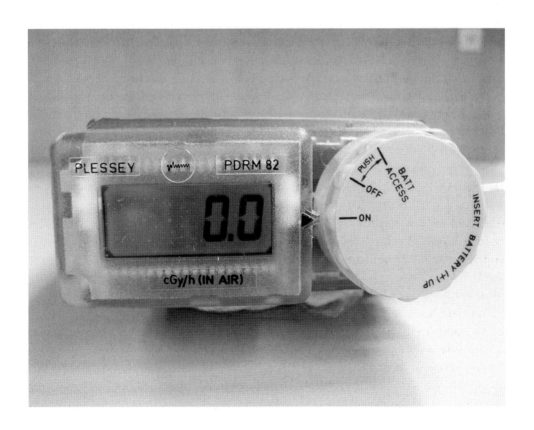

The rundown of the Civil Defence Corps in 1968 effectively ended the concept of rescue and for nearly a decade attention was directed to restructuring the regional government system. By the mid-1970s the Government issued a number of new pamphlets, this time focussing on survival. Leaflets described possible homemade shelters, usually consisting of one room in the house with a second 'inner refuge' within that room. One major difference was that you and your family would be expected to live for a minimum of two weeks before the state would help. The information also lacked some of the optimism displayed by earlier work, stating:

Even the safest room in your home is not safe enough, however.

'Protect and Survive' (1976 reprinted 1980).

The two-room system was designed to give enough living space for up to six people for an extended period and added protection for the first two to three days – post attack.

To obtain the best protection against external radiation in an average house it would be necessary to make best use of both distance and density. That would entail selecting the room in the house most distant from external walls and roof (distance from the roof is more important than distance from external walls) as a fallout room. …In addition it would be necessary to construct a further shelter (or inner refuge within the room itself, using whatever dense materials were available.

Civil Protection, Community Advisers Training Course (1986).

Positioning the fallout room could be problematic; shelters should only be built in the first four floors of a block of flats, clearly sound advice for fallout protection but not for blast and heat. Bungalows (PF 5) would also give less than adequate protection as there is no upper story to give distance between you and the fallout. Caravans (PF 2) also give little protection, and it was suggested in this case you look to your local authority for advice! However, guidelines in the main concentrated on the standard semi-detached house. It was suggested that all windows in the room were blocked up, preferably with bricks or concrete blocks although books, boxes of earth and furniture might be employed. Clearly some revisions had been carried out to earlier advice, as in 1956 Civil Defence literature suggested a piano as the ideal furniture type.

Because of the threat of radiation you and your family may need to live in this room for fourteen days after an attack, almost without leaving it at all.

'Protect and Survive' (1976 reprinted 1980).

The Inner Refuge

When the radiation threat from fallout was at its greatest, even the fallout room would not give adequate protection. It was, therefore, proposed that within your designated area you built an 'inner refuge'.

> *Make a 'lean-to' with sloping doors taken from rooms above or strong boards rested against an inner wall. Prevent them from slipping by fixing a length of wood along the floor. Build further protection with bags or boxes of earth or sand – or books, or even clothing – on the slope of your refuge, and anchor these also against slipping. Partly close the two open ends with boxes of sand or earth, or heavy furniture.*

'Protect and Survive' (1976 reprinted 1980).

Tables could also be employed, again surrounded with extra protection, as could the Second World War favourite, the under stairs cupboard. For those who were thinking ahead a purpose-built kit was available costing between £500–£800 with an additional £300 needed for the bricks to surround it. This kit was essentially a steel table designed to fit within the fallout room and capable of accommodating a family of four. Encouragingly:

> *This shelter will sustain the debris load resulting from the complete collapse of a normal two-storey house.*

'Domestic Nuclear Shelters' (1980).

Quite what the homemade version could withstand was not suggested. It quickly became apparent that unless you were prepared to spend quite large sums on purpose-built shelters your chances of survival were not very promising. Fallout rooms and inner refuges relied on one factor – completeness. With blast damage extending far out beyond ground zero the likelihood of houses keeping their roofs was, to say the least, optimistic, but not to worry:

> *If there is structural damage from the attack you may have some time before a fallout warning to do minor jobs to keep out the weather using curtains or sheets to cover broken windows or holes.*

'Protect and Survive' (1976 reprinted 1980).

It was clear that people would leave the safety of their shelter or inner refuge, through a mixture of curiosity, searching for food and water, or to flee the area. The risk of exposure in the first two days post-attack was a major concern, however not all survivors would escape the effects and it was important certain groups were protected. Youth would be paramount to the rebuilding of the nation; clearly the Government had an eye on this when issuing the following:

Visits outside the house may at first be limited to a few minutes for essential duties. These should be done by people over thirty where possible. They should avoid bringing dust into the house, keeping separate stout shoes or boots for outdoors if they can, and always wiping them.

'Protect and Survive' (1976 reprinted 1980).

Death

Whilst it is easy to view the suggested preparations with scepticism, it has to be remembered that if the unthinkable did happen the public would be expected to cope with many situations that were both unfamiliar and traumatic. Mentally this would have been devastating; the destruction of the community would lead to severe psychological conditions. The possibility of spending an unknown period of time in a room with little or no food and water, with dying members of your family, some maybe burnt beyond recognition, whilst others, including perhaps yourself, suffer bouts of diarrhoea and vomiting due to radiation poisoning is beyond the imagination.

You may have casualties from an attack, which you will have to care for, perhaps for some days, without medical help. Be sure you have your first aid requirements in your survival kit.

'Protect and Survive' (1976 reprinted 1980).

The first-aid kit would not cover the minor effects of warfare, never mind anything on the scale predicted from nuclear war. It was suggested that, as a minimum, household and prescribed medicines along with aspirins or similar tablets, plasters, bandages, cotton wool, disinfectant and Vaseline should be included. This was – rather optimistically – meant to tide you over until help became available:

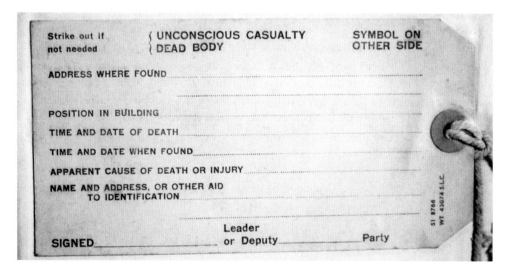

Body Label. The Home Office clearly thought of everything. Whether these would be distributed to every household at the start of hostilities is not clear. (Courtesy J.A. Parrish & Sons)

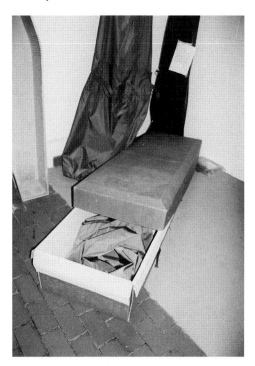

Cardboard Coffin. Coffins such as these were contained at most RGHQs. They were stored flat-packed using the minimum of space; the public, however, would not be so lucky. (Courtesy J.A. Parrish & Sons)

Listen to your radio for information about the services and facilities as they become available and about the type of cases which are to be treated as urgent.

'Protect and Survive' (1976 reprinted 1980).

The British Medical Council considered this would not happen as the shortage of drugs and supplies would mean prioritisation would come into almost immediate effect. The brutal reality is that the National Health Service, like many other major organisations, would be non-existent, and without it the disabled, chronically ill or drug dependant would quickly disappear, along with many of the older population. The bottom line is that the critical first few days would naturally sort out survivors from the terminally ill. The possibility of all family members surviving beyond the first week, especially those sheltering within the devastated areas, would be very slim indeed. This presents another major problem – the death of a family member.

If a death occurs while you are confined to the fallout room place the body in another room and cover it as securely as possible. Attach an identification.

'Protect and Survive' (1976 reprinted 1980).

As the fallout risk decreased, and providing no further attacks were forthcoming, then the disposal of the dead would become a major issue. Gone would be the usual ritual surrounding such events; in its place an attempt to minimise the health risks to the surviving shelter members:

> *You should receive radio instructions on what to do next. If no instructions have been given within five days, you should temporarily bury the body as soon as it is safe to go out, and mark the spot.*

'Protect and Survive' (1976 reprinted 1980).

At a county level this would have taken on major importance and presented some major logistical problems.

> *Following a nuclear attack, normal practices in disposal of the dead might have to be abandoned to avoid a major health hazard to the surviving population. It might be necessary to resort to mass burials or cremation.*

Civil Protection, Community Advisor Training Course Notes (1986).

Cremation of the bodies, whilst being the most effective measure against disease, would probably not happen for a number of reasons. The vast numbers involved would cause major logistical problems at a time when communications were at their least effective. The use of fuel, and this should be extended to wood as well as liquids, would probably be better served elsewhere and the surviving population would be less than willing to move rotten corpses. However, plans were made, local authorities were requested in peacetime to identify likely 'sites for temporary or mass disposal of human remains', probably parks and playing fields. Even this was problematic:

> *Burial sites should be chosen to avoid contamination of drinking water and should be clearly marked. Records of all those buried or cremated should be retained.*

Civil Protection, Community Advisor Training Course Notes (1986).

The horrors facing the population of this country in the event of a nuclear war were all too apparent. Over the years the Government produced information that was sometimes credible, sometimes laughable. The following extract sums up the level of credibility some information leaflets actually displayed:

> *On hearing the ALL-CLEAR*
>
> *This means there is no longer an immediate danger from air attack and fallout and you may resume normal activities.*

'Protect and Survive' (1976 reprinted 1980).

fourteen

Strategic Food Stockpile

How would millions of terrified, sick and injured people be fed? This chapter describes the networks that were in place for the storing and distribution of food, and the feeding of survivors of a nuclear attack.

The concept of storing food during a National Emergency is nothing new; during both the First and Second World Wars food was stockpiled in the face of dwindling resources, primarily through blockades and shipping losses in the Atlantic. A system of stores known as 'Buffer Depots' was set up around the country, holding strategic stockpiles of food and essential equipment. In times of critical shortage the stockpile would be introduced into the supply chain, and then be quickly replaced by goods imported from central handling depots, situated away from port areas and hopefully out of danger. Food control was further enforced by the introduction of rationing, a process which, on some food items, was still in force until mid-1954. Buffer Depots were strategically sited, requiring a number of criteria including good transport links, rail, road or canal, and being close enough to large population and industrial areas to be effective but far enough away so as to survive any attacks on those sites. By the end of the Second World War a massive network spread across the entire country with many specialised buildings storing different types of emergency food stockpiles. Many of these were utilised by the Government for the storage of the Strategic Food Stockpile (SFS), which was designed to be used after a nuclear attack.

Grain

One major component of the post-war food stockpile was grain. A number of monolithic grain silos had been built between 1939–45, capable on average of storing up to 5,000 tons of processed wheat or barley. Sites like those at Andover and Oxford follow the standard wartime pattern with a central grain elevator flanked by two wings containing three silos each. During the 1950s a number of new silos were built, this time more individual in appearance. One such site is Knapton, North Yorkshire.

Grain Silo. This site north of Oxford was built during the Second World War and could hold up to 5,000 tons of unprocessed grain. Many of these sites remained on the Strategic Food Stockpile register until 1994.

Built in 1957, it exhibits all the transport requirements, having a rail link and easy access to the main Scarborough to York road. Even with such large capacities the silo network was deemed inadequate. Placing of the sites, especially during the Cold War, had more to do with the economics of grain production than the supplying of grain after a nuclear attack. To counter this, grain was stored at other sites around the country including redundant aircraft hangars known as intervention sites. Strictly speaking these sites were used to help steady the price of grain between good and bad harvest years, however they were also earmarked as a strategic stockpile and would be used to cover any national emergency had it arisen. To give an idea of the scale involved, the eight sites, including the old Thor missile site at RAF Driffield, were still on the Ministry of Agriculture, Food and Fisheries (MAFF) register in 1999, having a total of 15 hectares of covered capacity. During the Cold War, especially during a build up to hostilities, many more covered sites would have been utilised.

Cold Stores

The ability to keep food cold, often below freezing, is a distinct advantage with one major drawback: power is needed if the food stored is not to spoil very quickly. Cold stores built during the last war were used continuously throughout the period of the Cold War giving on average over 7,000 cubic metres of storage space. Again these were situated on good transport links and were served by two separate generators to keep the store at the correct temperature. They were used by the Government to store such things as the famous butter and beef mountains, but would have very quickly become vital assets during any major conflict.

Knapton Silo. This site, with good road and rail links, built in the late 1950s would have been impounded at the start of hostilities. Any release of grain afterwards would have had to be sanctioned by the Regional Commissioner at the Skipton RGHQ.

General Purpose Stores

General stores were also maintained, first by the Ministry of Supply and later by the Property Services Agency, under contract to private firms. Over 200 depots were spread around the country in the 1950s containing supplies of food and equipment; by the 1980s this had been reduced to around 100 sites, but they were still mostly wartime structures. The food items stored through the 1980s were basic to say the least, all aimed at providing a high-energy diet rather than a balanced one. Flour, sugar, refined fats, yeast and boiled sweets all featured, although the sweets idea was abandoned due to difficulties storing them for prolonged periods of time. Packaged high-energy biscuits and cake mix were held at some depots, as were tins of meat. In total MAFF estimated 200,000 tonnes were still stored in 1995. Although the buffer depots were primarily used for wartime stockpiling they did see use in times of economic strife. One such example was the use of the Sterling Warehouse at Wootton Bassett, Wiltshire to stockpile sugar during the 1970s shortages, but on the whole the buffer depots stood silent apart from staff occasionally turning the sacks of flour and sugar. Other more general equipment was also stored at these sites including tents, plastic bowls and spoons, field cookers, and even, sometimes, mobile bakeries.

The stockpiles were considered a national resource and as such were not available to the local authorities, suggesting the Regional Government Headquarters staff would only release them in times of absolute crisis. However, the hardware also on site would be given over to the Local Authority to set up Emergency Feeding Centres. As the decades progressed more reliance began to be placed on food already in the supply system. The explosion of the supermarket concept starting in the late 1970s led to an increase of major food stockpiles at inland distribution centres, often with good rail and motorway access, and these would have been very swiftly requisitioned by MAFF and Home Office representatives. By 1986 the Home Office estimated that at least four to five weeks' worth of supplies were in this chain at any one time, if peacetime consumption was taken into account; but after an attack the population requiring feeding would presumably have dwindled somewhat.

Variety in Adversity

Whilst the Government planned to ensure some form of food stockpile survived it would not have been available to the general public for some considerable time. 'Protect and Survive' requested each household stockpile enough food for at least fourteen days in, or close to, the shelter room. This was to include sugar, jams, cereals, meats, fruits and fruit juices, all preferably tinned or well wrapped. And under no circumstances forget your tin and bottle opener! Both the pamphlet and subsequent information film also suggested your rations should be of sufficient variety to stop your family getting bored with the same diet.

However, the Home Office and MAFF foresaw a problem. As international tensions increased, especially when 'Protect and Survive' dropped on every doormat in Britain, the advice to stockpile food would cause widespread panic buying, increasing demand at food outlets. The answer was to introduce controls on long-life items, presumably by restricting the supply network at source. As the Home Office put it in 1986 '…to even out the spread of stocks more fairly and to improve survivability'. As the situation deteriorated and central control became a reality, the possibility of social unrest would increase, causing the whole system to collapse. It also had to be recognised that no

Buffer Depot. Everything from plastic bowls and spoons to boiled sweets and flour were stored at sites like this around the country. This one is situated at South Leigh, Oxon.

food from stockpiles would be issued until well after the attacks had ceased. Two basic reasons drove this, the effects of radiation poisoning would be very apparent by the third week, those suffering would probably not be supplied beyond very basic levels as the food stocks would be under tremendous pressure by this point. Also, any form of financial incentive to work would be ineffective; however, food would take on the role as the new currency, hence its being controlled from Central or regional government establishments, not local authorities.

Down on the Farm

The most important aspect of surviving any form of national emergency would be to produce food to a level that kept the majority of people alive. After a nuclear attack Britain would need its farmers like never before. Advice to the farming community on food production was in the main consistent throughout the Cold War and was, wherever possible, linked with current agricultural practice.

Home Defence and the Farmer

'Home Defence and the Farmer' (HDF), published in 1958, was the first publication to give all-round advice to farm-based food production, covering current thinking on coping with the effects of fallout on the farm. A number of Government departments were involved in its production, demonstrating the wider problems anticipated; these included the Agricultural Research Council and Medical Research Council. The pamphlet came at a time when many facets of British defence had shifted away from 'point attack' by fission weapons, including the stand down of the Gun Defended Areas and Rotor programme, now concerning itself more with the effects of fallout from fusion devices. Farms, by definition, were not strategic nuclear targets; however, the effects of fallout would be felt on those downwind of any explosion. This would cause major problems in both stock and, dependent on type, produce, so a comprehensive set of instructions covered most eventualities. Farms would also liase with local Civil Defence wardens, although by the 1970s this had been changed to a local farm warden who would be either a National Farming Union official or Senior Farmer.

'The Nation Would Need all the Clean Milk it Could Get'

As fallout spread downwind, large areas of pasture would become contaminated, affecting large numbers of the national animal stock and, whilst sheep were at risk as much as cattle, it was the latter which caused most concern. Milk would become increasingly important to the survivors and great consideration was given to restarting an uncontaminated supply as quickly as possible. The amount of fallout ingested by dairy cattle would be dictated by the condition of the pasture on which they grazed. Poorly managed pasture would encourage cattle to consume grass over a wider area and so eat more contaminants, whilst thicker growing grass would cut down on the area required. This said, if Britain were subject to a surprise attack, then the majority of animals outside would be exposed to fallout anyway.

The priority then was to move cattle indoors first. Other livestock were to be left outside either in a yard or small field, then milk them out or leave them with suckling calves and give just enough poor fodder to keep them alive, reducing the milk production. If at any point dairy cattle came into contact with contaminants, via fodder or water, the chances were the milk would be dangerous. When, in October 1957, pile number one caught fire at Windscale, large areas of Cumbria were cut out of the milk producing chain, so the Ministry was quite well versed in its advice over milk, having had an impromptu dry run. Then there was strontium 90, one of the many chemicals that made up fallout. Unlike others this makes its way into the bone of the animal and has a very long half-life; even when most fallout has decayed to safe levels the dairy herd could build up harmful levels of strontium, rendering the milk unsafe. Strontium in children's teeth became a major issue after studies during the 1950s demonstrated that the number of atmospheric nuclear tests being conducted were damaging health globally. The ideal situation with suspect milk, if it couldn't be checked for radioactivity, was to make it into butter or cheese, so that at least it could be saved from going off whilst waiting for the ministry to come and check it.

If milk, cheese or butter was found to be contaminated the Government advised the farmer to use it as feed for pigs and steers as 'radioactivity is unlikely to do them very much harm before they reach the age at which they are ready for the butcher' (HDF 1958). War office publication, 'The Nuclear Handbook for Staff Officers' (1963), mooted similar sentiments, saying the risk was low 'provided the animals are slaughtered before they become sick'. By 1986 MAFF were still issuing the same information, noting, '(it) would be safe to eat provided the offal were discarded'. Areas where the information did change included eggs; in 1958 it was better to get them checked rather than risk it and by 1986 it had been determined that most contaminants would be locked in the shell. Programmes of intensive testing, in both Britain and the United States, sometimes over long periods, were used to compile contamination information. It is clear that smaller animals were far easier to use in tests than cattle, a point demonstrated by a MAFF Circular (1977) on recovery rates from beta fallout particles in which mice were used to produce a recovery model; unfortunately recovery was suggested to be species specific. Farmers were also encouraged not to slaughter sick animals as 'to keep animals alive would help the Government to organise a fair meat distribution' (HDF 1958). Basically, unless animals were under cover and fed on uncontaminated fodder they, and their produce, would contain some risks. In a national emergency it would appear that those risks were acceptable.

The Growing Season

Fallout is caused by material being drawn up into the atmosphere as the fireball rises from a nuclear explosion; a ground burst would introduce the most dust and debris into the atmosphere. Dependent on the amount of weapons used and type of burst, this material could be significant enough to cause long-term climatic effects, the so-called 'Nuclear Winter'. This phenomenon became more apparent towards the end of the Cold War, presumably as a result of the wider environmental issues that became the focus of the 1980s 'Green Movement'. Any large-scale attack on the United Kingdom during the first half of the year would have had a devastating effect on any crops. Long periods of light depravation and reduced temperatures would cause widespread crop failures. Those that did survive would be at risk from fallout, taking in radiation through the leaves or roots, especially during the first week post-attack. The prospect of a harvest with next to no usable produce would become a distinct reality and coupled with an extremely harsh winter would, as the writers of 'Threads' put it, 'see most of the young and old disappearing from Britain'. The Government chose to acknowledge the concept but not substantiate it 'as yet the scientific basis for this theory is not firmly established' (Civil Protection, 1986).

Cereal crops close to harvest time would fare better as they have reduced water intake down to a minimum, but the risk of contamination would still be present, this time in the form of dust. For the operation of machinery (if it was still possible, for threshing would have exposed those undertaking the tasks to large amounts of contaminated dust) advice was at hand:

> *If you are doing a dusty job − ploughing or cultivating dry land, or threshing or grinding corn or stacking hay − a handkerchief or a simple dust filter should be worn over nose and mouth, and ears should be plugged with cotton wool. Afterwards the nose and ears should be thoroughly cleaned.*

'Home Defence and the Farmer' (1958).

Presumably tasks such as these would have been undertaken wearing something a little more protective in the 1980s. Other produce also had a potential risk. Root crops, when fully grown, would be safe as long as they were fully washed and peeled. Incidentally the Metropolitan District Emergency Feeding Plan published in 1985 estimated that it would take four people one hour to peel around 1 cwt of average quality potatoes. Green vegetables, such as lettuces, sprouts and cabbage, would need to be thoroughly shaken and the removal of the outer leaves would be essential, retaining only the heart, whilst peas and beans would need to be shelled before consumption.

Fish

Fish, by definition, after a nuclear strike, would only be a viable food source close to the point of netting. The same could be said for shellfish and other aquatic animals. MAFF considered the distribution and storage of the resource a logistical nightmare and suggested that 'fish are unlikely to provide a significant contribution to the nuclear survivors' diet'; however, information given to the local authorities did suggest it may have some worth. The biggest problem would, as always, be fallout. It was suggested that sea-fish would be fairly safe, but those which bottom fed in lakes and rivers probably would contain some form of contaminants. Another factor would be the ability to fish out at sea at all, as quite how much of the already EEC-depleted fishing fleet would still be intact after nuclear attack is questionable. The main ports would, by their very nature, have been severely damaged by conventional weapons at least, so any port around the country with any form of infrastructure left standing would have been immediately requisitioned. Also, fishing would have to take place well away from any river outflows as they would be carrying large amounts of contaminants off the land. Of course the Government is well qualified to discuss contaminated sea-life. Erik Martiniussen, in his paper 'Sellafield: Reprocessing Plant in Great Britain', chronicled the results of tests from a thirty-five-year study in 2001. The results have suggested that through the 1960s and '70s the levels of chemicals linked to nuclear activities in the Irish Sea had been higher than those released at Chernobyl, whilst some chemicals are still forty times the EC safe limit. So taking Government advice into consideration, fish would probably be the food of last resort.

It is still difficult to assess the effectiveness of the stockpile as many records remain closed, two examples being MAF 250/13 1955-1962: 'Plans for the distribution of meat in wartime'; and MAF 250/306 1967-1972: 'Chemical and biological warfare and its effects on food and agriculture'. Both are retained by the department; one can only wonder at the content.

Taking Control

The systems ready to be implemented changed, as did the system of Government, throughout the Cold War. For the purpose of explanation the following will concentrate on the 1980s unless stated otherwise.

After an attack the possibility of Central Government remaining in control would be, at best, extremely difficult; a move towards regional government would, at least in the short term, be more likely. In the case of the North East (Region 2) in the 1980s, MAFF Regional Offices (RO), such as York, would come under the direct control of Regional Government Headquarters 2.1 (RGHQ) at Skipton or 2.2 Hexham. Interestingly Civil Defence (1986) points out that only 'surviving offices' would be utilised, clearly being in the centre of a major town had its drawbacks. MAFF RO would liase with MAFF Divisional Offices (DO) who would in turn deal with the Local Authority Headquarters through a MAFF Local Agricultural Control Officer (LACO). The LACO would be no easy part to play and demonstrates the immense pressure some individuals would be under in such a dire situation. Each officer could expect to be responsible for between 700 and 800 farms; they would also be the middle-man between the RGHQ and Local Authority Headquarters. Prime duties included the control of animal systems including the structuring of a credible breeding stock, slaughter of sick and unproductive animals, and the movement and allocation of feedstuffs. Food manufacturing plants, processing plants, cold stores and grain facilities also would be controlled from this position as would be the use of fertilisers to bring on the maximum yields possible. In the 1980s this task would be assisted by the latest infrared satellite pictures that show fairly accurately what crop was growing where; in the 1950s and '60s this would have been infinitely more difficult. To assist in this monumental task wardens would be appointed, drawn from the farming community, to liase with around twenty farms, although in highland regions this number would have been lower.

The regional government would ultimately control all areas the LACO covered, regardless of local authority requests, including major stocks such as those identified at supermarket main depots, imported food which may arrive, released supplies from other RGHQs, supplies still situated on farms, especially harvested crops, and, finally, the Strategic Food Stockpile. The LACO would arrange for the supplies, as released, to be directed to a specific local authority, although this was unlikely to happen until the area concerned had completely run out of local supplies located in supermarkets, depots and warehouses. After that 'ministry stew' would be provided.

This is a very complicated network indeed with great onus being placed on the shoulders of a few individuals, as food would rapidly become the number one issue. Some areas of farmland would, undoubtedly, escape the direct effects of a nuclear burst and only see low levels of contamination. Also, travel may not be that difficult between one farm and another, but generally communications, at best, would be at a very basic level, and it would most certainly be difficult to ascertain the situation in some outlying areas weeks if not months after an attack. The network also relied on a level of completeness and if some links, especially the LACO, were missing for whatever reason, the prospects would have be very grim indeed.

Fourteen Days' Supply

The chances of the entire population taking the advice of 'Protect and Survive', or any other locally produced information, and stocking up with a minimum of fourteen days supplies, especially in urban areas, would in all reality be very slim indeed. Home Office Circular ES1/79 noted 'no arrangements could ensure every surviving household would have, say, fourteen days supply of food after an attack'. This could, of course, be affected by a number of situations; if Britain suffered a no-notice attack little or no time would be left to stock up. Even if tensions increased more gradually the rationing of supplies would, no doubt, be brought in, attempting to stem the inevitable panic buying and profiteering. The situation would be further exacerbated as shops and outlets discovered that any further stocks had been redirected to Government-controlled stockpiles. Either way most of the population would be hungry by week two of a major attack. The systems suggested to feed the survivors were in the main very optimistic, relying heavily on the survival of most of the peacetime infrastructure and above all the goodwill of the general population, something that would be in extremely short supply.

Emergency Feeding Centres

The Emergency Feeding Centre (EFC) infrastructure was the responsibility of the local authority, but the food was not; that would fall to the RGHQ, again demonstrating its perceived level of importance, post-nuclear strike. Advice in the early 1980s was quite comprehensive, covering many aspects of the feeding centre and had it all worked perfectly then all survivors would have been in safe hands; however, as with all best laid plans, the level of naivety was astounding. Prior to an attack the local authority feeding representative was tasked with identifying all the resources needed to effectively run EFCs, which would have been no mean feat. The list was to include all food bulk storage not already identified by the RGHQ as strategic, all canteens in the area, especially those located at schools, industrial sites, depots etc., as

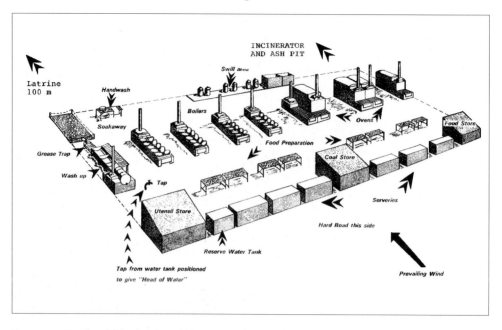

Emergency Feeding. This plan from 1986 suggests how to lay out a 1,000 meals-an-hour kitchen.
(© Courtesy Crown Copyright)

well as large restaurants and cafés. Then the staff to run the EFC had to be identified, primarily from the personnel at the chosen sites as well as any retired volunteers who may have once worked as cooks. Finally outdoor sites would need to be surveyed and selected in case the primary covered sites were damaged beyond use.

Once an attack had occurred it would be up to the individual, had they survived, to feed themselves for the minimum fourteen days. Conceivably it would take that long for the local authority, had they survived, to ascertain what the overall situation would be and where would be best to site the EFS. The Home Office information was quite specific at this point; there was to be no feeding effort until radiation had reduced to safe levels, so some areas would be beyond help. The local authority should also take into account the total population for any given area before committing to setting up the feeding centre. When it was decided to set up, the EFC equipment stored at the buffer depots would be released, including the 1.4 million plastic bowls and spoons that had been stockpiling since the early 1950s, and possibly a mobile bakery. The more standard equipment was the Soyer Boiler with a 45-litre capacity for boiling water and vegetables, stews and, naturally in times of dire crisis, tea. The No. 4 Field Cooker would also be available, which army relic could produce around 125 meals at a time, considerably speeding up the throughput of the centre. A number of insulated containers were also provided in case food needed to be transported any distance after preparation. Layouts for proposed centres were issued, covering 500 and 1,000-meal kitchens, ideally to be staffed by the Woman's Royal Voluntary Service (WRVS).

The problems here are self evident. The 1,000-meal kitchen is a good example of Cold War planning. Community Advisors were told that a 'speedy service' would

Millions of bowls and spoons were stockpiled at Buffer Depots around the British Isles. They hold one pint and would be distributed from emergency feeding stations.

be required to get through as many people as possible, targeting a maximum thirty minutes per sitting. To achieve this a team comprising the following was recommended: a supervisor, team leader, head cook, two assistant cooks and seven people to perform other kitchen duties such as washing up, food preparation and lighting fires. With the best will in the world people cannot work twenty-four hours a day, so it was suggested that three shifts be organised, keeping the centre operational constantly. So, each Emergency Feeding Centre had the capacity to produce 48,000 meals a day if it was running at peak performance. Putting that into some sort of perspective, the population of Salisbury was, at the end of the Cold War, 36,840. It is also 10,000 more than the current capacity of the Arsenal FC Stadium at Highbury, London. The control of such large numbers of people would have been a near impossible task, especially since most would be in a very poor physical and mental state by this time.

fifteen

'Mr Gorbachev – Tear Down this Wall'

The events of the late 1980s took the world by surprise and when Ronald Reagan demanded, 'Mr Gorbachev – tear down this wall', on a visit to Berlin in late 1987 he could hardly have imagined the monumental effects its opening would have. The winds of change started in 1988 when, at the United Nations, Mikhail Gorbachev announced that Soviet troops would be withdrawn from European countries; the people would now decide policy, not Moscow. This said, Gorbachev fully expected the fifteen countries that made up the Soviet Union to stay together, but in the event this could not have been further from reality. In this last chapter the knock-on effect of the Soviet Union's collapse will be described, but first the events leading up to the end of the Cold War will be laid out.

The USSR Collapse

For over forty years massive divisions of Russian troops and equipment had been stationed in Eastern Europe. This had served two purposes: firstly, it had kept any thought of reform out of the minds of the host country, and secondly, pressure had been kept on NATO. However, this was expensive and Gorbachev now needed to redirect military finances into his domestic reform programme. By early 1989 he had committed to removing over 50,000 troops out of client regime territories. Gorbachev also expected these countries to stay within the fold and follow the way of perestroika, pursuing a more open relationship between state and population, but without the threat of brutal put-downs, using tanks, the floodgates opened. Hungary saw the rebirth of democracy whilst in Poland 'Solidarity', under the leadership of Lech Walesa, was re-legalised. Poland went on to form a non-communist-led coalition, the first of the now faltering Warsaw Pact to do so.

The situation now gathered pace as Hungary opened its borders to Austria; thousands now started to move across the 'Iron Curtain' to freedom. East German families saw their opportunity and within three days over 13,000 had crossed to Austria. Importantly, Moscow had no problem with this, effectively giving the green

The wall comes down. The symbol of European division was breached on 9 November 1989 and signalled the beginning of the end for the Soviet Union.

light for escape. In an attempt to stop the loss of trained citizens, East Germany sealed its borders with Czechoslovakia, but the end was near. In a visit to East Berlin a few days later Gorbachev urged Erich Honecker to take up reform, and when this was met with disdain he announced it to a large staged rally; the crowd responded by chanting 'Gorby, Save Us'. Soviet troops still based in East Germany were ordered to stay in barracks; they were not to get involved in any crackdowns. The end for Honecker came a few days later when, in Leipzig, over 80,000 protesters gathered to demand reforms. The security police were ordered to open fire on the crowds but refused, instead Honecker was deposed, replaced by a younger man – Egon Krenz. All the West could do was stand by and watch as the East German state began to disintegrate. On 9 November 1989 the East German government announced that exit visas would be given to all those who wished to travel to the West. Within twenty-four hours tens of thousands had travelled through the wall to a rapturous welcome from West Berliners. By the end of the year both Bulgaria and Czechoslovakia had also shed their communist regimes. The year was to end in bloodshed as the last of the communist leaders, Nicolae Ceausescue, was toppled and executed on Christmas Day.

By the start of 1990 Gorbachev was experiencing pressure within the Soviet Union as the idea of independence spread. Lithuania now demanded a break from Moscow, but the crunch came in Azerbaijan. When civil war broke out between rival factions, Gorbachev panicked and sent in the troops; thousands were killed. The situation was now clearly spiralling out of control. To quell the impending collapse the abandonment of the one-party Soviet system was proposed. This met favour with Western leaders but hardliners in Moscow were not so impressed. On

29 May 1990 Boris Yeltsin was elected leader of the Russian Republic, even though he had renounced his Communist membership; the end was now clearly in sight. Throughout 1991 Soviet republics were in turmoil as Gorbachev faced opposition at home and humiliation abroad, culminating in a disastrous request for financial aid at the G7 meeting in London. On 18 August an attempted coup led by Gennardy Yanayev damaged Gorbachev's position irreparably. He was on holiday at the time and by the time he had returned to Moscow Boris Yeltsin was calling the shots, and on 25 December 1991 the Soviet Union was relegated to history as the Red Flag was lowered over the Kremlin for the last time. The Cold War was finally over.

Options for Change

In light of the new world order the British Government, at the time experiencing an economic downturn, published a fundamental review of its defence policy during 1990. It reversed the decision, taken in the 1980s, to support NATO's request for a 3 per cent annual growth in expenditure with a commitment to reduce combat readiness by around 30 per cent within the next five years. The review was called 'Options for Change'. At that time it was considered that the Soviet Union, albeit without the Warsaw Pact, still had the potential to threaten the West, and as such Britain would continue to honour its NATO commitments. British forces would now be utilised in a three-pronged arrangement, rapid reaction, main defence and augmentation forces. Just one year after this decision the world changed again, the Soviet Union crumbled away and Britain committed forces to the liberation of Kuwait. By 1993 the view that the new Russian confederacy, the Commonwealth of Independent States (CIS), could threaten the West was abandoned and the post-Cold War run-down gathered speed.

Throughout 1991–92 discussions moved away from replacements for Chevaline, Lance and WE-177 to disposal programmes and reductions of the nuclear capabilities. Chevaline was ready to be replaced by Trident, as the British deterrent stayed with the Navy; however, this was not to be the case for the Army and RAF. The Lance tactical missile system was withdrawn in 1992 and the 50th Missile Regiment disbanded. The Government announced in 1991 that there would be a 50 per cent reduction in the RAF's stockpile of WE-177; the first unit was dismantled in 1992 at AWE Burghfield. On 4 April 1995 the Government announced the whole stockpile would be removed by the turn of the century. The Navy WE-177 depth charges were removed to a central storage facility in 1992 and were decommissioned soon after. In the event the final WE-177 was decommissioned in 1998 ahead of schedule. All bombs were broken down to a component level whereupon some parts were recycled as scrap, however contaminated parts were destroyed. Interestingly, the fissile parts of the weapon were removed and kept for, as the Minister for Defence George Robertson put it to the house, 'defence purposes'. Obviously you cannot be too careful! The whole process has been estimated to have cost around £23 million.

Civil Protection Changes

By July 1991 the writing was also on the wall for nuclear-conflict-orientated civil defence, but the Government, whilst reducing the central budget, still required local authorities to contribute to emergency planning. Kenneth Baker also announced that the number of protected Local Authority Emergency Centres would be reduced from two in each county and one district HQ to just one county site. By 1992 this had changed again and the entire Regional Government Headquarters (RGHQ) network was disposed of by the Home Office. This included the two purpose-built structures at Chilmark, finished in 1986, and Ashdown Forest, finished in 1989, costing £2.1 million and £3 million respectively. On 10 July 1991 the decision was taken to restructure warning and monitoring on a more cost-effective footing and subsequently the UKWMO and ROC were stood down, much to the consternation of their members.

Radioactive Monitoring

The official stand down of the United Kingdom Warning and Monitoring Organisation and its field force, the Royal Observer Corps, masked a technological development that is still with us today. On 26 April 1986 a fire in the reactor room at Chernobyl quickly became the world's worst nuclear and indeed industrial accident; contamination spread over vast areas and was eventually picked up in Scotland and Wales. The incident demonstrated that whilst the United Kingdom had a comprehensive network of monitoring posts that could follow contamination, they had to be staffed if they were to be effective. By 1988 a series of automated sites had been set up independent from the UKWMO and ROC sites. This was upgraded in 1989 (RIMNET phase 1) and 1993 (RIMNET phase 2) and further improvements are likely.

RIMNET has one advantage over the UKWMO: it is fully automated. Radiation dose rate monitors situated at ninety-three sites across the British Isles, mostly on MOD sites, take hourly readings. These are automatically transferred to a central data collection point located at the Department for Environment, Food and Rural Affairs (DEFRA). From here the information is disseminated to the relevant departments, be they District Council, media, Meteorological Office or Department of Health. As with previous systems RIMNET has three states, Normal, Alert and Incident, followed by the customary red colour code.

So Are We Safe?

The slim-down of all aspects of both civil defence and military sites has been staggering since the collapse of the Soviet Union. Government phrases such as 'the peace dividend' and 'options for change' have masked the true scale of the situation, and some disposals may well yet prove to have been rather hasty in the 'new world order' that has emerged. One thing is clear – the world is far from safe. Throughout the Cold War the threat was easily recognisable; unless Britain was prepared to yield to the Communist yoke it would have to protect itself. But the Cold War was far more than protection. Lucrative defence contracts, even during times of financial downturn, kept the economy going. Throughout the 1950s an estimated one million craftsmen, technicians and scientists were employed on defence-related projects; by 1995 that had shrunk to just over 100,000. The leaps forward in technology included space flight, microwaves, computers, the Global Positioning System, telecommunications – especially mobile phones, and nuclear power; all had a level of British involvement or were invented here and now

RAF Fylingdales. The end of the 'Golf Balls', these unique structures were demolished in 1994. (Courtesy *Scarborough Evening News*)

have domestic applications in every home in the land. The defence industry itself has now become vulnerable to financial issues on a scale far removed from those early days. Contracts are now no longer the preserve of preferred companies and those who do win new projects are driven to find civilian applications to stay afloat. QinetiQ Ltd is the latest manifestation of this drive to make research and development pay rather than be supported. QinetiQ Ltd was formed on 1 July 2001 from various commercially viable departments of the Defence Evaluation and Research Agency, itself an amalgamation of the majority of the Government's research companies. So far the company, which for the moment is still wholly owned by the Government, has distinguished itself in a number of scientific fields. The benefits of fifty years of defence research are now being realised, via many civilian applications, and swelling the national coffers in the process, this clearly would not have been possible throughout the Cold War.

Defence partnerships with other sovereign states were, throughout the Cold War, something of a necessity, especially on complex weapons systems, and nowhere was this more apparent than in the aircraft industry. A number of projects, especially from the late 1960s, typified this partnership ideal; Concord was the most famous, but other aircraft were developed with the French including the Jaguar ground attack/fighter and the Puma helicopter. This led to the formation of Airbus Industries where a whole family of passenger aircraft now match American constructors in sales and operator badges. The first of the multi-national aircraft operated by the Royal Air Force – the Panavia Tornado, developed through the 1970s – saw Britain in partnership with Germany and Italy along with a number of smaller contributions from others. And with the next generation

Bempton. The ravages of the British climate are taking their toll on many structures around the country. This site is constantly battered by winds from the North Sea.

fighter, the Typhoon, the major contributors have been expanded to include Spain. Interestingly, the aircraft has been so long in development that the German government have considered pulling out on a number of occasions, their reason being the costs of reunification and the number of Russian-built aircraft inherited at unification, so in some respects the Cold War is still having an effect on defence spending.

But what of the Cold War sites described in this book? The air defence network has now been largely decommissioned as more effective and powerful radar equipment has come on line. The majority of these sites now stand silent and are slowly decaying. The famous 'Golf Balls', which were so prominent a feature on the North Yorkshire Moors that they became a tourist attraction, were demolished in 1994. And at this point it has to be remembered that these structures were unique. The American airbases around the country have largely been sold off, leaving just a few sites operational. Greenham Common is now a business park, having seen its runways and hardstanding ripped up and used as hardcore for the Newbury by-pass.

At Upper Heyford the majority of the base is scheduled for demolition in advance of new housing, but in the meantime is home to over 15,000 new cars in storage. A multitude of bunkers have found other uses such as secure stores for documents, and in the wake of September 11 some are now used as back-up stores for financial company records, the command centre at Greenham Common and RGHQ bunker at Chilmark being just two examples. The regional electricity headquarters at Keynsham near Bristol is now an office complex, whilst the central control at Becca Hall near Leeds is to become a conference centre. The buffer depots have been disposed of and the majority

The first peace march to the Atomic Weapons Research Establishment was over Easter in 1958; in 2004 protests were still staged in opposition to the Trident servicing programme.

demolished, as has been the fate of many of the smaller Civil Defence Controls like the four small sites in Bristol. The majority of county 'mains' and 'standbys' survive, often used as storerooms, primarily because they are beneath council-owned offices and have offered additional space. The 1950s War Rooms are slowly disappearing, although the one now owned by Reading University is in the care of the entomology department and is used as a DEFRA-registered insect repository. The Anti-aircraft Operations Rooms and Royal Observer Corps Sector HQs are a rather mixed story. Many sites have now been cleared; however, some have found new uses. No. 20 Group ROC HQ at York has become a scheduled monument, having the same statutory protection as Stonehenge, and is to be opened to the public as a museum, whilst No. 12 Group ROC HQ at Lansdown is now Command Training Centre run by Avon Fire Brigade. The RGHQ at Hack Green is now a museum dedicated to the Cold War, as is the splendid Kelvedon Hatch on the outskirts of London. And of the 800+ ROC underground monitoring posts? The majority still survive, but they are rapidly becoming damaged through a mixture of vandalism and neglect. Bempton CEW Rotor site is now suffering from storm damage. Not all are in danger; the ROC post at Wroughton airfield has become part of the Science Museum's exhibits and is regularly opened by Corps members who enthusiastically show the public around. The post at RAF Blakehill Farm has become a bat sanctuary and is surrounded by a nature reserve, and it is even possible to holiday at one site in the north of England to experience the Cold War first hand.

So is there a point to all this? Yes; the Cold War has and will affect the lives of everyone in this country for at least the next two decades. This is because we are

Hack Green. The legacy we leave our children.
Youngsters now learn through contact with
a once secret world. (Courtesy Hack Green
Secret Nuclear Bunker)

only now seeing the formation of Europe that should have happened fifty years ago.
NATO still exists, although it was designed to be a defensive organisation and has
gone on the offensive in recent years in the former communist state of Yugoslavia, and
it is likely to remain as long as America continues to make a financial commitment.
We are also destined to be drawn, from time to time, into conflicts that had their
origins in the Cold War. Nobody can escape the media headlines over 'Weapons of
Mass Destruction', yet the only reason the majority of states in the Middle East have
these is because either the East or West supplied the technology to them, usually in the
course of either containing communism or following the Soviet ideology. The world
is now, without doubt, a more unstable place, as terrorist groups have the capability
to use chemical agents and have done so, on occasion. These weapons may only affect
small numbers but the chaos is self evident; the only good thing is that Porton Down
and the British Government are probably the world's best when it comes to chemical
defence. Also, some aspects of the nuclear Cold War are still with us; this was graphically
demonstrated in 2004 when a march took place from London to Aldermaston, an
event that will probably be repeated until Britain becomes a completely nuclear free
country. But we need to consider one final point. Many of those sites visited whilst
this book was being researched are scheduled for removal, viewed by many as ugly
eyesores, monuments to a period in history best forgotten, but should we let them
slip into recorded history or should the majority be preserved? The author, being an
archaeologist, prefers the latter option, but it is up to the reader and general public at
large to decide. This book has attempted to cover the Cold War through British eyes;
we need to preserve artefacts and sites now if we are to pass on the Cold War legacy
to our children, so that they may understand how the world around them developed
and learn from our near fatal mistakes.

Glossary

A&AEE, Aircraft & Armament Experimental
   Establishment
AAOR, Anti-Aircraft Operations Room
ABMEW, Anti-Ballistic Missile Early Warning
ABM, Anti-Ballistic Missile
ABMM, Anti-Ballistic Missile Missile
ACDRU, Arms Control and Disarmament Research
   Unit
AEW, Airborne Early Warning
AFS, Auxiliary Fire Service
ATC, Air Traffic Control
AWDREY, Atomic Weapon Detection and Estimation
   of Yield
AWRE, Atomic Weapons Research Establishment
BAC, Bristol Aeroplane Company
BAJ, Bristol Aerojet
BAOR, British Army on the Rhine
BBC, British Broadcasting Corporation
BM, Ballistic Missile
BMEWS, Ballistic Missile Early Warning System
BPI, Bomb Power Indicator
BT, British Telecom
CDC, Civil Defence Corps
CEW, Centimetric Early Warning
CH, Chain Home
CHEL, Chain Home Extra Low
CND, Campaign for Nuclear Disarmament
COMARE, Committee on Medical Aspects of
   Radiation in the Environment
CRC, Control and Reporting Centres
CWP, Carrier Warning Point
DERA, Defence Evaluation and Research Agency
DIADEM, Direction Indicator of Atomic Detonation
   by Electronic Means
DOE, Department of the Environment
DOT, Department of Transport
ECCM, Electronic Counter-Counter Measures
ECM, Electronic Counter Measures

EFC, Emergency Feeding Centre
EMP, Electromagnetic Pulse
ESR, Essential Service Route
FAA, Fleet Air Arm
FMAU, Forward Medical Aid Unit
FMSP, Fixed Meter Survey Probe
GAMA, GLCM Alert and Maintenance Area
GCI, Ground Control Intercept
GDA, Gun Defended Area
GDT, Ground Defence Training
GLCM, Ground Launched Cruise Missile
GOR, Gun Operations Room
GPO, General Post Office
GZI, Ground Zero Indicator
HER, High Explosive Research
HO, Home Office
HTP, High Test Peroxide
ICBM, Intercontinental Ballistic Missile
ICDS, Industrial Civil Defence Service
IFF, Identification Friend or Foe
IRBM, Intermediate Range Ballistic Missile
JAEC, Joint Atomic Energy Committee
LACO, Local Agricultural Control Officer
LAEC, Local Authority Emergency Centres
LAFS, Local Authority Fire Service
LLAD, Low Level Air Defence
LOX, Liquid Oxygen
MAFF, Ministry of Agriculture, Food and Fisheries
MASH, Mobile Army Surgical Unit
MCC, Master Control System
MEC, Mobile Emergency Controls
MFC, Mobile Fire Column
MIRV, Multiple Independently-targeted Re-entry
   Vehicle
MLRS, Multi-Launch Rocket System
MOD(PE), Ministry of Defence (Procurement
   Executive)
MR, Maritime Reconnaissance

MSX, Message Switch Equipment
NAAFI, Navy Army Air Force Institute
NADGE, NATO Air Defence Ground Environment
NARS, North Atlantic Radio System
NATO, North Atlantic Treaty Organisation
NBC, Nuclear, Biological, Chemical
NGSRD, National Grid Strategic Reserve Depot
NRPB, National Radiological Protection Board
OR, Operational Requirement
OTHR, Over The Horizon Radar
PF, Protection Factor
QRA, Quick Reaction Alert
RAD, Radiation Absorbed Dose
RAE, Royal Aircraft Establishment
RAF, Royal Air Force
REC, Regional Emergency Committee
REM, Roentgen Equivalent Man
RIMNET, Radioactive Incident Monitoring Network
RN, Royal Navy
ROC, Royal Observer Corps
ROF, Royal Ordnance Factory
RPD, Rocket Propulsion Department
RRE, Royal Radar Establishment
RSG, Regional Seat of Government
RTS, Radar Tracking Station
SAC, Strategic Air Command

SACEUR, Supreme Air Commander Europe
SALT, Strategic Arms Limitation Talks
SAM, Surface to Air Missile
SFS, Strategic Food Stockpile
SHORAD, Short Range Air Defence
SLBM, Submarine Launched Ballistic Missile
SM, Strategic Missile
SOC, Sector Operations Centre
SRBM, Short Range Ballistic Missile
S-RC, Sub-Regional Control
SRHQ, Sub-Regional Headquarters
SSPAR, Solid State Phased Array Radar
START, Strategic Arms Reduction Talks
STOL, Short Take-Off and Landing
SX, System Exchange
TIR, Target Illuminating Radar
TTE, Telephone Trunk Exchanges
UKADGE, United Kingdom Air Defence Ground
    Equipment
UKWMO, United Kingdom Warning and Monitoring
    Organisation
USAF, United States Air Force
VTOL, Vertical Take-Off and Landing
WB, Warning Broadcast
WRVS, Women's Royal Voluntary Service
WWII, World War Two

Selective Bibliography

BAJ Coatings Limited. 1993. *Shadow to Shadow: A History of the Bristol Aeroplane Banwell Shadow Factory and Bristol Aerojet (BAJ) 1941–1991*, Eaton Press Ltd, Merseyside.

Baker, F. 1993. 'The Berlin Wall: Production, Preservation & Consumption of a 20th Century Monument', Antiquity 67.

Benn, T. 1987. *Tony Benn: Out of the Wilderness, Diaries 1963–67*, Arrow Books, London.

Bown, C. and Mooney, P.J. 1981. *Cold War to Détente 1945–80*, 2nd edition, Heinemann Educational Books, London.

British Transport Commission. 1952. British Transport Civil Defence Training Booklet, 2nd edition, British Transport Commission, London.

Brookes, A. 1982. *V-Force: The History of Britain's Airborne Deterrent,* Jane's, London.

Bud, R. and Gummett, P. (eds). 1999. *Cold War Hot Science: Applied Research in Britain's Defence Laboratories 1945–1990*, Harwood Academic Publishers, The Netherlands.

Central Office of Information. 1957. 'The H-Bomb: What about the millions of Survivors?', HMSO, London.

Central Office of Information. 1981. 'Civil Defence: Why We Need It', HMSO, London.

Central Office of Information. 1981. 'The Balanced View: Nuclear Weapons and Arms Control', Arms Control and Disarmament Research Unit, Foreign and Commonwealth Office, London.

Central Office of Information. 1982. 'Peace and Disarmament: A Short Guide to British Government Policy', Arms Control and Disarmament Research Unit, Foreign and Commonwealth Office, London.

Clarke, B. 2000. 'Peace Dividend Brings Archaeological Rewards', Antiquity 74.

Cocroft, W.D. and Thomas, R.J.C. Edited by Barnwell, P.S. 2003. *Cold War: Building for Nuclear Confrontation 1946–1989*, English Heritage, Swindon.

Cook, C. and Stevenson, J. 1996. *Britain Since 1945*, Longman, London.

Cooper, P.J. 1996. *Forever Farnborough: Flying the Limits 1904–1996*, Hikoki Press, Aldershot.

Dobinson, C.S., Lake, J. and Schofield, A.J. 1997. 'Monuments of War: Defining England's 20th Century Defence Heritage', Antiquity 71.

Dorrill, S. 2000. *MI6: Fifty years of Special Operations*, Forth Estate, London.

DTI. 2002. 'Managing the Nuclear Legacy: A Strategy for Action', Department of Trade and Industry, HMSO, London.

Freeze, G.L. 2002. *Russia, A History*, 2nd edition, Oxford University Press, Oxford.

Gander, T. 1984. *The Modern Royal Air Force*, Patrick Stephens, Wellingborough.

Gough, J. 1993. *Watching the Skies, The History of Ground Radar in the Air Defence of the United Kingdom*, HMSO, London.

Ground Zero Organisation. 1982. *Nuclear War: What's in it for You?* Methuen, London.

Higgins, H. 1993. *The Cold War*, 3rd edition, Heinemann Educational, London.

HMSO. 1956. Statement on Defence, 1956, HMSO, London.

HMSO. 1957. Defence: Outline of Future Policy, 1957, HMSO, London.

Home Office. 1956. Nuclear Weapons, 'Manual of Civil Defence', Vol. 1, Pamphlet No. 1, HMSO, London.

Home Office. 1949. Civil Defence, Basic Chemical Warfare, 'Manual of Basic Training', Vol. II, HMSO, London.

Home Office. 1952. Civil Defence, Welfare Section, 'Manual of Basic Training,' Vol. I, HMSO, London.

Home Office. 1957. Civil Defence, Elementary Fire-Fighting, Handbook No. 4, HMSO, London.

Home Office. 1957. Civil Defence, Light Rescue, Handbook No. 5, HMSO, London.

Home Office. 1960. Civil Defence, General Information (All Sections), Pocket Book No. 3, HMSO, London.

Home Office. 1976 (reprinted 1980). 'Protect and Survive', HMSO, London.

Home Office. 1979. 'UKWMO – Protecting by Warning', HMSO, London.

Home Office. 1981. 'Domestic Nuclear Shelters', HMSO, London.

Home Office. 1982. 'Domestic Nuclear Shelters: Technical Guidance', HMSO, London.

Home Office. 1988. 'Civil Protection', HMSO, London.

Isaacs, J. and Downing, T. 1998. *Cold War*, Bantam Press, London.

James, N.D.G. 1983. *Gunners at Larkhill*, Gresham Books, Henley-on-Thames.

Laming, T. 1993. *The Vulcan Story*, Arms and Armour Press, London.

Lowry, B. (ed). 1996. '20th Century Defences in Britain: An Introductory Guide', Practical Handbooks in Archaeology No. 12, Council For British Archaeology, York.

MAFF. 1959. 'Home Defence and the Farmer', HMSO, London.

Martiniussen, E. 2001. 'Sellafield: Reprocessing Plant in Great Britain', Bellona Working Paper, No. 05:2001.

McCamley, N.J. 2002. *Cold War Secret Nuclear Bunkers*, Pen & Sword, Barnsley.

Ministry of Defence, Public Information. 1981. 'A Nuclear Free Europe: Why it Wouldn't Work', E.G. Bond Ltd.

Ministry of Defence. 1995. 'Survive to Fight', revised edition, JSP 410, HMSO, London.

Ministry of Health. 1967. 'Emergency Home Care', London.

Minnion, J. and Bolsover, P. 1983. *The CND Story*, Allison & Busby, London.

Morgan, K.O. 1992. *The People's Peace: British History 1945–1990*, Oxford University Press, Oxford.

Newhouse, J. 1989. *The Nuclear Age: From Hiroshima to Star Wars*, Michael Joseph Ltd, London.

NRPB-R323. 2001. Management Options for Food Production Systems Affected by a Nuclear Accident: Task 5: Disposal of Waste Milk to Sea, National Radiological Protection Board, Didcot.

NRPB-W42. 2003. Review of Autopsy, *In Vivo* and Bioassay Measurements on Members of the Public in the UK, National Radiological Protection Board, Didcot.

Oulton, W.E. 1987. *Christmas Island Cracker*, Thomas Harmsworth Publishing, London.

Peacock, L.T. 1988. *Strategic Air Command*, Arms and Armour Press, London.

Popkess, Barry. 1980. *The Nuclear Survival Handbook*. New York: Collier Books.

Public General Acts and Measures. 1948. Civil Defence Act, 1948, 12 and 13 George 6, Chapter 5.

Public General Acts and Measures. 1986. Civil Protection in Peacetime Act, 1986, Elizabeth 2, Chapter 22.

Rhodes, R. *Dark Sun: The Making of the Hydrogen Bomb*, Simon & Schuster, New York.

Thompson, E.P. and Smith, D. 1980. *Protest and Survive*, Penguin Specials, Harmondsworth.

West, N. 1982. *A Matter of Trust: MI5 1945–72*, Weidenfeld and Nicolson, London.

Wilson, H. 1971. *The Labour Government: 1964–1970*. A Personal Record, Michael Joseph Ltd, London.

Wood, D. 1992. *Attack Warning Red: The Royal Observer Corps and the Defence of Britain*, 2nd edition, Carmichael & Sweet, Portsmouth.

Wright, P. 1987. *Spy Catcher*, William Heinemann, Australia.

Young. J. 1991. *Cold War Europe 1945–1989: A Political History*, Edward Arnold, London.

Public Record Office Documents

AIR 2/13675. Blue Streak: Underground Launching Site 1956–1958.
AIR 19/1014. Blue Steel Development 1961–1964.
DEFE 13/121. Siting of Thor Missiles in the United Kingdom 1958–1959.
AIR 19/1137. RAF Fylingdales: BMEWS 1962–1966.
MAF 99/1922. Buffer Depot Management Contracts 1950–1957.
HO 346/189. Hazardous Materials Transported by Road, Rail, Sea or Air 1959–1972.

Other Sources

A number of organisations have made their records available for this project, these are listed below.
Avon Fire Brigade
Bristol Aeroplane Company Museum
County & Metropolitan
Defence Estates
Defence Evaluation and Research Agency
Hack Green Cold War Museum
Hansard
Imperial War Museum
Kelvedon Hatch Cold War Museum
National Monuments Record (English Heritage)
Reading University
Royal Air Force Museum Hendon
Subterranaea Brittannica
University of Bath in Swindon
Thames Water
Wiltshire County Council
Yorkshire Air Museum

Index

If you are interested in purchasing other books published by Tempus,
or in case you have difficulty finding any Tempus books in your local bookshop,
you can also place orders directly through our website

www.tempus-publishing.com